CISTERCIAN FATHERS

GUERRIC

Liturgical Sermons

Volume One

Introduction and translation by
Monks of Mount Saint Bernard Abbey

CISTERCIAN PUBLICATIONS
Kalamazoo, Michigan

Ecclesiastical permission to publish this volume was received from Bernard Flanagan, Bishop of Worcester, 25 September, 1969.

© Cistercian Publications, Inc., 1970

Library of Congress Catalog Card Number: 75-148203

CISTERCIAN FATHERS SERIES: NUMBER EIGHT

GUERRIC OF IGNY

LITURGICAL SERMONS I

CONTENTS

Introduction	vii
The First Sermon for Advent	1
The Second Sermon for Advent	7
The Third Sermon for Advent	14
The Fourth Sermon for Advent	22
The Fifth Sermon for Advent	30
The First Sermon for Christmas	37
The Second Sermon for Christmas	42
The Third Sermon for Christmas	47
The Fourth Sermon for Christmas	54
The Fifth Sermon for Christmas	61
The First Sermon for the Epiphany	68
The Second Sermon for the Epiphany	76
The Third Sermon for the Epiphany	83
The Fourth Sermon for the Epiphany	91
The First Sermon for the Purification	99
The Second Sermon for the Purification	106
The Third Sermon for the Purification	113
The Fourth Sermon for the Purification	120
The Fifth Sermon for the Purification	127
The First Sermon for Lent	133
Sermon for the Saturday of the Second Week of Lent	140

EDITOR'S NOTE

The translation of the fifty-four sermons of Guerric of Igny presented here is based on the critical edition of the original prepared by two monks of Mount St Bernard Abbey, John Morson and Hilary Costello, who have also graciously supplied the introduction for this translation prepared by their confreres. Their critical edition of the Sermons will be published shortly by Editions du Cerf in their collection *Sources Chrétiennes*. With that edition there will be found an interesting account of the establishment of the critical text and a listing of the nine primitive manuscripts on which it is based. The editors note: "The manuscripts studied have agreed in confirming the authenticity of these sermons" and "they witness to a homogeneous text with unanimity such as we could hardly have expected."

The sermons will be presented in two volumes with an analytic index at the end of the second volume.

For the sake of convenience in locating references this English edition has retained the paragraph numbers as they are found in the edition of John Mabillon, which was reprinted in Volume 185 of Migne's *Patrologia, Series Latina*. The critical Latin edition did the same. However, following the critical Latin edition, the Fifth Sermon for the Purification, as it is found in Mabillon, has been omitted as inauthentic, and has been replaced by Mabillon's Sixth Sermon for the same Feast.

So far as we know this is the first time that many of the sermons of Guerric of Igny have appeared in English translation. We are grateful to the abbot and the monks of Mount St Bernard for their generous collaboration in the preparation of these volumes. We hope that the publication of this translation will not only make available to English readers the immensely fruitful theology and spirituality of this disciple of St Bernard but that it will make this truly lovable man and monk better known and loved.

M. Basil Pennington ocso

INTRODUCTION

THERE CANNOT BE many to whom the name "Guerric of Igny" means anything. Yet, with Bernard, Aelred and William of St Thierry, he has been called one of the four evangelists of Cîteaux. Each represents something of what is best in the twelfth century; St Bernard is in some sense the master of the other three; apart from this they have little in common. All came to the monastic life by very different ways. Since Guerric was the only one who lived at Clairvaux with Bernard for his abbot, we might expect him to have been the disciple in a way the others were not. Perhaps he was, but this is not to suggest that he was simply St Bernard's mouthpiece or interpreter. His approach to the mysteries of which he speaks is no less fresh and personal than that of an Aelred or a William.[1]

The *Exordium Magnum Cisterciense* compiled by Conrad of Eberbach at the end of the twelfth century, is not an historical source of the highest value, but it does outline the scenery for the drama of a great monastic revival, and it shows us what sort of reputation clung to the first abbot of Clairvaux and some of his followers. Two

1. Louis Bouyer has given a short appreciation of Guerric's teaching in *The Cistercian Heritage* (Mowbray, 1958) pp. 190–203. The fullest study since de Wilde's work (see note 8) has been made by Dom André Louf "Une Théologie de la Pauvreté Monastique chez le Bx Guerric d'Igny" in *Collectanea Ordinis Cisterciensium Reformatorum*, 20 (1958), pp. 207–22, 362–73. See also articles in the issue mentioned below (note 10).

chapters sing the praise of Guerric.[2] More to our purpose is a Life of Hugh, eventually abbot of Marchienne.[3] This contemporary of Guerric was his intimate friend before their ways separated. A letter written by Hugh Foliot speaks of Guerric, abbot of Igny, as one who exercised considerable influence beyond the enclosure of his monastery. It was Guerric, in fact, who persuaded the canons regular of St Denys at Rheims to postulate for Hugh Foliot as their abbot.[4] St Bernard refers to a Guerric, monk of Clairvaux, in two of his letters.[5] And it is highly probable, to say the least, that this is the future abbot of Igny. The reason for caution in this statement is that the name was rather common among the Flemish. If we add some indications from Guerric's own sermons, there is little more to say of biographical sources. There remain the charters of the diocese of Tournai, but these have a way of raising problems rather than solving them.

In 1890 the Abbé J. Beller published his *Life of Guerric of Igny*.[6] Historical sources being as slight as they are, it was a considerable achievement on this author's part to write fifteen chapters of which ten (219 pages) profess to be historical. There is a useful collection of *pièces justificatives* at the end of the volume. On the whole Beller's work is characterized by painstaking industry rather than by acute

---

2. The work is divided into *Distinctiones*. *Dist.* 2 is largely concerned with St Bernard; 3 and 4 with his immediate disciples. All references are to the critical edition by Bruno Griesser, *Exordium Magnum Cisterciense* (hereafter EM) (Rome: Editiones Cistercienses, 1961). The chapters devoted to Guerric are 8 and 9 of *Dist.* 3, pp. 163–6. All our references to EM will be to these two chapters unless otherwise stated. An English trans. will appear in vol. 30 of the Cistercian Studies Series.

3. *Vita Hugonis, Abbatis Marchianensis*, ed. E. Martène and U. Durand, in *Thesaurus Novus Anecdotorum*, vol. 3 (1717), col. 1709–36. References henceforward to VH.

4. Mabillon and E. Martène, *Annales Benedictini*, vol. 6 (1745), year 1149, pp. 422–423.

5. St Bernard, Letters 89 and 90; trans. B. James, *The Letters of St Bernard of Clairvaux* (London: Burns & Oates, 1953), Letters 92 and 93, pp. 137ff.

6. J. Beller, *Le Bx Guerric Disciple de Saint Bernard et second Abbé du Monastère de Notre Dame d'Igny de l'Ordre de Cîteaux au Diocèse de Reims* (Rheims, 1890). References henceforth to Beller.

Introduction ix

critical sense. It seems to have provoked five years later an article by Fr Michael Gatterer SJ critical of Beller and his sources but capable himself sometimes of utmost naïveté.[7] The thesis published by Dom Déodat de Wilde in 1935 was theological, and concerned with the life and work of Guerric only in its first twenty-five pages.[8] The history of the Abbey of Igny by the Abbé Péchenard is worth notice,[9] so also are some of the articles devoted to Guerric in the *Collectanea Ordinis Cisterciensium Reformatorum* on the occasion of the eighth centenary of his death in 1957.[10] The *Exordium Magnum* tells us that the second abbot of Igny was "full of days"[11] when he died, probably on the 19th of August 1157. In those days such an age might have been seventy and this would place his birth about 1087. Beller, followed in this by de Wilde, recognized Guerric as an acolyte in a charter of 1094 and as a canon in another of 1108.[12] If it were possible to accept these as reliable we should conclude that Guerric lived from five to fifteen years longer and might date his birth in the decade 1070–80. He was born at Tournai,[13] and was almost certainly educated in the humanities, dialectic and theology at the cathedral school. He could hardly have written as he did unless his faculties had been well trained and developed before he entered Clairvaux at a fairly mature age. From 1087 until 1092 this school was directed by the famous Odo of

7. M. Gatterer SJ, "Der Selige Guerricus und seine Sermones" in *Zeitschrif für Katholische Theologie*, 19 (1895), pp. 35–90. References henceforth to Gatterer.
8. Déodat de Wilde, *De Beato Guerrico Abbate Igniacensi Ejusque Doctrina de Formatione Christi in Nobis* (Westmalle, 1935). References henceforth to de Wilde.
9. P. L. Péchenard, *Histoire de l'Abbaye d'Igny de l'Ordre de Cîteaux au Diocèse de Reims* (Rheims, 1883).
10. *Collectanea O.C.R.*, 19 (1957). Historical articles: Raymond Milcamps and Alberic Dubois, "Le Bienheureux Guerric Sa Vie Son Oeuvre" pp. 207–21; Sr M. Aleth, "L'Abbaye Du Bx. Guerric N.D. d'Igny" pp. 300–17.
11. EM, *Dist.* 3, ch. 9, p. 165, l.31. The last figure always gives the line in Griesser's edition.
12. Beller, pp. 626; de Wilde, p. 9 and notes 4, 5.
13. VH, n. 16, col. 1723.

x   *Introduction*

Cambrai.¹⁴ Whether Guerric was actually taught by Odo or not, he is likely to have come under his influence indirectly and so may have established contact with the scholastic tradition which derived from St Anselm.¹⁵

Whereas Beller used some charters to establish dates in the life of Guerric, Gatterer rejected these as quite unreliable because of the frequency with which the name Guerric occurred. He noted for instance that there were three Guerrics recorded among the benefactors of the restored abbey of St Martin of Tournai in 1092.¹⁶ We may add that from 1094 to 1141 the name can be found in charters twenty-nine times in the forms Weric, Guiric, Guirric, Geric, Gerric, Gueric, Guerric (always with genitive inflection Werici, etc.).¹⁷ Twenty-three entries are known before the time at which our Guerric is thought to have gone to Clairvaux. Some of these may refer to him, but certainly not all of them, for sometimes the name appears twice on the same document. Thus in 1101 we find Guerric and Guirric.¹⁸ If one of them is ours it is impossible to say which, or whether he is identified with the Weric and Guirric who appear respectively in 1094 and 1100. Beller recognized Guerric as a canon in a charter of 1100. In fact the charter to which he refers does not make it clear whether the bearer of this name is a canon or not.¹⁹

It is impossible to prove conclusively that Guerric of Igny was a

14. Future Bishop of Cambrai, he is known as Odo of Tournai, also as Odo of Orleans because of his birthplace. Herman, *Liber Restaurationis Abbatiae Sanctae Martini Tornacensis*, n. 1; PL 180:41.

15. So H. Barre, *Saint Bernard Théologien, Analecta S.O.C.*, 9 (1953), p. 106. It is true that the author is speaking of a particular point of Mariology.

16. Gatterer, p. 36, note 6. The three names are recorded with different spellings by Albert D'Haenens, "Moines et Clercs à Tournai au Debut du XII Siècle" in *La Vita Commune del Clero Nei Secoli XI (e) XII: Atti Della Settimana di Studio Mendola*, 1959 (Milan, 1962), pp. 93–94.

17. Whatever we know of charters in the Tournai diocese comes from Dom Nicholas Huyghebaert OSB who has generously put the fruit of his research at our disposal.

18. March 9, 1101. Charter of Balderic for St Mary's of Tournai, unedited; twelfth-century chartulary in the cathedral archives.

19. July, 17, 1108. Charter of Balderic for his cathedral, original lost; twelfth-century copy in the cathedral archives: chartular C, cf. 9.

canon of the Chapter of Tournai. In the *Vita Hugonis* we read that he was *Magister Apud Tornacum*.[20] We should expect this to mean that he had charge of the cathedral school, possibly even of all cloister and foundation schools in the diocese.[21] However, another Hotfrid was Master in 1116, 1120 and 1121.[22] The phrase of the *Vita Hugonis* may mean that Guerric was Master before 1116 but abandoned this responsibility when, as we know from the same authority, he retired to a life of solitude and prayer. As far as the evidence of the list goes, it is just possible that he was Master between 1121 and 1125. Perhaps no more is meant than that he taught in the same school; or Hugh's biographer, writing nearly half a century later, may have made a mistake. It has been noted already that Odo of Tournai is likely to have influenced Guerric in the field of learning. But it is difficult to point to sources of Guerric's teaching in Odo's surviving works.[23] It is much easier to recognize this influence in the young man's decision to lead a solitary life. He must have known about the happenings at St Martin of Tournai, where Odo had been abbot from 1094 until he became bishop of Cambrai in 1105.

This was a time of crisis in the monastic revival of the eleventh and twelfth centuries.[24] At Tournai we catch a glimpse of the hesitations, false starts and groping towards an ideal. Odo, with a few followers, became a monk in 1092, and adopted the Rule of St Augustine. In order to safeguard his ideals against pressure from the

20. VH, n. 16, col. 1723.

21. Gatterer, p. 40, considered that he had the authority of Du Cange for the latter meaning. This is not evident either from the Maurist or the modern edition of the *Glossarium*, s.v. *Magister, Scholasticus*.

22. 1116: charter of Lambert, bishop of Tournai, for Saint Aime of Douai; Lille archives, Nord 1 G 194, item 1012: given by Lambert to Sainte Marie au-Bois, Paris, Bibl. nat, Picardie 291, item 61. 1121: Ghent State archives, deposit from Bishop's palace, Saint-Bavon collection, IV, n. 10. Only the last has been edited; Miraeusfoppens, *Opera Diplomatica* IV, p. 357.

23. E.g. in the principal work, *De Peccato Originali*, PL 160: 1071-1102.

24. For an account of the revival as it took form at Tournai see Ch. Dereine, "Odon de Tournai et la Crise du Cénobitisme au XII Siècle" in *Revue du Moyen Age Latin*, 4 (1948), pp. 137-54; also Albert D'Haenens, *art. cit.* (see note 16). For a more general picture, see B. Lackner, *Eleventh-Century Background of Cîteaux* (Cistercian Studies Series, 8).

nobles of Tournai, he changed to the full monastic Rule of St Benedict. Still unsatisfied, he tried to live the strict eremitical life. Opposition came this time from the bishop too, with the result that the adventurers returned to their monastery and followed a regime similar to that of Molesme. Even this did not last, and in 1095 the community finally adopted the Cluniac observances.[25]

The part played by the nobles of Tournai in this crisis in the history of St Martin's Abbey makes it certain that it was a *cause célèbre*. Guerric would seem to have acted against it. Like Odo he was a hermit at heart. But, unlike Odo, he did not gather a number of followers around him and retire into the desert. He, too, was in his way traditional. Whether he continued to teach in the school or not, he lived a solitary life in a small house near the church. Here he gave himself to reading, writing, prayer and meditation, interrupted only by an occasional visit from a privileged friend like Hugh.[26]

Meanwhile, the name of a certain Bernard of Clairvaux was becoming known far beyond the enclosures of that monastery. This son of a Burgundian nobleman had entered Cîteaux with a party of relatives and friends in 1112[27] to embrace a reformed observance of the Rule of St Benedict under the guidance of an English abbot, Stephen Harding. Cîteaux began to make foundations soon afterwards, and Bernard was put in charge of the fourth at the age of twenty-four, only three years after his entry into monastic life.[28] There is no evidence that the hermit of Tournai met the abbot of Clairvaux when the latter made a journey into Flanders[29] but he is likely to have heard much of him from two intimate friends who did. These were Hugh and Oger, destined to become abbots, one of Marchienne, the other of St Nicholas-du-Pré. St Bernard refers to a Guerric, a novice at Clairvaux, in his eighty-ninth letter, written to

25. Herman, *op. cit.* (see note 14). D'Haenens, *art cit.*, p. 97.
26. VH, *ibid.*
27. This is the date commonly accepted: *Bernard de Clairvaux* (Commission d'Histoire de l'Ordre de Cîteaux, 1953), pp. 39, 572. Cited henceforward as *Bernard de Clairvaux*.
28. *Bernard de Clairvaux*, p. 572.
29. *Vita Prima Sancti Bernardi*, bk. 4, n. 16; PL 185:331. A. Manrique, *Annales Cistercienses*, vol. 1, year 1131, ch. 1, n. 8.

Oger[30] and it is unlikely that this Guerric is any other than the future abbot of Igny. If we take this for granted, we must note that Oger became an abbot in 1126, but Bernard's letter was written before this time. In the same letter we hear of a recent work, *In laudibus Virginis Mariae*, often known as the homilies on the *Missus est*, written probably not earlier than the end of 1124.[31] So the novice to whom the letter refers was Bernard's subject, certainly before Oger's abbacy in 1126 and perhaps early in 1125. It is interesting to see how this compares with the evidence of the Tournai charters. There are two signatories with the name Guerric (or with an alternative spelling) in 1116, one in 1118, two in 1120, possibly one in 1122. We cannot be sure which of these, if indeed any, was Guerric of Igny; but the name does not occur again for eleven years.

Even if we make due allowance for the conventional character of the expressions in the *Vita Hugonis* and the *Exordium Magnum*, there is no reason to think that Guerric had been anything but a model cleric before his entry into the monastery. "With grace to aid him he kept the robe of innocence unspotted to the last." So writes Conrad.[32] The sentence by itself has little historical value. But neither for that matter has a sentence written in the first person by Guerric himself, which could be interpreted as meaning that he had led a corrupt youth. "After the waters of baptism I handled not just one corpse but one after another for every deadly sin I committed. That proverb which Peter the Apostle used was verified in me: the dog returns to its vomit; the newly-washed sow wallows in the mire."[33] If we accepted this as evidence it would be easy to deny the baptismal innocence of Bernard too[34]—not that Bernard or his biographers laid claim to it.

30. St Bernard, Letter 89:3; James trans., Letter 92, p. 138.
31. Arguments for the date of *In laudibus V.M.* have been given by D. Van Eynde OFM, "Les débuts littéraires de Saint Bernard," *Analecta S.O.C.*, 19 (1963), pp. 189–98.
32. EM, p. 164:3–4.
33. Ser. 14:4; cf. n. 7. These references without names are to the sermons of Guerric himself. The first number refers to the sermon and the following number after the colon to the section of the sermon.
34. St Bernard, *De Div.* 46; PL 182:669c.

The *Vita Hugonis* makes it clear that Guerric went to Clairvaux without any idea of staying there. He only wanted to derive spiritual advantage from a meeting with a famous abbot. Bernard saw the makings of a good monk in Guerric and urged him to stay. The result is told by Hugh's biographer in these words: "Entrapped by the abbot's conversation, he gave in to the persuasion that was brought to bear upon him. He had come only to pay his respects, not with any idea of taking up the monastic life. Then, without delay or looking back, the cleric became a monk, the master a schoolboy."[35]

Bernard seems to have shown little sympathy with Guerric's attraction to the strict eremitical life. He may actually have spoken the words attributed to him, or they may have been suggested to the writer by one of his sermons: "Alas for him that is alone: for if he should fall he has none to lift him up."[36] This did not conform well to the tradition of the Desert Fathers, as revived for instance by St Peter Damian and practiced by St Bruno with his followers. Yet Bernard's friendship with the Carthusians suggests that his stand against the eremitical life was a circumstantial one, designed to attract the would-be hermits to Clairvaux.[37]

Like so many of the Clairvaux community, Guerric was considerably older than his abbot. By human standards he was more mature and experienced. Novices were pouring into the community. New foundations began with Trois Fontaines in 1118; they were made faster than ever after the birth of Igny in 1128.[38] Among the contemporaries of the novice we can recognize such famous names as Bernard of Pisa, later Eugenius III, Henry Murdach, who was to be Archbishop of York, and Humbert, whom Bernard would

35. VH, n. 16; col. 1723.
36. *Ibid.*, words quoted from Eccles 4:10. Cf. St Bernard, *In Circumc. Domini.*
37. J. Leclercq, "Problèmes de l'érémitisme," *Studia Monastica*, 5 (1963), p. 197f.; J. Grillon "Bernard et les groupements eremitiques" in *Bernard de Clairvaux*, pp. 252-262. *Lettres de premiers Chartreux I (Sources chrét.* 88), pp. 100, 103.
38. L. Janauschek, *Originum Cisterciensium*, vol. 1 (Vienna 1877), pp. 14ff. Henceforth cited as Janauschek.

send to found Igny about three years after Guerric's arrival at Clairvaux. There were besides those whose chief interest for future generations would lie in their blood-relationship to St Bernard. During the thirteen years or so of Guerric's stay in this monastery the administration must have been very much in the hands of the Prior. Apart from Bernard's long periods outside,[39] his health had been so ruined by excessive fasts and other austerities that he had to live apart from his brethren.[40] But when he could not so much as attend choir he was far from idle. He must have addressed the community often. Even if his sermons, as we have them, are works written for publication,[41] we should expect them to reflect the spiritual teaching which he imparted to his monks. Guerric's time at Clairvaux coincided in fact with the zenith of Bernard's powers and his best literary output.

We should not expect to know much of the monk Guerric in the years before he became abbot of Igny. The *Exordium Magnum* has a story about an angel coming to attend upon him and dress him up for the occasion of his reading lessons at Vigils.[42] We have a little first-hand evidence if we may refer to Guerric the two passages in St Bernard's letters written to Oger, a regular canon of Mount-Saint-Eloi, near Arras: "You are looking for good news about the penitential life of our Guerric. I have to tell you that as far as we can judge by results, he is following a course pleasing to God and doing penance which is fruitful indeed."[43] "If you want to know about Brother Guerric—and I know you do—he is not a runner who has lost his way or a boxer hitting the air. All the same, he knows that the issue lies not with the boxer or the runner but with God's mercy. This being so, he asks your prayers, that God who made him a

---

39. Especially after 1130 because of the schism: *Bernard de Clairvaux*, p. 583ff. *Vita prima S Bernardi*, bk 2; PL 185:267–302.
40. *Ibid.*, bk. 1, nn. 39, 40; PL 185:250.
41. See the question discussed with regard to the sermons *Super Cantica* by J. Leclercq, *Receuil d'études sur S Bernard et ses écrits* (Rome, 1962), part 2, ch. 3, pp. 193–212.
42. EM, p. 164:6f.
43. St Bernard, Letter 89:3; PL 182:221; James trans., Letter 92, p. 138.

boxer and a runner will let him carry off the prize and pass the winning post."[44]

Igny

In 1127, St Bernard was asked to intervene in a quarrel that had arisen between Archbishop Reginald III of Rheims and the people of his diocese. As a token of gratitude for the success of his intervention Reginald offered Bernard a site for a monastery at Igny, between Rheims and Soissons. So Clairvaux made its fourth foundation.[45] Humbert, the first abbot, had been a Benedictine for twenty years at Chaise-Dieu in the diocese of Clermont; had entered Clairvaux soon after its foundation and been there about nine years.[46] We read in the *Vita Prima S. Bernardi* that he had been epileptic but cured as a result of St Bernard's prayers.[47] It took only two years to put up the first buildings of Igny and the Church was dedicated in 1130.[48] Five years later the community had expanded enough to found Signy, soon to be the home of William of St Thierry.[49]

Soon after this Humbert thought he had done as much as could be expected of him and wanted to return to the ranks at Clairvaux. Bernard would have none of it. Humbert may have thought that the indefinite absence of his Father Abbot in Italy gave him a reasonable opportunity, and back to Clairvaux he went. Bernard did not by any means share Humbert's view of the situation and wrote a letter threatening the abbot of Igny with excommunication, to say nothing of eternal punishment in hell.[50] However, Humbert got his way and Igny had to elect a new abbot. The runaway lived for

---

44. *Ibid.*, Letter 90:2; 222; James trans., Letter 93, p. 139.
45. Janauschek, p. 14.
46. EM, Dist. 3, ch. 4, p. 155:18ff. Péchenard, *Hist. de l'Abbaye d'Igny*, p. 35ff.
47. *Vita prima S Bernardi*, bk. 1, n. 48; PL 185:254. However, this passage was omitted from the second recension of the Life.
48. Péchenard, *ibid.*, p. 21f.
49. *Ibid.*, p. 45, Janauschek, pp. 33, 34.
50. St Bernard, Letter 141, PL 182:296; James trans., Letter 150, pp. 218f.

another ten years and was completely reconciled with his superior. His praises were eloquently spoken by the abbot of Clairvaux in a sermon specially devoted to this purpose.[51] When St Bernard came to die Humbert was seen in a vision coming to meet him.[52]

So Guerric the monk of Clairvaux became the second abbot of Igny in 1138.[53] There is a passage in the *Vita Hugonis* which suggests that Bernard influenced the choice considerably: "It was Bernard who had brought Guerric to the monastic life and Bernard favored his election as abbot. He knew no man living more holy than Guerric and so declared him the one candidate for office. Furnishing the new abbot with this testimonial he installed him in his stewardship at Igny."[54]

But this need not make us think that Guerric was imposed on the community. The monks of twelve years' standing would of course have known him at Clairvaux. Guerric himself says that the community chose him: " 'I am no physician and in my house there is no bread.' That is why I said from the start: 'Do not make me your leader.' It is not right for one to rule who cannot be of service. And how can he be of service who is not a physician and in whose house there is no bread? He has neither the art of healing souls nor learning to feed them with? I told you this, but you would not listen. You made me your superior."[55]

Guerric could have found better reasons for declining office than this alleged incapacity as a spiritual director. He may indeed have been about sixty years old, but then his long experience both before and after entry into Clairvaux must have been thought a valuable asset. However, it goes against the grain for such a man to have to urge others to live a life which he cannot live himself. His ill-health

---

51. *Id., In obiti domini Humberti*: PL 183:513-18.

52. *Vita prima S. Bern.*, bk. 5, n. 18, PL 185:362.

53. So A. Manrique, *Annales*, vol. 1, year 1138, ch. 4, n. 5. The date 1144 is given in the *Acta Sanctorum*, Oct. X. III *De B. Petro Monocolo* I, n. 4., ed. 1883, p. 54f. This date is discussed by Gatterer, p. 44, note 47, and by de Wilde, p. 17, n. 1.

54. VH, n. 16, col. 1723.

55. Ser. 36:1.

by now incapacitated him for the common life of the community and especially for manual work. In the sermon just quoted he goes on: "If I could not escape the burden, I had to look for a remedy. I listened to the advice of the Wise Man: 'Have they made you a ruler? Be among them as one of them.' But I couldn't even do this. Lack of wisdom forbids me being put over others; lack of health prevents me being one among them. I have not the depth of soul for ministering the word, nor the strength of body for giving good example."[56]

There is every indication that Igny flourished under Guerric. Vocations were plentiful and so were benefactors. Much land and money was given to the monastery during the first twenty years of its existence and several properties, presumably with granges, were established in the neighborhood.[57] In 1148 the second daughter-house was founded, Valroy in the diocese of Rheims.[58] It was none of this that was to make the abbot's name known to posterity, but the spiritual teaching committed to writing in his sermons. The *Exordium Magnum* gives an account of his death, chiefly in connection with some qualms of conscience over this writing.[59] He seems to have died on 19th August 1157.[60] More than six hundred years later his remains were taken into a new church and buried before the high altar. Then came the storm of the French Revolution. When the monastery had been restored in 1876 the body was exhumed and identified. The celebration of his feast on August 19th has been authorized for the monastery of Igny and for the diocese of Rheims.[61]

Preacher or writer

There is little hope of our finding anything written by Guerric other than the fifty-four sermons, all of them but the last assigned to

56. Ibid. Cf. EM, p. 164:29f.
57. Péchenard, *Hist. de l'Abbaye d'Igny*, pp. 76–80.
58. Janauschek, p. 117; Péchenard, *ibid.*, pp. 70f.
59. EM, Dist. 3, ch. 9; pp. 165f. See below, 75.
60. Beller, p. 323; de Wilde, p. 19, n. 2.   61. Beller, p. 331.

seasons and feasts of the year.⁶² Now we have to ask whether Guerric really preached these sermons and whether we have any means of knowing what he said as a preacher.

It was certainly part of his duty as abbot to preach to his community.⁶³ True enough the words of the *Exordium Magnum* in the story of a deathbed repentance suggest a literary composition meant to serve a spiritual purpose: "He remembered the book of sermons which he had compiled.... There is that book of sermons which I dictated at your request. I had the rashness and presumption to publish it without permission from the General Chapter."⁶⁴ However, if we are to use the authority of the *Exordium Magnum* at all, we have to take another sentence into account: "We have a clear and abiding testimony to the charm and richness of his doctrine. It is found in those sermons of his which he preached in the community chapter on the great feasts, sermons outstanding for their balance and spiritual value. The precentor of that monastery has preserved them in writing."⁶⁵

The sermons themselves are sometimes designed to give the impression that they are delivered orally. All the beginning of the Rogation sermon supposes that Guerric is simply doing his duty as abbot in speaking to the community. The last of the three on Sts Peter and Paul is said to be given on the day after the second, because a text of Scripture has not been adequately explained. The second for Our Lady's Birthday speaks of the one given the year before. The two do in fact link up.

Yet these indications have little value. We know that in the twelfth century the sermon was a *genre littéraire*, to which any work destined for publication might belong.⁶⁶ If this form was chosen it

---

62. It is unlikely that Guerric wrote the piece entitled *De Languore Animae Amantis* published by de Wilde (*op. cit.*, pp. 187-196). We have published this again in the light of further manuscript evidence. *Cîteaux*, 16 (1965), pp. 114-135.
63. This is supposed throughout. 64. EM, p. 166:3-9.
65. *Ibid.*, p. 164:26-20.
66. Gatterer failed to realize this throughout his study. In fact no one at that time seems to have grasped the real nature of the sermon's literary form. In J. Leclercq, *Receuil d'études*, II, see "Les sermons sur les cantiques ont-ils été prononcés?" pp. 193ff.

was part of literary artifice to refer to the circumstances and reactions of an imaginary audience.[67]

Guerric's sermons differ from St Bernard's and from St Aelred's in that, as we have them in their entirety, they could have been spoken to monks in chapter. Apart from some references to "these degenerate days" which are the commonplace of all preachers[68] we do not find those terrible denunciations of corruption in high places or excursions into political affrays which occur in the sermons of Bernard and Aelred.[69] Everything in Guerric is suitable for the edification of a monastic community. We cannot say the same of Bernard, and this is one reason for thinking that his sermons are a form of publication.[70]

Guerric may be contrasted with the same two abbots in another way. We have considerable evidence that Bernard revised and polished his text over a course of years,[71] and recent research has shown that Aelred did much the same.[72] Now we have found no such evidence for Guerric. The manuscripts show three recensions. These are quite clearly distinguished; but, with a single exception

---

67. Ser. 33:1; 46:1.

68. Ser. 5:2. Cf. *infra*, notes 91–95.

69. St Bernard, *Sermons on the Song of Songs*, 10:3; 23:2, 12; 33:14–16; 46:2; ed. J. Leclercq, H. Rochais, C. H. Talbot, I, pp. 49–50, 139–40, 146, 243–5; II, pp. 56–57: trans. K. Walsh, Cistercian Fathers, 4 and 7. St Aelred, *On the Feast of SS Peter and Paul*; ed C. H. Talbot, *Sermones inediti*, p. 129; De Oneribus, 11, PL 195:402f.

70. An outstanding example in St Bernard is furnished by the two sermons on the Song of Songs, 65, 66 (ed. Leclercq, *et al.*, II, p. 172–88) directed against the heretics of Cologne at the request of Evervin, Provost of Steinfeld. J. Leclercq, *Recueil d'études*, II, pp. 196f.

71. Demonstrated, *ibid.*, "Les étapes de la rédaction," pp. 213–44. This is confirmed by the findings of J. Leclercq and H. Rochais in "La tradition des sermons liturgiques de Saint Bernard," *Scriptorium*, 15 (1961), pp. 240–84. This article of 1961 is more recent than any of those reprinted in the *Recueil* published in 1962.

72. Compare with *On the Feast of SS Peter and Paul* (above note 69) the sermon published by Aelred Squire in *Cîteaux*, 11 (1960) pp. 104–110. See also Squire's article, "The literary evidence for the preaching of Aelred of Rievaulx," *ibid.*, pp. 165–77.

Introduction

the variants which distinguish them are slight.[73] The first recension alone is likely to have come from Guerric's own hand. Even if there is a series of variants within the first recension, it is by no means clear that they point to a revision made by Guerric himself.[74] In fact the idea that the sermons are a literary composition elaborated over a long period of time is not supported by any manuscript evidence.

If anyone wished to maintain that these were "live" sermons, he might argue that they correspond fairly closely to the days on which sermons had to be preached in chapter according to the Cistercian usages of the time.[75] All such days are represented except the feast of the dedication of the church. This omission is difficult to explain, since the Church at Igny had been dedicated eight years before Guerric's coming. Besides the sermons prescribed in the Usages we have two for Lent and one for the Rogation.

An argument on the other side is that the sermons, as we have them, are a work of finished literary elegance. We tell ourselves that Guerric could well have said those things to his community; but he could not have given them out in chapter just like that. We expect

---

73. The exception is as follows: *Alia tamen ratione sed tamen ineffabili et incomparabili felicitate princeps ille sedens in porta virginalis uteri panem Verbi coram Domino comedebat* (Ser. 28:6). This is an emended text and it is almost certain that the emendation was made after Guerric's lifetime. All the manuscripts of the first recension read: *Alia tamen ratione sed tamen ineffabili beatitudine et incomparabili felicitate verbo pascebatur anima illa, verbo ipsi in persona coniuncta, et incomparabili felicitate princeps ille sedens in porta virginalis uteri panem Verbi coram Domino comedebat*. This is not the place to discuss the theological question involved.

74. The Mss. of the earliest recension are: Paris, Bibl. nat. latin 18169, ff. 1–136, also 5317, ff. 96–187 (from Saint-Martin-des-Champs and Bonport respectively); Brussels, Bibl. roy II, 977, ff. lv–82 (from St-Ghislain). There is also Lille 98, ff. 1–145ᵛ (from Loos). The last belongs to the first recension but shows a number of variants. It could possibly represent an original unrevised text. We may discuss more fully elsewhere the 9 manuscripts, grouping three recensions, on which the coming edition is to be based. Meanwhile Dom Jean Leclercq has given some account of all manuscripts of Guerric which he knows to exist: *Recueil d'etudes, I*, "La collection des sermons de Guerric d'Igny," pp. 159ff.

75. *Die Ecclesiastica Officia Cisterciensis Ordinis des Cod. 1711 von Trient*, ch. (XC) LXVII; ed. Bruno Griesser, *Anal. S.O.C.*, 12 (1956), p. 230.

that, if a preacher is to hold his audience, his utterances must have a certain spontaneity. If not the ideas, at least the details of the expression must be impromptu. If we find balance, alliteration and rhythm studied to perfection, then we have not the real thing. But there is an obvious danger here of projecting our ideas and preferences of the twentieth century back into the twelfth.

We must suppose that Guerric spoke to his community on most of the days for which we have his sermons, if not on all of them. Now if, at the same time, he produced a corpus of sermons which was a finished literary composition, we should expect these to correspond notably, perhaps even in substance, with what he had spoken aloud. The compiler of the *Exordium Magnum* was near enough to Guerric's time to know what was normal procedure. We have in fact the "book of sermons which I dictated at your request."[76] This means that the book was written on wax tablets by a secretary at the author's dictation. When the work had been thoroughly corrected it was transferred on to parchment (*quaternuli*).[77] These were not bound together so long as it was thought that further correction might be necessary.[78] Yet there are reasons to think that the finished work differed but little from what the abbot had said in the Chapter House. So thought Conrad of Eberbach, for it is hardly possible that he meant something quite different by the words: "those sermons of his which he preached in the community chapter on the principal feasts, preserved in writing by the precentor of that monastery."[79]

It is not often that sermons of this kind can be dated. There are at best two probable indications in Guerric's collection. At the beginning of the third sermon for SS Peter and Paul the preacher hesitates to comment on the words "until the day give out its breath and the shadows lengthen."[80] He gives as one reason that St Bernard—"our master, the Holy Ghost's interpreter"—has given the hope that he will expound them in the course of his sermons on the Song of

76. EM, p. 166–7f. 77. *Ibid.*, 11.
78 J. Leclercq, *op. cit.*, p. 163 and note 1.
79. EM, p. 164:27f. 80. Ser. 46:1.

Introduction   xxiii

Songs. Now the Abbot of Clairvaux did in fact deal with this text in his twenty-second sermon, which should probably be dated before the discussion of Gilbert Porreta's Trinitarian doctrine in 1148, but soon after the journey to Toulouse in 1145.[81] So Guerric seems to have written his third sermon on SS Peter and Paul—*Donec aspiret dies . . . Erratis, fratres, in me*—before this time. One objection can be raised against this argument, but it does not seem decisive. Guerric is concerned with the text, quoted at the end of his previous sermon, as it is found in *Song of Songs*, 4:6. Bernard indeed did comment on the exact words, but took them from 2:17.

There is another possible chronological indication in the Rogation sermon. Guerric has several interpretations of the three loaves.[82] When he speaks of "the heretic's empty daring," which has gone so badly astray, he may be speaking of Abelard; but the drift of the whole passage, confined as it is to the mystery of the Trinity,[83] suggests rather Gilbert Porreta. If in fact he has Gilbert in mind, then the sermon should be dated after the Council of Rheims in 1148.[84]

Style

Guerric as an artist in words has recourse to most of the tricks in vogue among his contemporaries, such as alliterations and inversions. They are rarely if ever carried so far as to disgust the reader. The play upon words *prosperare, prosper, prospera, prosperum, prosperabitur, prosperabuntur*, in the second sermon for Advent[85] reveals him in his most frivolous mood. He yields nothing to St Bernard or any other in his control of scriptural language. If there

---

81. Ed. Leclercq, *et al.*, II, pp. 225ff. C. H. Talbot, "The archetypes of Saint Bernard's sermons Super Cantica," *Scriptorium*, 8 (1954), p. 221 and note 8. Cfr. J. Leclercq, *Recueil d'études*, II, pp. 241f.
82. Ser. 36:3f.
83. *Ibid.*, n. 3.
84. Guerric is likely to have made St Bernard's view of Gilbert's teaching his own. See St Bernard, *Sermon Eighty on the Song of Songs*, nn. 5ff., ed. Leclercq, *et. al.*, II, p. 280–2.
85. Ser. 2:2.

is a text or a phrase in the Bible which suits his purpose just for the moment, it will not fail to come to his pen.

Guerric is versatile enough to pass from his usual calm doctrinal meditation to something quite dramatic, as for instance a complaint made by the suffering Christ to his Father with the consoling promise given in return.[86] The sermon on the Prodigal Son is a literary masterpiece with its vivid description of his welcome home and then the lengthy exhortation to the penitent sinner whom he represents.[87] In his second sermon for the Purification, Simeon is made to talk to the Child in his arms with a tenderness which continues to move us without ever becoming insipid.[88] Hearts which have been burdened with the penance of Lent and the sorrow of Good Friday—"our bones have been humbled by the penance and mourning of Lent, more indeed by the sorrows of his passion"—clamor with their burning desire for the consolation of the risen Christ on Easter morning.[89] Of all the sermons the one in which the descriptive and dramatic art appears to best advantage is the second on the Assumption of Our Lady; so much so that the author thinks it necessary in his introductory words to excuse the style of treatment which he has chosen. Mary, at the point of death, languishes with love, saying that she cannot be consoled until her Jesus "kiss me with the kiss of his mouth." She is surrounded by angels who have come to comfort her. All that they can do is to be her faithful messengers and tell him, however well he knows it already, that she is languishing from love.[90]

But these passages are highlights. There is little or nothing of the thunder and lightning which may occasionally rumble and flash from St Bernard. It is true that Guerric can use irony. When he has

86. Ser. 31:3f.

87. Ser. 21:2ff. It may be of interest to contrast this with a passage from John of Fécamp on the Prodigal Son: *Lessus poenitentiae*; in J. Leclercq and J. P. Bonnes, *Un maître de la vie spirituelle au XIIe siècle: Jean de Fécamp*, pp. 224-26, stanzas 29-47. John gives the penitent's aspirations all in the first person, with but little interpretation of detail. There is a difference of literary form here. Both are influenced by St Augustine. Guerric is nearer to his master's sermon; John to his soliloquy.

88. Ser. 16:3.   89. Ser. 33:1.   90. Ser. 48.

Introduction xxv

described the lifelong austerity of the Baptist he addresses those who would make the spiritual life easy: "But now thanks be to God for giving us—if in fact he has—victory without a battle, pardon without repentance, justification without good works, holiness without toil, an abundance of the delights of the flesh and the spirit at the same time." He can be severe, as in the later parts of these third and fourth sermons on St John the Baptist.[91] He denounces sin or the purely nominal Christianity of the world outside the monastery.[92] In the first sermon for Advent there is a terrifying list of the stages of sin, beginning with contempt for God's messengers, and ending thus: "be taken by sudden death; be beaten in eternal damnation."[93]

Yet in spite of this, what runs throughout Guerric's sermons is a restraint all the more impressive for its tenderness and a leniency arising out of a heartfelt concern for his brethren's spiritual good. Several times the tone of condemnation is followed by that of apology. In the second Easter sermon he has spoken at some length of resistance to grace, then adds: "But in you, brethren, we look with confidence for something better and more conducive to your salvation."[94] In the last Purification sermon he stresses the need of purification in this life, but goes on: "Brethren, you too have sinned; but you have been washed clean."[95] Moreover, the style is so elegant without ever becoming unduly involved or obscure, that we may think Conrad of Eberbach chose his epithets well: *luculentissimi— discretissimi—vere spiritales*.[96]

---

91. Ser. 43:3; 42:5f; 43:4.
92. Ser. 14:2.
93. Ser. 1:3.
94. Heb 6:9; Ser. 34:5. Cf. 38:2, 5.
95. Ser. 19:5. This is really Guerric's fifth sermon for the Purification. Purif. 5 as given in PL 185:79–89 (*Adorna...Ad nos, fratres*) is the single sermon in this collection which is spurious. It is found in none of the manuscripts used for the critical edition. The question has been discussed by J. Leclercq, *Recueil d'études*, I, pp. 167–70.
96. EM, p. 164:26. Cf. André Fracheboud, "Le charme personnel du Bx Guerric," *Collectanea O.C.R.*, 19 (1957), pp. 223–8.

Personality

It is difficult to know from a man's writings what he was like to meet and live with. Guerric regularly protests his own incapacity[97] and even directs his criticisms of contemporary monastic life against himself.[98] This is, of course, the kind of convention which is most frequent in introductory passages, and it is difficult to believe that anyone would take it by itself as a guarantee of true humility.[99] What is more compelling is the restraint and balance of judgment which appear on every page. One can hardly think that the sermons were written by a man who had it in him to be unbalanced or aggressive. Certainly they come from someone who grasped thoroughly the nature and purpose of the monastic life, who surveyed and presumably himself traveled the way to union with God.

It has just been seen that Guerric's leniency led him to testify to the high degree of his brethren's virtue. They needed no correction from him. It would of course be the height of credulity to accept these utterances as historical testimonies to the level of monastic observance at Igny.[100] A monk of any experience, hearing these commendations, would immediately ask himself for which member of the community the abbot had intended the reproofs which had gone before. Igny was a large community under Guerric and was nearly thirty years old at the time of his death. Applicants to the novitiate were not subjected to so searching a scrutiny as is found

97. Sers. 36:1; 39:4; 40:1; 46:1.
98. Ser. 14:2f.
99. Yet this is what Gatterer did: pp. 86–87. De Wilde had to consider the graces with which Guerric might have been favored in prayer. He was far more realistic and cautious in his understanding of Guerric's humble disclaimers expressed in the first person: pp. 155–6. Cfr. A. Fracheboud, *art. cit.*, 228–32.
100. Thus in Ser. 24:6 Guerric inveighs against ill-feeling among brethren. Then he continues: "Why do I say this... Because I suspect such evil... Not because there is anything like this among you; rather as a precaution lest there ever should be." Gatterer (p. 47 and note 60), perhaps with an entire lack of sense of humor, accepted this as an historical testimony to prevailing charity among the brethren.

Introduction xxvii

necessary in our own day. Human nature would not be in a fallen state if a community under such circumstances consisted of nothing but saints. Yet the presumption is that the level of spirituality and of observance at Igny was high. The abbot, under God, is the making of his community. There was the far-reaching influence of Bernard upon all his monastic filiations; besides, at the time of Guerric's death, there were senior monks at Igny who could remember Bernard's rule at Clairvaux itself. Others had entered Igny under Humbert, the more junior had been under Guerric alone. The ideals of primitive Cîteaux had not had time to fade. It was still the Golden Age of the Cistercian Order.

After reflecting in this way upon Guerric and his influence, we find a charming bathos in the story of the deathbed repentance, as it is told in the *Exordium Magnum*.[101]

The General Chapter had issued this decree: "On the lawfulness of dictating new books. No abbot, monk or novice shall be allowed to compile new books unless permission has been given for a particular case in the abbots' General Chapter."[102] We have no evidence for the existence of this decree before a collection of 1151, when most of Guerric's sermons may have been committed to writing; but it is likely that it was known earlier. Neighboring abbots, including Bernard himself, by this time four years dead, must have known something of Guerric's literary activities, but no complaint had ever been made. The story makes it clear that the abbot's conscience had never been troubled about his sermons before this time. But he would not be satisfied until the brethren had brought his book of sermons and burnt it. He was an old man and may perhaps have been too much out of touch with things to know that there were other copies.[103] In his dying condition it is unlikely that he could see what was being burnt. Whatever exactly happened—and of course the story may have been made up to

---

101. EM, Dist. 3, ch. 9.
102. *Instituta generalis capituli* according to Ms. Laibach 31, ed. Canice Noschitzka soc. *Anal. S.O.C.*, 6 (1950), p. 34.
103. EM, *loc. cit.: in aliis quaternulis*. The phrase does not mean "in four other manuscripts" as has been thought by Gatterer and others.

excuse the existence of the sermons for a later generation—we still have Guerric's work. "This was how God arranged things for our good. He would not have his Holy Church, least of all the Cistercian Order, deprived of the grace which was to come to it from such a wealth of learning."[104]

DOCTRINE

It is time to introduce Guerric's doctrine as it bears upon the life of union with God. Most of this can be presented only in a summary form, with footnotes designed for readers who may care to verify statements or to trace antecedents. We will develop at length only one characteristic idea: the prominent theme of *Enlightenment*. Something will be said at greater length with a view to placing it in a traditional theology of light.

Scripture

Guerric does not undertake a formal commentary on Scripture. His aim is to preach a sermon proper for the day and in practice he draws upon texts found in the day's liturgy. Even so, he says, it is beyond him to explain the Scriptures or even worthily to recall the explanations given by others.[105]

The "law of the Lord" is a garden. We eat its old fruit, well stored, or pluck the new, according as we draw upon the prophets or upon the apostles and evangelists.[106] Our reading will not help us unless it is assiduous and persevering.[107] It is in the midst of silence that the Almighty Word will come down from his royal throne,[108] and the waters of Siloe which flow in silence will make fruitful a soul that is at peace.[109] The model of this silence is the Word made flesh, silent in the womb of Mary, the Prince himself sitting in the

---

104. Ibid.   105. Ser. 46:3.   106. Ser. 54:2.
107. Ser. 22:5.   108. Ibid., Ser. 4:2. Cf. Ser. 17:2.   109. Ser. 22:5.

Introduction

eastern gate and eating the bread of the Word before the Lord.[110] When God comes to our souls—that "middle advent" which can take place here and now—the place of Scripture which was dry and sterile can suddenly yield a rich harvest.[111] The brothers may remember that even while they persevered in their manual labor, Jesus sometimes came and joined himself to them and opened the Scriptures, so that they understood verses which had been obscure.[112]

Following Origen, the senses of Scripture, suggested by the three loaves of the Rogation sermon,[113] are the historical, allegorical and moral.[114] But we have here also the so-called anagogic sense, pointing to a fulfillment.[115] In fact there is a double *anagogia*, one mystical, the other eschatological. Christ, by his resurrection, effects in us the first resurrection, by which the soul rises from the death of sin; and this in its turn is both the type and cause of the second resurrection by which the body is to be freed from corruption.[116]

If Scripture is historical or allegorical, telling us what has been done for our salvation, and also moral, telling us what we must imitate in our own lives, there is no artificial transition from one sense to another. The moral sense of Scripture is a proper and necessary "interiorization."[117] "What is a mystery for your redemption is also an example for your imitation."[118] What Dom Déchanet has said of William of St Thierry and his contemporaries is very true of Guerric. "However free, the twelfth-century moral

110. Ser. 28:5f. H. De Lubac, *Exégèse médiévale*, vol. I (Paris: Aubier, 1959), p. 599 and note 3. Thomas Merton, *The Christmas Sermons of Bl. Guerric of Igny* (Trappist, Ky.: Gethsemani, 1959), pp. 23f.

111. Ser. 4:1; cf. 3:4.

112. Ser. 35:4; cf. 33:2.

113. Ser. 36:4.

114. Origen, texts discussed by De Lubac, *Exégèse*, I, pp. 198–207.

115. John Cassian, *Conferences*, 14, ch. 8; *Sources Chrétiennes*, 54, pp. 189ff.; trans. E. Gibson in *The Nicene and Post-Nicene Fathers*, Series 2, vol. 11, pp. 437f.

116. Ser. 34:1. Cf. 19:5. See De Lubac, *Exégèse*, I, pp. 624f.

117. De Lubac, I, p. 555 and note 3; cf. pp. 586–591.

118. Ser. 27:4. Cf. 18:1.

interpretation of Scripture rests solidly upon dogma and an author such as William is much too traditional to attempt to separate the story of his mystical life from the Christian mystery."[119]

Mystery and sacrament

Allegorical sense, or mystical, is "the sense which is related to the mystery which is the single reality, at first hidden in God, then revealed to men as it came into being in Jesus Christ."[120] The heart of this mystery or sacrament,[121] is the sign once offered to Achaz and now given to us: Christ conceived of a Virgin.[122] He who is born in eternity for the blessedness of the angels, is born in time not for them but for our renewal.[123] The ancient of days has become a little child. Ancient because he is the Word, eternal and incomprehensible,[124] it is said of him now: "An abbreviated word, yet in such a way that in it every word which makes for salvation is summed up."[125] He is the Word who in eternity has needed no other nourishment than the Word; now he is the Prince sitting in the gate of the Virgin's womb, eating the bread of the Word before the Lord "in another way yet with unspeakable beatitude."[126] Guerric says this of him as man; but for fear that the "in another way" should suggest that he is less than the Father, someone has interpolated as subject "that soul which was united to the Person of the Word."

119. J. M. Déchanet in the introduction to William of St Thierry, *Exposition on the Song of Songs*, in *The Works of William of St Thierry*, vol. 2, Cistercian Fathers Series, 6, p. XIV.

120. De Lubac, *Exégèse*, 1, p. 397. See also Odo Brooke, "Faith and Mystical Experience in William of St Thierry, *Downside Review*, 82 (1964), p. 99.

121. Ser. 14:2.

122. Ser. 28:1-4.

123. Ser. 6:1; 8:1. Merton, *op. cit.*, pp. 4-7.

124. Ser. 6:1.

125. Is 10:22f.; Rom 9:28. Ser. 10:3. Cf. 16:5; St Aelred, *When Jesus Was Twelve*, n. 13; *Sources Chrétiennes* 60, p. 76; trans. Theodore Berkeley in *The Works of St Aelred*, vol. 1, *Treatises*, Cistercian Fathers Series, 2. See De Lubac, *Exégèse*, 2, pp. 188-197.

126. Ser. 28:6.

Introduction xxxi

Just as Christ was born for our renewal, so he was crucified that the man of sin in us might be crucified. "He crucified the world to Paul and Paul to the world."[127] "For our Redeemer chose this way of suffering to work out our salvation and give it its form, to the end that the mystery of redemption should provide a pattern of justification."[128] His resurrection too is a cause and type of what happens to us, first in soul, then in body: "Christ both brings about for us the first resurrection by the mystery of his own resurrection and by the example of that same resurrection of his will bring about for us the second."[129] He has ascended above the heavens; if we will allow him he will spread his wings like an eagle and carry us upon his shoulders.[130]

Form

Any idea that Christ's death and resurrection may be mere examples of what is to happen to us is excluded by the recurrence of the verb "to bring about." Whether "to form," set beside it, means anything other than exemplary causality, must be determined from its use elsewhere. In fact, *forma, formare, informare* are key-words for Guerric, suggested sometimes by the Pauline text: "My little children, with whom I am again in travail until Christ be formed in you."[131]

Mary, in the second sermon for her birthday, is said to have known her Son, first in the form in which she gave birth to him. This was far removed from knowing him in the form in which he is begotten by the Father.[132] Between the form of flesh and the form of the Word there is another, a spiritual form shown in his flesh: "the form, that is to say, of the life he lived in his body in order to convey his message to those who were to believe in him."[133] We

127. Ser. 30:2.   128. *Ibid.*, n. 5.   129. Ser. 34:1; cf. 35:1.
130. Ser. 37:4–5. On the sanctifying power of the mysteries of Christ read *de Wilde*, pp. 70–94: ch. 3, "De mysteriis Christi."
131. Gal 4:19. Ser. 27:5; 28:7; 47:2, 3.
132. Ser. 52:1.   133. *Ibid.*

read soon afterwards that this middle form is for our example.[134] But something is to be effected in us according to the example; and for this the corresponding verb *formare* is used: Christ is to be formed in us.[135]

It has been evident that the mysteries of the life of Christ in his Birth, Passion, Resurrection and Ascension, are examples for us, but much more. The question must arise: how much Guerric may mean when he says of Christ's life as a whole that it is a form according to which Christ is to be formed in us.

The source of the terminology is undoubtedly St Paul's word to the Philippians: "though he was in the form of God ... he took the form of a servant."[136] It does not directly bear on our question whether the use of the Greek *morphe* was influenced by Platonic philosophy. There is a phrase in the *Republic* where it is asked whether the Supreme Being can change himself and appear in one form and another. The answer is given as negative.[137] The passage of Philippians might almost have been designed as the true and adequate answer to the question.

Even if St Paul is Guerric's source, we need to know further what *forma* could have meant for Guerric. Its meaning in the Latin of the West has been determined by St Augustine more than by anyone else. To understand *forma* in St Augustine we must look to Plotinus and ultimately to Plato.

This is not the place to develop such an argument at any length. In a word, Plato's theory of ideas reduces all causality to formal.[138]

---

134. *Ibid.* 135. *Ibid.* 136. Phil 2:6f.
137. Plato, *Republic*, 2, 380Df.; trans. P. Shorey (Loeb Classical Library), vol. 1. (New York: Putnam, 1930), p. 189: "Do you think that God is a wizard and capable of manifesting himself by design, now in one aspect, now in another, at one time changing and altering his shape in many transformations and at another deceiving us and causing us to believe such things about him; or that he is simple and less likely than anything else to depart from his own form?"
138. The places of course are well known: *Euthyphro*, 6; trans. H. Fowler, *Plato* (Loeb Classical Library), vol. 1 (New York: Macmillan, 1914), pp. 21f.; *Phaedo*, 100, leading up to the proof of the immortality of the soul at 105e; trans. *id.*, pp. 343ff.; *Republic*, 6 508B–509B; trans. *op. cit.*, vol. 2, pp. 101ff.;

Introduction xxxiii

For the most part Plotinus says little to modify the Platonic system,[139] but we are bound ultimately to conclude that he adds both efficient and final causality to formal.[140] The result is that for St Augustine the words *forma* and *formare* sum up all the divine causality.[141] How familiar this was to the Middle Ages can be seen in writers like John of Fécamp and occasionally in St Bernard.,[142] It is true that Guerric uses the words *forma* and *exemplum*, which of their nature need mean no more than a model to which one must conform. Yet they are used in such a tradition and context that they

and finally the metaphor of the cave-dwellers in *Republic*, 7, 514a–517a; trans., *ibid.*, pp. 119ff. It must be recognized that whether in Plato or Plotinus, the word is not *morphe*, as in St Paul's passage to the Philippians, but *eidos* or *idea*.

139. See for instance Plotinus, *Ennead*, 6, 5, 6; trans. S. Mackenna and B. S. Page, *On the One and Good, being the Treatise of the Sixth Ennead* (London: Medici Society, 1930).

140. *Ennead*, 1, 8, 2; trans., A.Armstrong, *Plotinus* (Loeb Classical Library), vol. 1 (Cambridge, Mass.: Harvard University, 1966), pp. 281ff. See W. R. Inge, *The Philosophy of Plotinus*, vol. 2 (1941), pp. 118–122.

141. St Augustine, Sermon 117, *On the words of the Gospel of St John: In principio erat Verbum:* PL 38:662f. *The Problem of Free Choice*, bk. 2, nn. 44f.; PL 32:1264f.; trans. M. Pontifex (Ancient Christian Writers, 22), (Westminster, Maryland: Newman, 1955), pp. 125ff. The same idea influences his commentary on 2 Cor 3:18 found in *On the Trinity*, bk. 15, n. 14; PL 42:1068: trans. A. Haddan, *Basic Writings of St Augustine*, ed. Oates (New York: Random House, 1948), vol. 2, pp. 848ff. Rudolf Eucken undoubtedly exaggerated when he said that Plotinus had influenced Christian theology more than any other thinker; so did W. R. Inge, even when he added the qualifying phrase "since St Paul"; but their remarks contain a large element of truth, which underlines the argument briefly sketched here. See Inge, *op. cit.*, vol. 1, p. 12.

142. John of Fécamp, *Confessio theologica*, 1, 132–137; ed. J. Leclercq and J. P. Bonnes, *Un maître de la vie spirituelle au XII siècle: Jean de Fécamp* (1946), p. 114. For St Bernard see M. Standaert, "La doctrine de l'image chez Saint Bernard," *Univ. cathol. Lovan.*, *Sylloge excerptorum e dissertationibus ad gradum doctoris...*, vol. 14, section 4 (1947), pp. 114–118. Fr Standaert studies texts of St Bernard only, taking no account of tradition established by St Augustine, to say nothing of Plotinus and Plato. Yet his conclusion is in line with that given above. See the use of *forma*, etc., exemplified in St Augustine, St Bernard, William of St Thierry and Isaac of Stella: André Fracheboud, "L'influence de S. Augustin sur le Cistércien Isaac de l'Étoile." *Collectanea O.C.R.*, 11 (1949), p. 275 and note 4.

c

connote and suggest a more far-reaching causality. It is reasonable to think that for Guerric all the actions of Christ are efficacious by virtue of their union with the principal events of his life; that like them they are sacraments or mysteries which are able to effect in us what they signify.[143]

Mary's work in us

Guerric is likely to have been familiar with the words addressed to Mary in a sermon known under the name of St Augustine: "If I call you the form of God, you are worthy of it."[144] Guerric himself says of her: "Mary consummated the mystery. She herself like the Church of which she is the type (*forma*) is the mother of all who are reborn to life."[145] Whatever the causality indicated by the word *forma* in the passage already studied, and further expressed by the words *formare*, *informare*, it is communicated by Christ to Mary. The teaching on the three forms is found in the Second Sermon for the birthday of Our Lady. We read that it is her desire to form her Only-Begotten Son in all those who are sons of God by adoption: "Although they have been brought to birth by the Word of Truth, nevertheless she brings them forth every day by desire and loyal care until they reach the stature of the perfect man, the maturity of her Son, whom she bore and brought forth once and for all."[146]

The first sermon for the same feast begins with the classical contrast between Mary and Eve. The paragraph is indebted to yet

143. De Wilde, using an argument of a different kind and more fully developed, seems to have arrived at virtually the same conclusion: ". . . a spiritual form that is more than merely exemplary, truly something more, namely a certain active principle by which the soul is informed."—*op. cit.*, p. 37. For all its Lutheran connotations, it is yet impossible here not to recall Dietrich Bonhoeffer's striking meditation on the form of Christ in us: *Ethics* (London: SCM, 1960), pp. 17-23, 162.

144. Pseudo-Augustine (Ambrose Autpert?), Sermon, *Adest . . . dies valde venerabilis*, for the Feast of the Assumption of the Blessed Virgin Mary, n. 5; PL 39:2131.

145. Ser. 47:2.   146. Ser. 52:3.

another sermon attributed to St Augustine, which was read in the Office of the day, in which the theme of the second Eve is developed.[147] Guerric hails Mary as the new mother who has brought new life to those who have grown old in sin.[148] Elsewhere he calls Eve the "mother of prevarication" and Mary the "mother of redemption."[149] The title given to Eve, "mother of all the living," belongs by right to Mary.[150] We are told exactly why, "she is in fact the mother of the Life by which everyone lives, and when she brought it forth from herself she in some way brought to rebirth all those who were to live by that life. One was born, but we were all reborn, since in that seed which holds the power of rebirth we were all already then in him."[151] St Paul continually gave birth to his sons, until Christ should be formed in them, by preaching the word of truth. Mary does the same, in a way that is more sublime, and brings her nearer to God, by giving birth to the Word himself.[152]

This idea of Mary regenerating us by giving birth to Christ could give rise to much speculation. It is enough for us to notice what is explicit in Guerric. We come back to the sermon on the three forms of Christ. St Bernard restricted Mary's direct activity in our regard to her mediatory intercession.[153] Guerric, having spoken so clearly of her spiritual motherhood,[154] says that she desires to form her Only-Begotten in us and gives birth to us day by day.[155] To say

147. Pseudo-Augustine, Sermon, *Adest . . . optatus dies*, for the Annunciation of the Blessed Virgin Mary, nn. 1f.; PL 39:2105.

148. Ser. 51:1.   149. Ser. 18:1.

150. Ser. 47:2.   151. Ibid.

152. *Ibid.*, n. 3. De Wilde, pp. 95–100. Precise limits are set to the meaning of Mary's spiritual maternity in Guerric's teaching by Claude Bodard, "Le Christ, Marie et l'Église dans la prédication du Bx Guerric de l'Igny," *Collectanea O.C.R.*, 19 (1957), pp. 284–288.

153. Taught especially in his Sermon of the Nativity of the Blessed Virgin Mary, *De Aquaeductu*; PL 183:437ff. See H. Barré, "Saint Bernard, docteur marial," *Analecta S.O.C.*, 9 (1953), vol. 2, pp. 112–113.

154. Ser. 51:1.

155. Ser. 52:3. De Wilde wrote at length on Mary's part in our formation: pp. 100–112. When he came to comment on the crucial text, he was prudent enough to restrict himself to the statement: "To form Christ in us, as we say, is to express his spiritual form in our souls."—p. 100.

the least he is preparing the way for a theology which will attribute to Mary a real and present activity in the communication of grace.

Motherhood

"The bridegroom, I say, has breasts, lest he should be lacking any one of all the duties and titles of loving kindness. He is a father in virtue of natural creation or of the new birth which comes through grace, and also in virtue of the authority with which he instructs. He is a mother too in the mildness of his affections, and a nurse because he is so attentive to the care such a duty imposes."[156] Guerric assigns the attribute of motherhood to God. Since we learn from Scripture that this was communicated to the chosen people and to the Christian Church,[157] it is to be expected that the Church's motherhood should have been recognized from the beginning of Christian tradition.[158] It emerges also from the contrast between the Church and the Synagogue,[159] particularly from an allegorical interpretation, borrowed by Guerric and St Bernard from St Jerome, of the two harlots judged by Solomon.[160] She is the true mother who at all costs desired the child's life.[161] We are nourished at her breasts.[162] The undisciplined and quarrelsome distress her, like the twins struggling in Rebecca's womb.[163] The second Christmas sermon has an enlargement upon the theme of Isaiah: "Give praise then, you who could not bear a child."[164] . . . O virgin and mother, in utter purity conceiving, they are your gift from the Son who was given you."[165]

A traditionalist like St Bernard was so conscious of the Church's motherhood that he declined to recognize that Mary had a spiritual

---

156. Ser. 45:2.   157. Is 54; Gal 5:26f.
158. St Hippolytus, *De Christo et Antichristo*, ch. 61; PG 10:780f. St Cyprian Letter 8, To martyrs and confessors; PG 4:254c.
159. Ser. 7:1f.   160. Ser. 8:4.   161. Merton, *op. cit.*, p. 17.
162. Ser. 45:1.   163. Ser. 28:7.   164. Ser. 7:1.
165. *Ibid.* Bodard, *art. cit.* (note 152), pp. 289–292.

Introduction xxxvii

motherhood in our regard.[166] He need have had no fear, if he had been able to investigate tradition still more closely. We can recognize Mary, our mother, and as such a type of the Church, at Cana, on Calvary, in the Apocalypse.[167] In the earliest known commentary on the woman clothed with the sun, St Hippolytus used of the Church words which in their literal sense could only apply to Mary.[168] This tradition of Mary as type of the Church continued into the Middle Ages, or at least was then rediscovered. We have noticed already that Guerric says of Mary: "She herself, like the Church of which she is the type, is the mother of all who are reborn to life."[169] The same idea introduces an exhortation to join Simeon and welcome the child Jesus in the temple, brought there by Mary, who here is symbolic both of the Church and of grace. "Let him come into the temple with Simeon and receive in his hands the child which his mother Mary brings, that is, let him embrace with his affections the Word of God which Mother Church offers. . . . However, not only is the Church a mother to those who hear but much more is grace a mother to those who pray. Prayer will give you the Child to embrace. . . . For him, whom the Church offers to our ears by its preaching, grace brings into our hearts by its enlightening; and it makes him the more present and the more delightful inasmuch as it conveys naked truth to the understanding. The Truth which is Christ Mary gives us to embrace clothed with flesh; the Church, clothed with words; grace, naked in the inpouring of the Spirit."[170]

The last and perhaps the most astonishing word on motherhood is that we are to share with Mary her motherhood of Christ. It is the outcome of an old and long tradition;[171] if Mary is the type of the

---

166. Cf. H. Barré, *op. cit.*, pp. 106f.; although he attributes the saint's silence on this point to his devotion to Mary as his Lady.
167. A. Feuillet, "La Messie et sa Mère d'après le chapître xii de l'Apocalypse," *Rev. Biblique*, 66 (1959), pp. 55–86. See especially p. 82.
168. See note 158.   169. Ser. 47:2.
170. Ser. 17:2. Cf. Bodard, *art. cit.*, pp. 289–292: *Fondamentalment donc l'attitude de l'Eglise Mère est mariale.*
171. Based on such passages as Mt 12:46–50; Lk 11:28; it is found in Origen, *Selecta in Gen.*; PG 12:124c; St Augustine, Sermon 192, for the Feast

Church, she is the type of the soul: but the idea has rarely been developed at such length or in so tender accents as by Guerric. It arises first out of Solomon's judgment of the two harlots: we are to imitate the one who was found to be the true mother. We are mothers of the child who has been born not only for us but in us. "Keep watch then, holy mother, keep watch in your care for the new-born child until Christ is formed in you who was born for you; for the more tender he is, the more easily can he perish for you, he who never perishes for himself."[172]

The fullest treatment of the last motherhood theme is the conclusion to the second sermon on the Annunciation[173] where Mary's virginal conception is said to have a moral. "What is a mystery for redemption is also an example for you to imitate."[174] We are to conceive God in our heart; indeed the Apostle tells us that we must carry him in our body.[175] "O faithful soul, open wide your bosom, expand your affections, admit no constraint in your heart, conceive him whom creation cannot contain[176] . . . you also, blessed mothers of so glorious an issue, attend to yourselves until Christ is formed in you."[177]

Enlightenment

The points so far selected and summarized should provide a context in which one may now study in fuller detail God's work in the soul as Guerric conceives it. However, his concept of progress in the knowledge of God can hardly be appreciated, unless something is

---

of Christmas, n. 2; PL 38:1012; trans. M. Muldowney, *Sermons on the Liturgical Seasons* (New York: Fathers of the Church, 1959), pp. 32f.; *Holy Virginity*, n. 5; PL 40:399; trans. J. McQuade, *Treatises on Marriage and Other Subjects* (New York: Fathers of the Church, 1955), p. 148; Venerable Bede, *On Luke* (11:28), bk. 4; PL 92:480 and CCL 120, p. 237, with other places cited there.

172. Ser. 8:5.   173. Ser. 27:4f.   174. *Ibid.*, n. 4.
175. *Ibid.*   176. *Ibid.*

177. *Ibid.*, n. 5. On the soul's motherhood of Christ see de Wilde, pp. 38–42; Bodard, *art. cit.*, pp. 282f.; Merton, *op. cit.*, pp. 15–22.

said of its larger background: a traditional theology of enlightenment.

"The soul goes ever on, and grows increasingly accomplished in the wisdom which comes from the study of being. The nearer it progresses to the sight of God, the better does it understand that the divine nature cannot be seen." If God is beyond vision, we see him best by not seeing him. It was in a "resplendent darkness" that John said: "No man has seen God at any time."[178] So spoke St Gregory of Nyssa in a text taken almost word for word from Philo.[179] In one of his homilies on the Song of Songs, St Gregory described three stages of the Bride's knowledge: in light, in cloud, in darkness.[180]

We read of this way of knowing God by not knowing him, this theology of darkness or way of denial (*apophatic*), very early in Christian mystical tradition, and it also has some foundation in non-Christian as well as in Christian and inspired sources. It made its way over the East in the diffusion of the writings of pseudo-Dionysius and more slowly over the West after these had been translated into Latin. Its final development by St John of the Cross has made it classical and familiar to every student of Christian spirituality. The negative way is certainly known to St Gregory the Great, who thus concludes one of his outstanding passages on contemplation: "And when it tastes that inward sweetness, it is on fire with love, it longs to mount above itself, yet it falls back in a broken state to the darkness of its frailty. And advancing in high perfection, it sees that it cannot yet see that which it ardently loves, which yet it would not love ardently did it not in some sort see the same."[181] He says a little later: "And if it does not as yet apprehend what it is, it has

---

178. St Gregory of Nyssa, *Life of Moses*; PG 44:376f., *Sources Chrétiennes* 1 bis, nn. 162f., p. 81.

179. Philo, *On the Posterity of Cain and his Exile*, 5, 14f.; SC, *ibid.*, notes 2, 5; trans. F. Colson and G. Whitaker, *Philo* (Loeb Classical Library), vol. 2 (Cambridge, Mass.: Harvard, 1950), p. 335.

180. St Gregory of Nyssa, *Commentary on the Song of Songs*, homily 11; PG 44:1000f.; trans. H. Musurillo, *From Glory to Glory* (New York: Scribner's, 1961), pp. 246ff.

181. St Gregory the Great, *Morals on the Book of Job*, bk. 5, n. 58; PL 75:711C; trans. J. Newman (*Library of the Fathers*) vol. 1 (Oxford: Parker, 1844), p. 286.

surely learned what it is not."[182] Then he concludes his mystical interpretation of the experience of Elias on Horeb: "But the Lord is said not to be in the 'wind of quaking' and in the fire, but it is not denied that he is in the 'still small voice' in that verily where the mind is hung aloft in the height of contemplation, whatever it has power to see perfectly and completely is not God. . . . . Then only is there truth in what we know concerning God, when we realize that we cannot know anything fully concerning him."[183]

Guerric of Igny comes near to a theology of darkness in his third sermon for the Epiphany. The good Christian, he says, rejoices in the light God has given him, but sees still how much he is in darkness, and asks to be enlightened yet more. "For the more his lamp is enlightened, the more truly is his darkness revealed to him by the lamp itself."[184] The sentence resembles that of St Gregory of Nyssa quoted by way of introduction to this section, although Guerric does not refer expressly to the knowledge of God. You have gone far, he says, in the way of enlightenment if you know what is lacking to you. The wise of this world are quoted—evidently Socrates, known through Cicero—to the effect that "the first degree of knowledge is reckoned as knowing one's own ignorance." More to the point is the contrast between our knowledge in this life and that of the face-to-face vision: for here there is always question of the knowledge of God: "We see for the most part as in a mirror, a confused reflection. But this itself is very far removed from the true clarity and the clear truth which accompany face-to-face vision."[185] The contrast is typified in the blind man who was cured to the extent of seeing trees walking; but, when the Lord's hands were laid upon him again, he saw all things clearly.[186] From this point, however, Guerric develops the theme in another direction, being concerned only with the knowledge of his sins.[187] So he leads up to the

182. *Ibid.*, n. 62; 713C; p. 289. 183. *Ibid.*, n. 66; 716A, p. 292f.
184. Ser. 13:1. 185. *Ibid.*
186. *Ibid.*, n. 2. Ser. 46:4, is also suggestive of the theology of darkness: "To be sure what is called a shadow in comparison with manifest truth is for the most part something of unspeakable glory and splendor . . . these glories are shadows. . . ."
187. *Ibid.*, n. 3. For the meaning of darkness in Guerric see de Wilde, pp. 115f.

distinction between the enlightenment of faith and that of justice. With the two distinctions which follow, of knowledge and of wisdom, we have the scheme of the fourfold enlightenment which we shall soon have to consider.[188]

Since St Gregory the Great influenced the Western Middle Ages more than any other Father of the Church, we might have expected that the theology of darkness or negation in the knowledge of God would have continued and developed. Yet in point of fact the whole purpose of these introductory paragraphs has been to lead up to the assertion that the spirituality of the eleventh and twelfth centuries was indebted to Gregory in other ways certainly, but not to any great extent in this. The characteristic Cistercian teaching—if indeed there is such a thing—is by way of contrast a theology of light rather than of darkness. Although we are told repeatedly that man's knowledge of God in this life is as "in a mirror dimly" still the statement is by way of affirmation.

It can hardly be said that Guerric develops the theology of darkness of St Gregory the Great. This is understood more easily if it is remembered that such a theology never had the place in Gregory the Great's teaching which it had in that of Gregory of Nyssa. The Western doctor speaks of the God whom we desire as the *incircumscriptum lumen*.[189] This phrase is actually borrowed by Guerric; and as applied to God in himself, it would of course have found its place easily enough in the Eastern school.[190] But for St Gregory the Great, our knowledge of God is light. It is characteristic that the treatment of contemplation in the fifth book of the *Moralia* begins thus: "For the soul's 'eating' is its being fed with the contemplations of the light from above."[191] Of the soul which has undergone its purgation he says: "It is then enlightened by the bright coruscations of the boundless light swiftly flashing upon it."[192]

188. *Ibid.*
189. St Gregory (this name alone means St Gregory the Great), *Morals*, bk. 6, n. 59; bk. 10, n. 13; PL 75:763C, 928B; trans. Newman, pp. 359, 588.
190. Ser. 13:4.　　　191. St Gregory, *Morals*, bk. 5, n. 14; 686B, p. 251.
192. *Ibid.*, bk. 24, n. 11; PL 76:292; trans. Newman, vol. 3 (1847), p. 57.

xlii   *Introduction*

If Gregory the Great did so much to influence the moral and spiritual theology of the Middle Ages, he by no means stood alone. The way of negation taught by St Gregory of Nyssa passed through Evagrius of Pontus to St John Cassian; but the emphasis and the terminology in Evagrius and Cassian were not the same as in Gregory. They spoke not so much of darkness as of indetermination. According to Evagrius prayer is the suppression of thoughts.[193] This may mean the suppression of the imaginary and the sensible; for we are told also that we must go by way of the immaterial to the immaterial.[194] However Evagrius is to be understood, the teaching of Cassian takes the form of opposition to the anthropomorphite heresy, which attributes to God a human form,[195] and it leads him to describe thus the highest kind of prayer. "This (state of prayer) is not merely not engaged in gazing on any image, but is actually distinguished by the use of no words or utterances; but with the purpose of the mind all on fire as produced through ecstasy of heart by some unaccountable keenness of spirit, and the mind thus being affected without the aid of the senses or any visible material pours itself forth to God with groanings and sighs that cannot be uttered."[196] The words of Evagrius or Cassian may be thought of as representing a transitional stage between the theology of darkness of St Gregory of Nyssa and the theology of light, itself ancient but

---

193. Evagrius of Pontus, *On prayer*, ed. I. Hausherr, *Les leçons d'un contemplatif: La Traité de l'Oraison d'Evagre de Pontique*, n. 70. See the article "Contemplation" in DS II (2). Evagrius is treated by J. Lemaitre under the heading: *Mystique catastatique ou mystique de la lumière* (1830f.); Gregory by J. Daniélou under: *Mystique de la ténèbre* (1872f.)

194. *Ibid.*, n. 66. See also nn. 4, 11, 55, 56, 57, 61, 69, 119, 120. Also, *Praktikos*, PG 40:1275c; trans. J. Bamberger, Cistercian Studies Series, 4. The same thought underlines the theological discussion in a letter by Evagrius, n. 8 of those attributed to St Basil; PG 32:245–268; trans. R. Deferrari, *St Basil: The Letters* 61, 62 (Loeb Classical Library), vol. 1 (New York: Putnam, 1926), pp. 47ff. See the idea of indetermination as taken up by St Gregory, *Morals*, bk. 5, nn., bk. 6, n. 59; PL 75:712f., 763; trans. Newman, pp. 288f., 359.

195. John Cassian, *Conferences*, 10, ch. 2-5; *Sources Chrétiennes* 54, pp. 75–79; trans. E. Gibson, *Nicene and Post-Nicene Fathers*, series 2, vol. 11 (Grand Rapids: Eerdmans, 1955), pp. 401ff.

196. *Ibid.*, ch. 11; p. 93; trans. p. 408.

finding a new expression in the writings of the great Latin doctor, St Augustine.

St Augustine was aware of the limitations of our contemplative knowledge of God, yet his emphasis and his expression differed from those of his predecessors. Conscious of man's striving as well as of God's uplifting, he thought of the soul as flung back by the splendor of blinding light, returning to itself, and so going down from the mountain of contemplation to the valley of human concerns. "With the flash of a trembling glance, it arrived at that which is.... But I was not able to fix my gaze thereon; and my infirmity being beaten back, I was thrown again on my accustomed habits, carrying along with me naught but a loving memory thereof."[197] The description and sequel are very similar in the contemplation at Ostia: "And while we were thus speaking and straining after it (the region of unfailing plenty), we slightly touched it with the whole effort of our heart and we sighed and there left bound the first fruits of the Spirit; and returned to the noise of our own mouth, where the word uttered has both beginning and end."[198] Augustine appears as a teacher of the way of light and affirmation (*cataphatic*) especially in a passage of the *De Trinitate*. Having enumerated all the things which God is not, he brings the soul to the realization: "Behold and see, if you can, that God is truth. For it is written that 'God is light'; not in such a way as these eyes see but in such a way as the heart sees when it is said, he is truth. Ask not what is truth, for immediately the darkness of corporeal images and the cloud of phantasms will put themselves in the way, and will disturb that calm which at the first twinkling shown forth to you, when I said 'Truth.' See that you remain if you can in that first twinkling with which you are dazzled, as it were by a flash, when it is said to you, 'Truth.' But you cannot, you will glide back into those usual and earthly things."[199]

197. St Augustine, *Confessions*, bk. 7, n. 23; PL 32:745; trans. J. Pilkington, *Basic Writings of St Augustine* (New York: Random House, 1948), vol. 1, p. 105.
198. *Ibid.*, bk. 9, n. 24; 774; trans. p. 141.
199. *Id.*, *On the Trinity*, bk. 8, n. 3; PL 42:949; trans. A. Haddan, *Basic Writings*, vol. 2, pp. 774f.

St Augustine is concerned in the passages to stress not the dark but the fleeting, indeed momentary character of man's sublime intercourse with God. St Gregory the Great had, of course, read St Augustine, and seems to recall his phrases more than once. "For not even in the sweetness of inward contemplation does the mind remain fixed for long, in that being made to recoil by the very immensity of the light it is called back to itself."[200] "The effort therefore of the mind is driven back, when directed towards it, by the bright encircling of its boundless nature. . . . It accordingly falls back at once to itself and having seen, as it were, some traces of truth before it, is recalled to a sense of its own lowliness."[201] "This silence is therefore well described as having been made not for a whole but for a 'half-hour' because contemplation is never perfected here, however ardently it be begun."[202]

The theme of the fleeting character of the highest contemplation, often indicated by the use of *raptim, rapere, rapidus*,[203] also the symbol of the half-hour of the Apocalypse, was to become a commonplace in the following centuries. In passages such as those which we quote from Guerric the language is biblical throughout, but for its application he is indebted to the tradition established by the early Fathers. Thus, for instance, he speaks of the monks intent on their psalmody: "The Bridegroom takes you, absorbed in his praises with accents of exultation and thanksgiving, into the place of his admirable tent, even to the house of God, that is, the unapproachable light in which he dwells."[204] We also find here St Augustine's descent or return to ourselves: "As long as we are with the Father of lights, with whom there can be no change, no swerving from his course, we know nothing of night, we enjoy a blessed daylight. When we

200. St Gregory, *Morals*, bk. 5, n. 58; PL 75:711C; trans. Newman, vol. 1, p. 286.
201. *Ibid.*, bk. 24, n. 12; PL 76:292CD; trans. vol. 3, p. 57.
202. *Ibid.*, bk. 30, n. 53; 553C; p. 401. On the half-hour cf. *On Ezekiel*, bk. 2, homily 2, n. 4; PL 76:957A.
203. E.g. in John of Fécamp, *Confessio theologica*, 3, 6; ed. J. Leclerqc and J. Bonnes, *Un maître de la vie spirituelle au XIIème siècle*, p. 147.
204. Ser. 54:3.

fall thence we relapse into our own darkness."[205] He contrasts the fleeting contact with the lasting vision, saying of our faith: "It will be brought to its consummation when the naked truth of things will be seen as present and we shall contemplate face to face what now is scarcely seen for a fleeting moment now and then as a confused reflection."[206] Of the symbolic half-hour, he says: "So too there are not lacking clouds which will raise up our spirits to higher things, provided our hearts are not too lazy and tied to earth, and so we will be with the Lord if only for half an hour." As with St Augustine these clouds are the inspired writers, and their words may be the occasion of our uplifting: ". . . your minds and hearts have been borne aloft as on a cloud to sublime things and on occasion carried beyond even these, so that they merited to behold, in however small a degree, the glory of God."[207]

The Fathers just mentioned help to explain why the spiritual theology of the twelfth century was predominantly one of light and affirmation. Yet an influence equally powerful and in the same direction came from Origen. His Scriptural commentaries especially were known in the Latin versions made by St Jerome and Rufinus. We have a summary account of the Igny library with its original manuscripts, as it was found in the early eighteenth century, and it is true that Origen is not mentioned.[208] Yet if we may judge from Cistercian libraries more or less well preserved to our own day, we should expect the Alexandrine doctor to have been well represented there. Certainly he was at Signy, and it is at least probable that the Signy manuscripts were copied from originals which belonged to Igny, the mother-house.[209]

205. *Ibid.*   206. Ser. 12:5.
207. Ser. 2:3. For the half-hour see Ser. 46:6.
208. E. Martène, *Voyage littéraire*, vol. 1, part 2, p. 87. Quoted by M. Dimier, "Les premiers cisterciens étaient-ils ennemis des études?" *Studia monastica*, 4 (1962), p. 83.
209. On books of Origen at Clairvaux see A. Wilmart, "L'Ancienne Bibliothèque de Clairvaux," *Collectanea O.C.R.*, 11 (1949), pp. 117f. At Pontigny, C. H. Talbot, "Notes on the Library of Pontigny," *Analecta S.O.C.*, 10 (1954), pp. 114, 119, 129f., 148f. At Signy, J. Déchanet, *The Works of William of St Thierry*, vol. 2, Cistercian Fathers Series, 6.

Origen taught that the devils held in their possession the ignorant, but suffered their worst torments when a Christian gave his whole attention to the word of God.[210] If we are cleansed, it is by light sent from heaven,[211] and one of the stages in our spiritual progress is an understanding of the reasons for the incarnation.[212] The final stage is expressed in these words: "For this whole course is therefore undertaken and pursued, that we might come to the river of God, that we might be close to the source of wisdom and be watered by divine knowledge, and thus purified in every way we might merit to enter into the land of promise."[213] To rest with John on the heart of Jesus is to contemplate the treasure of wisdom and knowledge hidden there;[214] and to be refreshed from the breasts of the Bridegroom is to draw upon the source of wisdom and knowledge.[215] The first object of knowledge (*gnosis*) is the Blessed Trinity; the second the soul herself.[216] The Bride asks to be taken into the Bridegroom's cellar; for there is no such wine to be had elsewhere; its ingredients are the teachings of wisdom and knowledge.[217]

Wisdom, Knowledge and Love in the Cistercian Writers

Origen's influence helps to explain why knowledge of God is expressed in terms of light rather than of darkness. It also accounts for a tradition which issues in what we may call the intellectualism of the Cistercians. This appears in William of St Thierry (to select one from countless examples) in his explanation of the spiritual life: *animalis, rationalis, spiritualis*. This is the viewpoint from which St Bernard was able to assert: knowledge is life, love is sense.[218] As for Guerric and his disciples: they never forgot that perfection in this

---

210. Origen, *On Numbers*, homily 27, n. 8; *Sources Chrétiennes* 29, p. 531.
211. Ibid., n. 12, p. 545.   212. Ibid., p. 543f.   213. Ibid., p. 555.
214. Id., *Commentary on the Song of Songs*, bk. 1; PG 13:87AB.
215. Ibid.; 100B.   216. Ibid., bk. 2; 126B.   217. Ibid., bk. 3; 155B.
218. William of St Thierry, *Exposition on the Song of Songs*, Preface, nn.1 9f.; *Sources Chrétiennes* 82, pp. 92ff.; trans. C. Hart, Cistercian Fathers Series, 6; St Bernard, *De Diversis*, 116; PL 183:741C.

life and happiness in the life to come involved an intimacy of love; nor would their frequent use of the Song of Songs have been compatible with any mistaken notion on this point. They knew well St Gregory's formulae: "by love we see and own the likeness of our Maker presented to our contemplation;"[219] "love itself is knowledge;"[220] but to use these Gregorian principles in order to develop the thought of Origen belonged rather to the genius of a William of St Thierry.[221] It has been well said that the theme of William's entire commentary on the Song of Songs is: *Amor Dei intellectus est.*[222] The merging of a two-fold tendency is clear enough in the account which St Bernard gives of wisdom; it is both knowledge and love.[112] A disciple of Guerric said that the Bride's eyes were knowledge and love.[224]

Yet we shall see, like others familiar with the texts of Origen, Guerric was often content to repeat that spiritual progress meant growing in knowledge and wisdom; that God would draw a soul closer to himself by throwing ever more light upon the mysteries hidden in the Sacred Scriptures. Thus he describes God's coming to the soul after its patient prayer and waiting: "For if you sing wisely in the way of integrity, coming he will come and will bring to light what is hidden from you so that you may understand the mysteries of the Scriptures you do not at present know."[225]

219. St Gregory, *Morals*, bk. 10, n. 13; PL 75:927D; Newman trans., vol. 1, p. 558.
220. *Id.*, *On the Gospel*, homily 27, n. 4; PL 76:1207A. Cf. St Bernard, *De Diversis*, 29, n. 1; PL 183:620C.
221. William of St Thierry, *Exposition on the Song of Songs*, nn. 57, 76, 144; SC 82, pp. 150–152, 186–190, 302–304; Hart trans., CF 6, pp. 46, 63, 114.
222. J. Déchanet, in a note on the last place cited in SC 82.
223. St Bernard, *On the Song of Songs*, 69:2, PL 183:1113; ed. Leclercq *et al.*, vol. 2, p. 203; trans. Walsh, CF 7. See R. Kereszty, "Die Weisheit in der mystischen Erfahrung beim hl. Bernhard von Clairvaux," *Cîteaux*, 14 (1963), pp. 126–129. This valuable study (cited henceforth by the name Kereszty alone) has been published in three parts in the same volume of *Cîteaux*, pp. 6–24, 105–134, 185–201.
224. "Liber Amoris," *Cîteaux*, 16 (1965), pp. 125–126.
225. Ser. 3:4.

xlviii   *Introduction*

If it be asked, then, what Guerric has taken from Origen, the first answer which suggests itself will be that he has acquired the habit of finding God's highest gift summed up in two texts of St Paul: "... Christ Jesus in whom are all the treasures of wisdom and knowledge."[226] "To one indeed is given through the Spirit the utterance of wisdom, and to another the utterance of knowledge according to the same Spirit."[227]

Enlightenment and Mortification

This insistence on spiritual enlightenment is not of course to deny that mortification is essential in the spiritual life as Guerric conceives it; indeed as he must so conceive it if he is to be faithful to tradition. St John the Baptist, in the four sermons for his Nativity, is constantly presented to us as the model of penitents. The fourth and fifth Purification sermons bear striking witness to his belief in Purgatory, but they are concerned with purgation here as well as after death.[228] With St Paul we must mortify not only the flesh but also the vices which may continue to reign in the heart.[229] The cost of our receiving the angel's blessing is that, like Jacob, we should limp with a withered thigh.[230] In the past Guerric's teaching on mortification has been reinforced by the attributing to him St Bernard's twenty-eighth sermon *De Diversis*.[231] Indeed it was characteristic of the nineteenth century that any student of Guerric should overload the scales in this sense. Gatterer's summary statement, *Guerricus ist demnach ein allgemeiner Bussprediger*, hardly gives a just impression of the abbot of Igny.[232] True enough, the German professor had more

226. Col 2:3.
227. 1 Cor 12:8. On the "mystique de la lumière," its sources, its application to Guerric and to St Bernard see A. Decabooter, "L'Optimisme de Guerric d'Igny," *Collectanea O.C.R.*, 19 (1957), pp. 254–256.
228. See de Wilde, pp. 117f.
229. Ser. 30:5. A single aspect of Guerric's teaching on renunciation has been studied by Dom A. Louf: "Une théologie de la pauvreté monastique chez le Bx Guerric d'Igny," *Collectanea O.C.R.*, 20 (1958), pp. 207–222, 362–373.
230. Ser. 41:1.   231. Gatterer, p. 72, note 161.   232. *Ibid.*, p. 75.

Introduction

to say than this: but his predilection for an emphasis on penance may well justify us in insisting upon Guerric's more positive, indeed more characteristic, contribution to monastic spirituality.

Purgation, Light, Contemplation

If the enquiry into Guerric's theology of light is to be pursued, it may well be asked with what precisely are we concerned: with God's action upon the Church or upon the individual soul; if the latter, whether we are considering the relations of the ordinary faithful with God or rather a privileged state called contemplative. Perhaps it is best to answer that we are interested in God's self communication to men generally. His action upon the Church is for the benefit of individual souls, and will be reflected more or less clearly in his dealings with each one. If some are called to higher ways in prayer and to more intimate communion with God, this is but the development under God's special influence of his elementary gift of faith. One hardly needs to surround this idea with all the safeguards which seemed necessary thirty years ago. We should be placing our author well out of his period and context if we were to refer to "infused contemplation" in a technical sense and then shrink from the conclusion that he spoke of a general invitation to such a state.[233]

Foundation of the Three Ways

Three inspired books succeed one another in the sacred pages: Proverbs, Ecclesiastes and the Song of Songs. St Bernard begins his sermons on the last with a reference to all three and suggests that they correspond to the stages of spiritual progress.[234] He is recalling

---

233. This is how de Wilde wrote, p. 154; and it may well have seemed necessary in the nineteen-thirties.
234. St Bernard, *On the Song of Songs*, 1:2; PL 183:785f.; ed. Leclercq *et al.*, vol. 1, pp. 3f.; trans. Walsh, CF 4.

a tradition which goes back to the earliest Christian commentaries. Origen teaches that three things are to be learned: moral reform, knowledge of the created wonders which surround us, contemplation of that supreme Being and Good which they reflect. These "disciplines," *praktike, physike, theorike,* correspond to the three books of Scripture. The text "The God of Abraham, the God of Isaac, the God of Jacob" is then expounded[235] in such a way as to point to the same three-fold distinction. Here is the foundation of the classical three ways of the spiritual life: purgation, illumination, union.

Purgation: Disciplina

Although Guerric does not mention them explicitly, he does tell us that in the first place light from God follows our humble submission to teachers and the correction of our faults. "And even if you have advanced on the way of the Lord so that the road you follow is straight and your life is ordered by gentleness, you have indeed advanced, but you have not yet reached your destination unless the word of God is a lamp to your feet and a light on your path."[236] Nor is it just a matter of one stage succeeding another in time. It has well been said that for St Bernard the moral-ascetic and the contemplative aspects of spiritual development are parallel and mutually supporting from the beginning to the end of the course.[237] For Guerric, the two processes are also fused: the way of purgation is itself the way of enlightenment: "The commandment is a lamp, and teaching a light and the reproofs of discipline the way of life ... you will incline your ear to masters and acquiesce in their reproofs and advice and give yourself to the task of learning ... knowledge of the law frees from traps."[238] In fact we must always be getting correction and instruction like schoolboys. A phrase used elsewhere,

235. Origen, *Commentary on the Song of Songs,* Prologue; PG 13:73f., 76.
236. Ser. 4:4.
237. Kereszty, p. 22 and note 68. Cf. our critique of Gatterer above, p. xlviii and note 232.
238. Ser. 4:4.

disciplinam sapientiae et Christianae scholam philosophiae, is in the language of a long accepted tradition.[239]

Illumination: Scientia

The theme of light is prominent as might be expected, in the Epiphany sermons. "A new-born child cries on earth;" but of this same infant we go on to read, "while in the heavens he creates a new star so that light may witness to light, a star to the sun."[240] The Church constantly represented by Christian writers as the wild goat, scanning the details of all before it from its mountain crag—"keen of sight to penetrate Christ's mysteries"[241]—is represented in this second Epiphany sermon as obeying the divine call, "Arise, be enlightened, Jerusalem, for your light has come;"[242] coming, that is, for the enlightenment of her faith. There follows a Pauline thought, already dear to St Ambrose: this Church is mother of the Gentiles; the Jerusalem so enlightened is to bring forth to God children of light.[243] This light which has come from the Father of lights and shines in the face of Christ Jesus, is the beginning of that eternal life which is to know the one true God and Jesus Christ whom he has sent. The knowledge which we have now by faith is a pledge of something to come.[244] Guerric follows St Ambrose yet again in the development of a Pauline idea: the ring placed on the finger of the prodigal son is a pledge.[245] The greater gift to come is direct knowledge by vision. There follows a prayer introduced by the word *interim*, often used of the present life, the time of waiting for the consummation.[246] The prayer is not only for faith and

239. Ser. 22:4. 240. Ser. 12:2.
241. Ser. 44:3. Cf. Origen, *Homilies on the Song of Songs*, 2, n. 11; *Sources Chrétiennes* 37, p. 98. See J. Morson, "The English Cistercians and the Bestiary," *Bulletin of John Rylands Library*, 39 (1956), pp. 161f.
242. Ser. 12:1. 243. *Ibid.*, n. 3. See also Ser. 7:1.
244. *Ibid.* 245. Ser. 21:2.
246. So in Ser. 6:2ff. Cf. St Bernard, *Sermons on Psalm* 90, 9:7; 10:1, 3 (four times), 4; *De Diversis*, 18:1 (three times), 2 (twice), 3; PL 183:220D, 222f., 223C, 587f.

knowledge, but also for charity which is their fulfillment: "In the meantime increase our faith, leading us on from faith to faith, from brightness to brightness, as by your Spirit, that from day to day we may enter more deeply into the treasure of light, so that faith may become more all-embracing, knowledge more full, charity more fervent and spread further abroad until through faith we are led to the vision of your face."[247]

The following sermon brings us to four stages of spiritual progress, each of which is called light. The light of faith being presupposed as the first, the others are equivalent to the traditional purgative, illuminative and unitive ways. "You granted us the light of faith, grant us also the light of justice, the light of knowledge, the light of wisdom, too."[248] The outcome will be "that you may cast off the darkness of this world and arrive at your home country of eternal brightness, where your darkness will be like midday and night will be lit up like day."[249] All the earth will be filled with the majesty of that "unbounded light" known to Guerric from St Gregory. The progress through the four stages is now described more fully: "Let us then who are already in the light through faith go forward from it and through it towards a more ample and a more serene light, first that of justice, then that of knowledge, finally that of wisdom. For what we believe through faith has to be worked out or merited in keeping with our faith through justice, afterwards understood through knowledge and finally contemplated through wisdom."[250] We are to believe, then to act, to understand, to contemplate. If faith is the light which it should be, it will not endure the presence of sin. The actions performed under this light are themselves "works of light." Guerric follows St Gregory when he says that they are the "lamps burning in the hands of those who do them as they wait the coming of the Bridegroom."[251] Guerric's teaching on faith cannot be set out here at greater length. He devotes the greater part of another sermon to commenting on the Pauline definition: "Faith is the substance of things to be hoped for, evidence of things that appear not."[252]

247. Ser. 12:3. 248. Ser. 13:3. 249. Ibid., n. 4. 250. Ibid.
251. Ibid. 252. Heb 11:1; Ser. 25:3ff. See de Wilde, pp. 119f.

Our author is still one with Gregory in recognizing that there are many in the Church with faith and justice radiant, but with the understanding darkened, knowledge dimmed almost to nothing. They cannot speak to you of the mysteries of faith; the Bible is sealed to them, not because they cannot read but because they have no sense for the discernment of good and evil, true and false.[253] The remedy is suggested by a text of the prophet Hosae: "Sow for yourselves justice . . . and thus illumine yourselves with the light of knowledge." We shall not find it in our Bibles, for it is a reading of the Septuagint and probably of the old Latin version, likely to have been familiar to Guerric from his reading of St Ambrose or St Jerome. It tells us that the practice and merit of justice will enkindle the light of knowledge.[254] Of the several gifts embraced by such knowledge, one man receives this from the Spirit, another that; but it is most rare for all to be given together. In language largely biblical they are listed thus: "to one he gives knowledge of mysteries, to another understanding of the Scriptures, to another the interpretation of tongues, to another power to test spirits, to another that ability so necessary as it were in the taste, to distinguish and judge between virtues and vices, so that vices may not deceive under the appearance of virtue."[255]

Contemplation: Sapientia

Happy the man who is allowed to go yet further and attain to wisdom, which Guerric defines as follows: ". . . wisdom, that is, a savor and taste of things eternal so that he can be still and see and while he sees taste how sweet is the Lord; and if what the eye has not seen and the ear has not heard and what has not entered into the heart of man is revealed to him through the Spirit—this man indeed I will say is enlightened magnificently and gloriously, like one who gazes

---

253. Ser. 13:5.   254. *Ibid.*

255. *Ibid.*, n. 6. For a further study of Guerric's concept of knowledge and comparison with that of St Augustine and St Bernard, see de Wilde, pp. 122–130. On "La Lumière de la science" see also A. Decabooter, *art. cit.* (note 227), pp. 256–258.

on the Lord's glory with face unveiled and over whom the Lord's glory often rises."[256] In him is fulfilled what the Spirit said through the prophet, the text on which Guerric has based this sermon. "Arise, be enlightened, Jerusalem, for your light has come, and the glory of the Lord has risen over you."[257] We shall not be blamed if we have not received this gift, but there is no excuse for not desiring it. Even though it is a gift, some preparation is called for on our part. Just as the light of knowledge is enkindled by frequent reading, provided that this be done in the light of those good works which constitute justice, so this light of wisdom is set on fire by prayer.[258]

Wisdom, then, is the consummation of a life of faith and virtue. St Bernard can be quoted to the same effect, provided that, as already noted, we do not tie ourselves down to the idea of a strict chronological succession. "Indeed wisdom follows after virtue which is, as it were, the stable foundation on which wisdom builds her house."[259]

After reading Guerric to this point, it is superfluous to repeat that wisdom is enlightenment. William of St Thierry follows Origen closely in his exegesis of the *osculum oris sui;* but eventually replaces *illuminari* with *sapere* as the operative word.[260] Guerric for his part quotes the Pauline text *revelata facie gloriam Domini speculantes.*[261] These seem striking words indeed to use of anything given to man in this life. Yet so they are used as originally spoken by St Paul, of the knowledge accorded to the Christians, free and transformed by the Spirit, in contrast to the darkness of unbelieving Jews, still trusting in the Law. In St Bernard they sometimes mean the beatific vision, but when he uses them of man's knowledge of God in this life, he feels that they need a fuller explanation than is under-

---

256. *Ibid.*, n. 7.   257. Is 60:1.   258. Ser. 13:7.
259. St Bernard, *On the Song of Songs*, 85:9; PL 183:1192C; ed. Leclercq et al., vol. 2, p. 313; trans. Walsh, Cistercian Fathers 31.
260. William of St Thierry, *Exposition on the Song of Songs*, n. 36; Sources Chrétiennes 82, p. 120; trans. Hart, Cistercian Fathers 6.
261. ". . . with unveiled face, beholding the glory of the Lord."—2 Cor 3:18.

Introduction lv

taken by Guerric, or for that matter by St Paul.²⁶² The text will be found again in Guerric to describe the loftiest contemplation, with or without the phrase *revelata facie*.²⁶³ In this Epiphany sermon they explain the function of wisdom.²⁶⁴

The association of wisdom with taste can be traced as far back as Origen,²⁶⁵ and indeed has its foundation in some texts of the Old Testament.²⁶⁶ For Latin Fathers who confined their attention to the words of their own language (*sapere, sapor, sapientia*) the connection became etymological.²⁶⁷ Hence wisdom, which for Guerric is so clearly enlightenment, becomes also *saporem et gustum aeternorum*, that is, love and satisfaction of desire in the spiritual order. To understand what this means for Guerric we must remember that he is familiar with the teaching that has come down from the Greek Fathers through St Gregory the Great: that desire for God and the satisfaction of that desire increases together.²⁶⁸ This is what the

---

262. St Bernard, *De Diversis*, 41:11; PL 183:659BC. M. Standaert has studied the places in which St Bernard uses 2 Cor 3:18 of the knowledge of God either in this life or in the life to come (e.g., *Sermon on St Victor* 2:4; *Office of St Victor*; PL 183:375C, 778D; ed. Leclercq *et al.*, vol. 3, p. 506; trans. M. Cawley, *The Works of Bernard of Clairvaux*, vol. 1, Cistercian Fathers, 1, p. 176): *loc. cit.* (note 142), pp. 105–107.

263. Ser. 19:6; 46:4.

264. On the relation of wisdom to intellect and will in SS Augustine and Bernard see de Wilde, pp. 137–139. Not being a scholastic Guerric is but little concerned with faculties. Unlike St Thomas Aquinas, who will treat of wisdom first as an intellectual virtue and then as a gift of the Spirit, Guerric does not ask whether it resides in the intellect, or, if so, whether it is premised by a disposition of the will. See *Summa theol.* 1–11, q. 57, a. 2; 11–11, q. 45, a. 2.

265. Origen, *Commentary on the Song of Songs*, bk. 3; PG 13:151f.

266. E.g., Prov 9:1–5; Sir 24:29.

267. St Isidore of Seville, *Etymologia*, 10, 240; Pf. 82:392C. St Bernard, *On the Song of Songs*, 85:8; PL 183:1191D; ed. Leclercq *et al.*, vol. 2, p. 312; trans. Walsh, Cistercian Fathers 31. William of St Thierry, *The Nature and Dignity of Love*, n. 28; PL 184: 397CD; trans. Cistercian Fathers 15. For texts of St Augustine and John of Fécamp see J. Leclercq and J. Bonnes, *op. cit.* (note 142), p. 99, note 3. See the matter treated by Kereszty with apt quotations and references: *art. cit.*, pp. 186–189.

268. St Gregory of Nyssa, *On the Song of Songs*, homily 6; PG 44:885–888; trans. Musurillo, *op. cit.* (note 180), pp. 196f.; *Life of Moses*; 404A; SC 1 bis, n.

lvi   Introduction

Greeks called *epectasis:* a noun formed from the verb used by St Paul: stretching out to the things that are before me.[269] Guerric expresses this idea in a sermon for Palm Sunday: ". . . . now satiate yourself, if indeed you can be satiated with unspeakable joy, which satiates desire in such a way as to cause greater and happier hunger."[270]

That wisdom is both enlightenment and the satisfaction of desire is very clear from Guerric's words already quoted: "wisdom, that is, a savor and taste of things eternal so that he can be still and see while he sees, taste. . . ."[271] The approximation, and even the apparent identification of wisdom and love is something which Guerric has in common with his contemporaries.[272] Elsewhere the fire which warmed the breast of the aged Simeon is said to be both love and wisdom. This is followed by an interpretation, taken from St Jerome, of Abishag the Canaanite girl who warmed the cold body of king David. "O tinder of Love . . . a delightful torture of happiness, like the burning glow of health refreshed. . . . How much more carefully and tenderly did this fire warm an old man than did Abishag, the Shünammite, King David . . . unless maybe Abishag was this same fire, namely Wisdom in whose embrace not only are the cold warmed but the dead also brought back to life."[273]

This figure of life-giving warmth is associated once more with spiritual resurrection, understanding (*intellectus*), wisdom (*sapientia*)

233, p. 107; trans. pp. 147f.; St Gregory the Great, *On the Gospel*, homily 36, n. 1; PL 76:1266AB. John of Fécamp, *Confessio theol.* 3, *op. cit.*, 528f.; ed. J. Leclercq and J. Bonnes, p. 159. St Peter Damian, *Rhythmus de gloria Paradisi*; PL 145:982C; on which see J. Leclercq, *The Love of Learning and the Desire for God* (New York: Fordham, 1961), pp. 73f. St Bernard, *First Sermon for All Saints*, n. 11; PL 183:459A. William of St Thierry, *Exposition on the Song of Songs*, n. 56; SC 82, p. 150; trans. Hart, CF 6. St Aelred of Rievaulx, *The Rule for Recluses*, n. 33; SC 76, p. 164; trans. M. P. Macpherson, in *The Works of Aelred of Rievaulx*, vol. 1, *Treatises*, Cistercian Fathers 2.

269. Phil 2:13.   270. Ser. 32:2.   271. Ser. 13:7.

272. St Bernard, *De Diversis*, 73; PL 183:695B. William of St Thierry, *Exposition on the Song of Songs*, nn. 72, 136; SC 82, pp. 180, 288; trans. Hart, CF 6, pp. 60, 109.

273. Ser. 15:2. Cf. St Jerome, Letter 52, nn. 3f.; PL 22:528–530; St Bruno, Letter 1, n. 7; SC 88, p. 72.

and divine contemplation in Guerric's last Easter sermon. Here he follows St Gregory, and a sermon known to him under the name of St Augustine, in giving a spiritual interpretation to the raising of the dead boy by Elisha. It seems clear that *intellectus* is meant to take the place held by *scientia* in the texts we have studied already. At the same time there is mention of the *charismata septiformis gratiae*. This does not mean that our author has a theology of the seven gifts. He is chiefly interested in the pair, knowledge (or understanding) and wisdom to which St Paul and Origen have given a place of their own in our spiritual tradition. Guerric reminds us then how, when the Prophet had lain upon him, the boy yawned seven times and at last opened his eyes. The warmth of the Prophet's body means the first communication of the Holy Spirit, given by Christ, the true Elisha. "More fully however and more obviously does he advance toward resurrection when by a desire and certain hunger for justice he begins to yawn often... This yawning is a spreading wide of the affections that they be the more able to contain the breath of life, so that after other spiritual gifts the spirit of understanding and wisdom may be infused and open the eyes to contemplate God."[274]

Transformation into the Image

Guerric's theology of light receives a further elaboration in his teaching on the "middle advent." It is an idea which he has in common with St Bernard and many others; but it is interesting to see how he chooses to develop it.

Christ came into the world at the Incarnation; he is to come again as Judge. Lest his first coming should prove to have been in vain for us, and lest he should have to come again in anger, he comes to us now.[275] This coming is no less hidden than the first. Both Bernard and Guerric speak of it in terms borrowed from Origen; we are not

---

274. Ser. 35:5. See de Wilde, pp. 126f. On wisdom and contemplation as the normal term of progress in the monastic life, see A. Decabooter, *art. cit.* (note 227), pp. 258f.

275. Ser. 2:3.

conscious of the Lord's coming or of his going, but only of his presence. "Only while he is present is he light to the soul and mind." "In that light invisible he is seen, inconceivable he is understood."[276] The enlightenment of the middle advent does indeed culminate in love: "... when God, the Love of the lover, is grasped even in the senses, when the Bridegroom embraces the Bride and they become one in the Spirit."[277] But the words immediately following explain what is meant by transformation into the image of God. It is the highest capacity given to man in the present life; it is a certain vision: "and she is transformed into the same image in which, as in a mirror, she sees the glory of the Lord."[278] Guerric's authority for this use of the Pauline text seems to be St Augustine, who said that a mirror shows the image of the reality but no more. It follows that the purpose of the image of God in ourselves was to make us fit for such sight of him as a mirror could give.[279] Among St Bernard's various expositions of God's image in man there is one which is very close to this Augustinian concept as found in Guerric: the image is intended to be a means to the knowledge of God.[280] The notions of the image and the mirror call for some account of Guerric's teaching on the knowledge of God as given in his third sermon for the feast of SS Peter and Paul. He is commenting on the text of the

---

276. Ibid., n. 4. For unperceived coming and going see St Bernard, *On the Song of Songs*, 74:5; PL 183:1141; ed. Leclercq *et al.*, vol. 2, p. 242; trans. Walsh, CF 31; *De Diversis*, 41:11; PL 183:659cd. Cf. Origen, *Homilies on the Song of Songs*, 1:7; SC 37, p. 75.

277. Ser. 2:4.

278. Ibid.

279. St Augustine, *On the Trinity*, bk. 15, n. 14; PL 42:1067; trans. S. McKenna (Washington: Catholic University, 1953), pp. 469f.

280. St Bernard, *De Diversis*, 9:2; PL 183:566A; cf. *On the Song of Songs*, 24:5; PL 183:896f.; ed. Leclercq *et al.*, vol. 1, pp. 156f.; trans. Walsh, CF 4; *On Loving God*, n. 6; PL 182:977f.; ed. Leclercq *et al.*, vol. 3, pp. 123f. The variations of St Bernard's doctrine on the image have been studied and co-ordinated by M. Standaert, *op. cit.* (note 142); see especially pp. 75, 80, 93. For the teaching of William of St Thierry on the "likeness" as the perfection of God's "image" in us, enabling us to know him, see Odo Brooke, "Faith and Mystical Experience in William of St Thierry," *Downside Review*, 82 (1964), pp. 92–103, especially p. 98.

Canticle: "Until the day breathes and the shadows flee."[281] The "shadow" is the medium of ordinary knowledge in the mind, what the scholastics will call a "species."[282] Of these shadows it is said ". . . which are born in our minds from other things as if in a mirror."[283] "For the soul forms for itself a shadow of the thing of which it thinks,"[284] but this shadow-medium will represent either material and worldly reality or else divine. Our idea of God is but little reliable. Indeed, it is not even a shadow of God himself, but only something substituted, unless it should happen that the day should breathe upon us. "Yet a shadow cast by the things of God is very dubious, however keenly our mental vision be sharpened to perceive it; or rather it is not a shadow of the thing itself but something else takes its place, except when that day breathes."[285] Even with this special grace, it is no more than a shadow we see. To look upon the face of Truth itself will never be for these bodily eyes, nor for this present life. So we come back to the image and mirror of the Advent sermon. "Although it is luminous and glorious it is still a shadow, as when on the surface of a mirror that has been wiped clean and is in the light there appears the brilliant likeness of a most brilliant object."[286] Guerric goes on to quote St Paul: "Now we see in a mirror dimly, but then face to face."[287] But two things are necessary if we are to see through the mirror. First its surface must be cleansed of every bodily image and shadow. Then he who dwells in light inaccessible must turn our way and deign to show himself through the shadow of the image.[288] But even this knowledge through a shadow is a shining light for one who has the mirror within him clear. Guerric applies to it the same Pauline text that inspired the thought of his earlier sermon: "It is given to us, all alike, to catch the glory of the Lord as in a mirror, and so we become transfigured into the same likeness, borrowing glory from

---

281. Song 4:6. For Guerric's teaching on the "shadow": de Wilde, pp. 141–146.

282. For the psychology of *species* in sense knowledge cf. William of St Thierry, *Exposition on the Song of Songs*, n. 94; SC 82, p. 218; trans. Hart, CF 6.

283. Ser. 46:3.   284. Ibid.   285. Ibid.
286. Ibid.   287. 1 Cor 13:12.   288. Ser. 46:4.

that glory as the Spirit of the Lord enables us."[289] Even though St Paul's phrase *revelata facie* is this time omitted, the text is striking enough as conclusion to an account of our knowledge of God in this life.

What we have just read about a medium of knowledge in the second sermon for Advent and the third for SS Peter and Paul corresponds to the teaching of William of St Thierry on the *imago, speculum* or *aenigma*, always needed in this life.[290] However, speaking in one place of the Bridegroom and Bride divided from one another only by the wall of this mortality, William uses words which might be taken as a paraphrase of the "with unveiled face, beholding the glory of the Lord": "Beyond the glass and the riddle," he says, "he shows himself to a certain extent in himself."[291]

The earlier treatment of the mirror and image recalled a passage in the *De Trinitate* of St Augustine. This sermon on the "shadow" is reminiscent of some pages in the third book of Origen's *Commentary on the Song of Songs*. The Alexandrine doctor does not use the word, as Guerric does, in the sense of a psychological medium of knowledge, but in association with his similar treatment of the "mirror" of 1 Corinthians, 13. We have been under the shadow of the Law, then under the shadow of Christ. Even the shadow of Christ is imperfect knowledge and points to a consummation. "So that after this, if we pass through this way which is Christ we can come to this, that we see him face to face whom we had previously seen, as it were, in a shadow or a riddle."[292] The time of shadow will end with the world: "after the consummation of the world we will then see Truth not through a mirror or a riddle, but face to face."[293] A last and significant word must be taken from Guerric's fifth Purification sermon: ". . . what is granted but rarely and to rare souls to experience as in a mirror and a confused reflection

---

289. Ibid.
290. William of St Thierry, *Exposition on the Song of Songs*, Preface, nn. 21–23; SC 82, pp. 94–100; trans. Hart, CF 6, pp. 15–18.
291. *Ibid*, n. 154; p. 326; trans. p. 126.
292. Origen, *Commentary on the Song of Songs*, bk. 3; PG 13:153BC.
293. Ibid.

(*aenigma*), that is, to be before the Lord in Jerusalem."[294] This is something between faith and vision as is clear from the following paragraph: ". . . advancing from the vision which is through faith to that which is in a mirror and an image and finally from that which is in the image of the form to that which will be in the very truth of the face or in the face of truth."[295] Once again, through the image and the mirror we are said to see God's glory, not indeed "face to face" but still with an unveiled face. For faith, God is veiled; for contemplation the veil is lifted from his face. Here are the three stages: "For if you constantly attend to the presence of the Lord, veiled though it be, through faith, eventually you will contemplate his glory also with face unveiled, albeit in a mirror and image. But when the days of purification are completed and what is perfect comes, you will stand before the Lord in Jerusalem dwelling with his face and looking upon him face to face without end, to whom be benediction and glory for ever and ever. Amen."[296]

John Morson OCSO
Hilary Costello OCSO

294. Ser. 19:6.   295. *Ibid.*   296. *Ibid.*

SERMON 1

THE FIRST SERMON FOR ADVENT

"WE ARE WAITING for the Savior."[1] Such waiting is truly a joy to the righteous, who are waiting for the hope of blessedness, the glorious coming of our great God and Savior Jesus Christ.[2] "What am I waiting for," a righteous man may ask, "but the Lord?"[3] "I know," he says, turning towards him, "that you will not disappoint me after such a wait as mine.[4] Already my being is with you;[5] for our nature, taken from amongst us and offered on our behalf, is glorified with you. This gives us hope; for all flesh will come to you,[6] the members following their Head, so that the holocaust may be complete."

But a man can wait for the Lord the more trustfully if his conscience is so at rest as to let him say: "Every smallest possession of mine, Lord, is entirely yours, for I have treasured up in heaven all my powers, either by giving them to you or by renouncing them for you. At your feet I have laid down all that is mine, knowing you will be able not just to keep it safe,[7] but to restore it to me multiplied a hundred-fold and to add to it eternal life." How blessed are you, poor in spirit, who in accordance with the advice of the Wonderful Counsellor, lay up for yourselves treasures in

---

1. Phil 3:20. This text was read daily at Lauds during Advent.
2. Tit 2:13.
3. Ps 38:8. The Vulgate enumeration of the psalms is used throughout as being that with which Guerric was familiar. This enumeration can be found in the Douay and Confraternity of Christian Doctrine translations.
4. Ps 118:116.   5. Ps 38:8.   6. Ps 64:3.   7. 2 Tim 1:12.

heaven,[8] lest your hearts become corrupt by remaining on earth with your treasure. "For," he says, "where your treasure is there your heart is also."[9] Let your hearts go then, let them go after their treasures; let your attention be fixed on high and your expectancy hang upon the Lord, so that you can justly say with the apostle: "Our abiding place is in heaven, from where we are expecting the Savior to come."[10]

O hope of all peoples,[11] everyone who waits for you shall not be disappointed.[12] Our fathers waited for you—all the righteous from the beginning of the world hoped in you—and they have not been disappointed.[13] For they have now received your mercy in the midst of your temple[14] and make joyful choir to praise you, singing: "Blessed is he who comes in the name of the Lord;[15] trustfully have I waited for the Lord and he has turned towards me."[16] They recognize the divine majesty humbled in the flesh and say: "Look, this is our God; we have been waiting for his coming and he will save us. This is the Lord; we have been relying on him and we shall be joyful and happy in the salvation he will grant us."[17]

2. For just as the Church awaited in the holy ones of old the first coming, so in us she is expecting the second. Just as she steadfastly hoped in the first for the price of her redemption, so she hopes in the second for the reward of her earnings. This looking forward in hope raises her above earthly concerns; her eyes are fixed with joyous longing upon those of heaven. There are some, impatient to find happiness in the affairs of this present life, who neglect the Lord's advice and make every effort to snatch the prizes this world offers. But blessed is the man whose whole hope rests in the Lord's name and who takes no notice of spurious and empty foolishness.[18] He will shrink from the contamination of their ways,[19] because he knows that it is better to become humble with the meek than to share out ill-gotten gains with the proud.[20] He will find comfort in

---

8. Mt 6:20.
9. Mt 6:21.
10. Phil 3:20.
11. Gen 49:10.
12. Ps 24:3.
13. Ps 21:6.
14. Ps 47:10.
15. Ps 117:26; cf. Mt 21:9.
16. Ps 39:2.
17. Is 25:9.
18. Ps 39:5.
19. Wis 2:16.
20. Prov 16:19.

saying to himself: "The Lord is my share, so I will wait for him. The Lord is good to everyone that trusts him, to a soul that seeks him. It is good to stand by quietly, ready to greet the Lord.[21] Though, true enough, my soul has longed for your salvation, Lord, still I trust in your word.[22] As it says in Scripture: 'Hope long delayed grieves the soul and desire unfulfilled brings it weariness,'[23] still your promise is there to strengthen it. In this the soul does not have just a bare hope; it overflows with hope, hope mounting upon hope as trial comes upon trial, delay upon delay. I am absolutely sure that in the end he will appear and will prove not to have deceived me; so in spite of the delay he imposes I shall go on waiting for him confidently, because he certainly will come and will not be later[24] than the most timely day."

When will this day be? When the full number of all these brethren of ours has been reached[25] and the time of mercy set aside for penance is completed. Listen to Isaiah, who often gained entry to the heavenly council chamber; he tells us with what design the Lord puts off the judgment for a time: "The Lord delays so that he can be merciful towards you, and thus he will be honored for having spared you. The Lord is a God of judgment; blessed is everyone who waits for him."[26]

3. So, if you are wise, give an eye to yourself and see how you are using this delay. If you are a sinner, do not be heedless but take the opportunity to repent. If you are holy the time is given you to progress in holiness, not to slip away from the faith. For if the evil servant said in his heart: "My Lord's coming is delayed," and began to behave brutally towards his subordinates, even indulging in feasting and carousals with drunken companions, it will be a day he did not know, a day he hoped would never come, upon which the Lord of that servant will return and mark him out and give him a place among the hypocrites. There it is that there shall be weeping and gnashing of teeth.[27] The wickedness and infidelity of this

---

21. Lam 3:24–26. 22. Ps 118:81. 23. Prov 13:12.
24. Cf. Hab 2:3. 25. Rev 6:11. 26. Is 30:18.
27. Mt 24:48–51.

servant seem to speak with that voice of disgust and despair which we read of in Isaiah. When the Lord delays for a while there are disbelievers and mockers to whom it seems fit to insult the messengers he so frequently sends: "A rule about this, a rule about that," they say, "a rule about this, a rule about that; wait for this, wait for that; wait for this, wait for that, a little bit here, a little bit there."[28] But as to the penalty that will come upon these miserable men the prophet is not silent. A little further on he adds: "The word of the Lord will come to them" (what they themselves said to the prophets): "A rule about this, a rule about that, a rule about this, a rule about that, wait for this, wait for that; wait for this, wait for that; a little bit here, a little bit there. They will sally out and fall back again, beaten, snared and taken."[29] That is to say, they will sally out by apostasy; fall into evil ways; be ensnared in delights that bring death, in temptation that leaves neither the will nor the power to escape by repentance; be taken by sudden death; be beaten in eternal damnation. "Man," says Solomon, "does not know what his end will be; in a dark moment he is taken, suddenly like a hooked fish or an ensnared bird."[30]

So, in case our faith should cool or our patience become sultry through the delay of our hope, and we start to side with those who believe for a time but fall away in time of trouble,[31] he who grants faith, tests what he has granted and crowns what he has tested, cries to us from heaven: "Let him who would believe, not be in a hurry[32] to see what he believes." For if we hope for something we do not see, then we exercise patience in waiting. Through Hosea the Lord gives an order to the Bride whom he has taken to himself in troth: "You will be waiting for me many days, but you are not to take any other husband or lover."[33] This is the proper way of waiting for the Lord, keeping his troth. Even though we may miss the consolation of his presence we must not look about adulterously but wait in suspense for his return. The Lord says this in the same prophet: "The people will wait in suspense for my return."[34]

28. Cf. Is 28:10.   29. Is 28:13.   30. Eccles 9:12.   31. Lk 8:13.
32. Is 28:16.   33. Hos 3:3.   34. Hos 11:7.

Fitting it is indeed that the people should be in suspense, as it were, between heaven and earth, unable as yet to grasp heavenly affairs but preferring even so not to have any contact with those of earth. And if at any time they should make contact with them, it is only with the very tips of the fingers—I mean the most outward parts of the soul—and then on account of the necessities of corrupted nature which we are forced to minister to as long as creation is subject, however unwilling, to such external formalities.[35] It is commonly said: "He is unfortunate who is waiting in suspense;" but I would say: "He is most happy who is waiting in such suspense as this." The reason why my soul chooses this suspense and my bones such a suspended death[36] is to make them persevere in their suspension from this cross until I merit to die upon it.

4. O Lord Jesus: when you were about to exercise that power which was yours of laying down your life, and the sort of death by which you would will to do it still remained in your own choice, you chose to hang from the cross, so that being raised up over the earth you might draw us to yourself and hang us also above earthly concerns. But you suffered to be laid down only at death, so that we also might persevere until death on the cross and ascend from there to heaven all the more easily, stepping as it were off the topmost rung. Grateful thanks to you, Lord Jesus; there it is we are; there it is we wait for you; not for Elijah, to come and bring us down, but for Eli, that is to say, Our Lord, to come and take us up.[37]

"A little bit here, a little bit there."[38] If you should give a rule about this or a rule about that, I for one have made a single act of belief in all your rulings—but do you help my lack of belief,[39] so that I may wait for you, ever wait there for you unmoved, until I see what I believe. For I believe that I shall see the Lord's favor in the land of the living.[40]

Do you believe this too? Then wait for the Lord, behave courageously, strengthen your heart and bear with the Lord.[41] Woe upon

---

35. Rom 8:20.
36. Cf. Job 7:15.
37. Cf. Mt 27:46f.
38. Is 28:13.
39. Cf. Mk 9:24.
40. Ps 26:13.
41. Ps 26:14.

those who have lost patience and turned aside into crooked ways.[42] And what will they do when the Lord starts examining them? For, although he does command that he should be awaited with patience, in another place he promises that he will be coming quickly. On the one hand he is giving some idea of the great persistence needed, on the other he is strengthening the faint-hearted, terrifying the improvident, and rousing up the lazy. "Look," he says, "I am coming quickly and bringing with me rewards to bestow on everyone in proportion to his labors."[43] Further, to Jerusalem he says: "Your salvation shall soon come; why should you be consumed with grief?" The time truly is short,[44] though it may well seem very long to any of us who are in turmoil, whether from labor or from love. Both these then are necessary: first of all to make us fear the Judge who is near at hand, and, maybe for me, maybe for you, is in the very doorway;[45] and then to give us long-suffering patience should he prolong the delay. But certainly he shall come,[46] that Lord of ours, our dread and our desire, the rest and the reward of his laborers, the sweetness and embrace of his lovers, the blessedness of all, our Savior Christ Jesus, who lives and reigns throughout endless ages. Amen.

---

42. Sir 2:16.
45. Mt 24:33.
43. Rev 22:12.
46. Cf. Hab 2:3.
44. Cf. 1 Cor 7:29.

SERMON 2

THE SECOND SERMON FOR ADVENT

"BEHOLD THE KING is coming, let us hasten to meet our Savior."[1] Solomon put it very well when he said: "As cold water to a thirsty soul, so is good news from a far country."[2] He certainly brings good news who announces the coming of the Savior, the reconciliation of the world and the good things of the world to come. How welcome the feet of them that preach peace and bring good tidings.[3] There are many of them, not one. Many, I say, but with one mind. In a long succession from the beginning of time messengers have come to us with one message, one word: "He comes, yes, he is coming."[4] "Where have these messengers come from?" you ask. Scripture tells us: "from a far country."[5] Because they come from the "land of the living"[6] and

1. For the opening theme of this sermon Guerric uses the antiphon or refrain of the invitatory used at the vigils or matins of the First Sunday of Advent: *Ecce venit rex: occurramus obviam Salvatori nostro.* Guerric's sermons are inspired by the liturgy not only in occasional texts, but very extensively in regard to their themes and the Scripture passages that are employed.

2. Prov 25:25.

3. Guerric here employs the fourth responsory from the vigils of the common office for apostles and evangelists: *O quam pulchri (super montes) pedes: (Annuntiantium pacem, annuntiantium bona)* (Cistercian Antiphonary).

4. Ezek 39:8. *Ecce venit* is a constantly recurring theme in the Advent liturgy.

5. Cf. Josh 9:6.

6. The phrase "the land of the living" (*terra viventium*) occurs not only in the Psalms (26:13, 141:6) but also in the Canticle of Hezekiah (Is 38:11) which is sung at Lauds on Tuesday. It is also found in the proto-gospel of Isaiah (53:8) which is read during the Advent offices.

7

there is a great distance between that and this land of the dying; between ourselves and them, there is still a great chasm.[7] From there then the Prophets were sent to us and angels too. For if they went about here in the body they were caught up there by the Spirit when they were to be sent so that they might hear and see there what they were to announce here. Such messengers are waters of refreshment[8] and a draught of saving wisdom to a soul athirst for God. For such a soul the herald of the coming and of the other mysteries of the Savior draws and proffers water with joy from the springs of the Savior.[9] And the soul is heard to reply to the messenger, be it Isaiah or any other of the Prophets, in the words of Elisabeth. It has drunk of the same spirit as she has and says: "Whence is this that my Lord should come to me? Behold as soon as your salutation sounded in my ears the Spirit in my heart leapt for joy, earnestly desiring to hurry off to meet God its Savior."[10]

2. And really, brethren, we should go to meet the coming Christ with joy in our heart. Even at this very moment he should be saluted from afar, or at least we should return his greeting who orders deliverance for Jacob.[11] "You shall not be ashamed to salute a friend," says Wisdom.[12] How much more ought you to return a greeting? O Salvation of my face and my God,[13] what an honor that you should have saluted your servants. How much the greater that you should have saved them? Our salvation would not have been whole and entire had you only ordered deliverance and had not really given it. But you have given it not only by greeting with the kiss of peace in your Incarnation those you had previously saluted with words of peace, but, more, by effecting their salvation through your death on the Cross.

Let us therefore rise up with joyful eagerness and hasten to welcome our Savior. Let us adore him and salute him at a distance,[14] crying out to him: "Deliverance, Lord, deliverance; Lord, grant us days of prosperity. Blessed are you who will be coming in the name

---

7. Cf. Lk 16:26.   8. Cf. Lk 16:24.   9. Is 12:3.
10. Cf. Lk 1:43f.   11. Ps 43:5.   12. Sir 22:31.
13. Ps 42:6.   14. Cf. Lk 1.7:12.

of the Lord.[15] Welcome to you who come to deliver us: blessed be you who come to better our lot. Grant us days of prosperity then, Lord, you who come so favorable and beneficent to the human race; set out, proceed prosperously and reign.[16] May the Father, God of our salvation, make your journey a prosperous one."[17] "He shall prosper in the things for which I sent him,"[18] says the Father, but not in accordance with the prayers of the carnally-minded, nor with the desire of Peter who did not want him to suffer.[19] And whatsoever he shall do shall prosper,[20] not to satisfy the rash wishes of men but for their true salvation. Vain is the deliverance of men,[21] but salvation is of God[22] who has effected our salvation in his own blood, pouring it out in payment, offering it as refreshment.

Come then, Lord, save me and I shall be saved.[23] Come and smile upon us and we shall find deliverance.[24] We have waited for you, be our stronghold, our deliverer in time of trouble.[25] In this fashion did the prophets and holy men, with great desire and longing, run to greet the Christ who was to come, hoping if possible to see with their eyes what they foresaw in their hearts. Hence the words of the Lord to his disciples: "Blessed are the eyes that see what you see; I tell you there have been many prophets and holy men who longed to see what you see and never saw it, to hear what you hear and never heard it."[26] Abraham, our father, was full of joy to see the day of Christ. He saw it—but in the lower regions—and rejoiced.[27] In that day the coldness and hardness of our hearts will be greatly punished—I mean [3.] if we do not look forward with joy of spirit to the anniversary of Christ's birth which, we are promised, we shall, God willing, see very soon. In fact Holy Scripture seems to insist we have such joy so that our spirit, lifted out of itself,[28] may run to meet the arrival of Christ in transports of joy, and, straining forward impatient of delay, may strive to pierce the future even now.

15. Ps 117:25f.
16. Ps 44:5.
17. Ps 67:20.
18. Is 55:11.
19. Mt 16:22.
20. Ps 1:3.
21. Ps 107:13.
22. Ps 3:9.
23. Jer 17:14.
24. Ps 79:4, 8, 20.
25. Is 33:2.
26. Lk 10:23.
27. Jn 8:56.
28. Lam 3:28.

I say this because I believe that when we are admonished in many places in Scripture to meet the coming of Christ it is not only the second coming that is referred to but the first also.[29] In what way, you ask. Because just as in the second coming we will go to meet him, our bodies rising up in exultation, so we must greet his first coming with hearts straining with desire and leaping with joy. For you know that in the resurrection, when we have put on new bodies, as the Apostle says, we shall be caught up in the clouds to meet Christ in the air, and so we shall ever be with the Lord.[30] So too there are not lacking clouds which will raise up our spirits to higher things provided our hearts are not too lazy and tied to earth, and so we will be with the Lord if only for half an hour.[31] Unless I am mistaken you know from experience what I say. For when the clouds sent out a sound,[32] that is to say, when the voices of prophets or apostles sounded in the Church, your minds and hearts have been borne aloft as on a cloud to sublime things and on occasion carried beyond even these, so that they have merited to behold, in however small a degree, the glory of God.[33] Then, I doubt not, you recognized the truth of the word the Lord rains down from that cloud he daily sets as a means of ascent for us:[34] "The sacrifice of praise shall glorify me; and there is the way by which I will show him the salvation of God."[35]

In this fashion it may happen that before his actual coming the

29. The theme of the two comings, or rather of the three comings (see further on in this same paragraph) of Christ is common in the Advent Sermons of the Cistercian Fathers; e.g., St Bernard's Sermons for Advent, especially the third and fifth. Helinand of Froidmont who often quotes St Bernard in this instance departs from him in distinguishing four comings: see PL 212:481ff.

30. 1 Thess 4:17.   31. Rev 8:1.   32. Ps 76:18.   33. 2 Cor 3:18.

34. Ps 103:3. Frequently where we have the first person plural in the text here (us), many of the manuscripts have the second person plural (you). See the critical edition.

35. Ps 49:23. There is undoubtedly here a reference to the daily celebration of the Eucharistic sacrifice. The Cistercian Fathers do not often treat of the Eucharist *ex professo* (with the significant exceptions of William of St Thierry's *De Sacramento Altaris* and Isaac of Stella's *De Officio Missae*), yet from the passing references in their writings it is readily seen that the role of the Eucharist in Christian life was well understood and appreciated by them.

Lord may come to us, and before he arrives for the world in general he may pay us a friendly visit. "I will not leave you orphans," he says, "I will come to you."[36] And indeed, be it for a man's merit or ardent striving, that coming of the Lord to the individual is frequent in this middle time between his first coming and his final coming, conforming us to the first, preparing us for the last. He comes to us now of course so that his first coming will not have been in vain nor his last in anger against us. In this coming he is intent to reform our spirit of pride, making it conform to his humility which he manifested in his first coming, so that he might also refashion our lowly body, making it like to his glorious body[37] which he will manifest when he comes again the second time. Without any doubt that intimate visitation which imparts to us the grace of the first coming and pledges the glory of the second is to be desired with all longing and sought after with every care. For "God loves mercy and truth; the Lord will give grace and glory,"[38] granting grace through his mercy, conferring glory through his truth.

4. And just as in the order of time, so too in the degree of its likeness this spiritual coming is midway between the two corporeal comings, like a mediator it participates in both. The first coming was hidden and lowly; the last will be public and glorious; this one is certainly hidden but no less wonderful. I say hidden not because it is unknown to the one visited but because he comes to him secretly. This is why the soul filled with glory exults, saying to itself: "My secret is my own, my secret is my own."[39] But not even the one to whom he comes can see him before he enters into full possession of him. As holy Job says of himself: "If he comes to me I will not see him; if he departs I shall not understand."[40] Coming he is not seen, departing he is not understood; he who while he is present and only while he is present is light to soul and mind. In that light, invisible he is seen, inconceivable he is understood. On the other hand how wonderful this coming of the Lord even though it is hidden.

36. Jn 14:18.
37. Phil 3:21.
38. Ps 83:12.
39. Is 24:16.
40. Job 9:11.

Into what a sweet and happy state of absorbed admiration of himself does he plunge and keep the soul contemplating him; all the inward man exclaims: "Lord who is like to you?"[41] Those who have experienced it know of what I am speaking: would that those who have not experienced it would really desire to do so, in such a way however that rash curiosity might not cause them to be overwhelmed by glory as searchers of majesty[42] but rather that filial love might be strengthened in them by grace as longers after their loved one. For the Lord lifts up the meek and brings the wicked down even to the dust,[43] resists the proud and gives his grace to the humble.[44]

Since then the first coming brought grace and the last will bring glory, this one indeed partakes both of grace and of glory; for in it, through the consolation of grace, we are given a foretaste of future glory. In the first the God of majesty is seen as one despised, in the last he will be seen in awe-inspiring might. In this one he is wonderful and lovable: the lustre of grace that renders him lovable demands admiration, not disdain; the splendor of glory that makes him wonderful brings consolation, not fear. Of the first coming Isaiah wrote: "We have seen him and there was no sightliness that we should be desirous of him;"[45] concerning his final coming even the just man was in dread: "And who shall stand to see him?"[46] But the Apostle writes of this one: "But we all, beholding the glory of the Lord, are transformed into the same image from glory to glory as by the Spirit of the Lord."[47]

Utterly wonderful and lovable it is when God, the Love of the lover, is grasped even in the senses, when the Bridegroom embraces the Bride and they become one in the Spirit,[48] as she is transformed into the same image in which as in a mirror she sees the glory of the Lord.[49] How blessed are they who because of their burning love have already merited to receive this privilege. Blessed too are they whose holy simplicity leads them to hope for it sometime. The

---

41. Ps 34:10.   42. Prov 25:27.   43. Ps 146:6.
44. Jas 4:6.   45. Is 53:2.   46. Mal 3:2.
47. 2 Cor 3:18. 48. 2 Cor 3:18.   49. 1 Cor 13:12.

Sermon 2:4

first already enjoy relief from labor in the fruit of their love: the others, whose merit is perhaps the greater as their relief is less, bear the burden of the day and its heat,[50] awaiting their coming reward. And so, my dear brethren, we who have not had experience of such a wonderful consolation are in the meantime encouraged by firm faith and a pure conscience to wait patiently for the coming of the Lord.[51] That faith, with as much joy as fidelity, says with Paul: "I know whom I have believed and I am certain he is able to keep that which I have committed unto him against that day,"[52] against the coming, that is, of the glory of the great God and our Savior Jesus Christ,[53] to whom be glory for ever and ever. Amen.

---

50. Cf. Mt 20:12.   51. Jas 5:7.   52. 2 Tim 1:12.
53. Tit 2:13.

SERMON 3

THE THIRD SERMON FOR ADVENT

"BE PREPARED now Israel to meet the Lord, for he is coming"[1]. And you too my dear brethren be prepared as well; for the Son of Man will come when you least expect him.[2] He is coming, nothing is more certain than that; but when he will arrive—nothing is less certain. Right up to the last moment we will not know the actual time the Father in his almighty power has appointed.[3] Even the angels who stand before him have not been given the privilege of knowing that day or hour.[4] Our last day most certainly must come to us; but it is very uncertain when it will come, where we will be or whence it will come. All we can say is that it is knocking at the door for the old, and lies in wait for the young. O that they would keep careful guard over themselves who see death so ready to enter, nay rather who see it already entering. For has it not already entered, at least to some extent, a body grown senile and decrepit? Yet in many who are already half-dead one can see worldly desires still alive. The limbs are growing cold and the fire of avarice still burns within; life is coming to its end and ambition still strains ahead. Because our youth or health perhaps appear to promise some more years ahead of us death is not often before our eyes, but this is just the very reason why, if we are wise, it should be in our thoughts, lest that day come like a thief in the night[5] and find us unprepared and unready. It is lying in wait for us

---

1. Amos 4:12.   2. Lk 12:40.   3. Acts 1:7.
4. Mt 24:36.   5. 1 Thess 5:2.

and we should fear it all the more for its being hidden, for we can neither see it nor get warning of it. There is therefore only one thing that makes us safe: never to think that we are safe. For fear makes a careful man always prepared until at length fear can give way to security and not security to fear. The wise man says: "I shall keep myself from my iniquity,[6] seeing that I am powerless in respect to my death." He knows that the just man, if he is surprised by death, will be at rest.[7] In fact that man triumphs over death who was not overcome by iniquity during his life.

Brethren, how beautiful and blessed it is not only to be without fear of death but with the assurance of a good conscience to triumph over it; in the spirit and words of Martin;[8] to rebuke the foul beast if he dares to present himself, to open joyfully to the Judge when he comes and knocks.[9] At that hour you may see unfortunates like me tremble, begging for a truce and having it denied them; wanting to buy the oil of penance for a sorrowing conscience and not having enough time;[10] desirous of turning aside those ghostly specters and not being able to do so; anxious to hide away in the body from angry wrath and being forced to go forth. He will go forth, his spirit shall go forth and the sinner shall return into his earth[11] whence he was drawn. "In that day all their thoughts shall perish."[12] It is only human, I know, to be distressed about the moment of our passage from the earth. Even the perfect wish not to be stripped but rather to be further clothed.[13] And although their conscience does not in fact reproach them, yet since that is not where their justification lies,[14] they must of necessity fear the unknown judgment. But whether it be attachment to this life, or lack of holiness, or fear of

6. Ps 17:24.   7. Wis 4:7.

8. The reference is to St Martin of Tours who is usually considered to be the first great monk of the West. Jacques Fontaine has recently published a critical edition of Sulpicius Severus' classical *Life of St Martin: Sources Chrétiennes*, 133 (Paris: Cerf, 1967). An English translation prepared by Bernard Peebles was published in volume seven of the Fathers of the Church Series (New York, 1949), pp. 101–140. Martin's encounters with the Devil are found in Chapters 6 (p. 111), 21 (p. 131) and 24 (p. 136).

9. Lk 12:36.   10. Cf. Mt 25:8ff.   11. Ps 145:4.
12. Ps 145:4.   13. 2 Cor 5:4.   14. Cf. 1 Cor 4:4.

the judgment that troubles the soul[15] the just man says: "You, O Lord, will remember mercy,[16] and you will send your mercy and your truth and will deliver my soul from the midst of the young lions,[17] and I who was up till now sore distressed, in peace in the selfsame I will sleep and will rest."[18]

God called the earth and it heard him with trembling.[19] For when he made known judgment from heaven, at the very sound of it the earth trembled and then, purified by its terror, was at rest.[20] Blessed are they who so purge themselves of all the dross of sin[21] during this present life that at the moment of death they need no more than the purification effected by fear. As for me, a useless and negligent servant, it will go well if I am saved through fire, all the wood, hay and stubble[22] that I have heaped up for myself consumed by the flames; or if I escape, only half-burned. And indeed, by comparison with the evil of damnation, it is a good thing to be saved by fire; without any doubt it is much better to be made perfect by the mere cleansing of fear; and best of all not to be disturbed even by fear.

2. For that reason be ready, O true Israel, to meet the Lord, so that you may not only open to him when he comes and knocks,[23] but may run to meet him, eager and joyful, while he is still far off, and, confident about the day of judgment, pray earnestly that his kingdom may come.[24] If you want to be found ready then, take the advice of Wisdom and prepare justice for yourself before the judgment.[25] May you be prepared to do every good work[26] and no less prepared to suffer every evil so that your lips may sing without any reproach from your heart: "My heart is ready, Lord, my heart is ready, ready with your help to do good, ready to suffer ill, and so ready for both that I will sing and give praise in my glory,[27] that is, I will rejoice and glory whichever comes." And at once the just man

---

15. Ps 41:7.
16. Hab 3:2.
17. Ps 56:4f.
18. Ps 4:9.
19. Ps 49:1; Bar 3:33.
20. Ps 75:9.
21. Is 1:25.
22. 1 Cor 3:12ff.
23. Cf. Lk 12:36.
24. Mt 6:10.
25. Sir 18:19.
26. Tit 3:1.
27. Ps 107:2.

rouses himself in this matter, saying: "Arise psaltery and harp,"[28] that is, my heart and my body,[29] to rejoice in the living God.[30] The heart is meant on account of its spiritual activity, the body because of its passions. For the heart relishing the things that are above is a psaltery giving forth heavenly music; the body suffering things of earth is a lyre producing worldly music. So it is that elsewhere David, offering his devoted service to God, says: "I am ready to keep your commandments,[31] and so ready that I am not troubled when temptation breaks in on me and persecution rages. Let my rival pursue me,[32] my servant curse me,[33] my own son seek my life,[34] even so I am not troubled about not keeping the commandments of evangelical perfection. I will render good for evil to those who return evil for good;[35] will be solicitous for the safety of those who persecute me, mourning their death; will bear with the reproaches of my servant, not permitting my honor to be vindicated by a friend." Here is evangelical perfection before the evangel: charity, patient and kind,[36] even towards enemies whom it endures. And because he was so prepared he went confidently to meet his Lord. "Without iniquity," he says, "have I run and directed whatever was perverse in me so far as I was able."[37]

Therefore do rise up to meet me coming to meet you, for I cannot reach your heights unless, stooping low to the work of your hands, you stretch out your right hand.[38] Rise up to meet me and see if there be in me the way of iniquity.[39] And if you do find it there unknown to me, remove it from me, and, having compassion on me with regard to your law, lead me in the eternal way,[40] which is Christ.[41] He is the way by which we journey, the eternity at the

---

28. Ps 107:3.

29. This is reminiscent of a passage in Bernard of Clairvaux's *Apologia* (no. 14) where employing Ps 80:3 he finds in the two instruments the same analogy to man's spirit and body. See *The Works of Bernard of Clairvaux*, vol. 1, trans. M. Casey (Cistercian Fathers Series, 1).

30. Ps 83:3.	31. Ps 118:60.	32. 1 Sam 16–27.
33. 2 Sam 15–18.	34. 2 Sam 16:5ff.	35. Ps 7:5; 37:21.
36. 1 Cor 13:4.	37. Cf. Ps 58:5f.	38. Job 14:15.
39. Ps 58:6; 138:24.	40. Ps 118:29; 138:24.	41. Jn 14:6.

journey's end; he is the spotless way, the blessed dwelling-place.

3. However, I think that even before you reach that blessed dwelling, if you have prepared for the Lord a spotless way he will quite often deign to tread the way with you,[42] making smooth the path before you,[43] so that your heart may be enlarged and you may run in the way of his commandments.[44] The beginning, you may say, is strait and narrow.[45] For wisdom walks in the way of justice, as she herself says.[46] And he that possesses justice shall lay hold of her and she will meet him as a mother welcomes the son who cherishes her.[47] She goes about seeking such as are worthy of her and she shows herself to them cheerfully in her ways and meets them with all prudence.[48] If you complain she seldom if ever meets you, consider whether you have perhaps soiled your way. For it is written: "The foolishness of a man soils his way; he finds fault with God in his heart."[49] Yet God stands at the gate and knocks, in order that if a man opens to him he may share with him the delights of the heavenly banquet.[50] The spouse says: "A knock on the door, and then my true love's voice: Let me in, my sister, my spouse.[51] Open your heart to me and I will nourish it; open your mouth and I will fill it."[52] "I have opened my mouth," says David, "and have drawn my breath."[53] Now the breath of our mouth is Christ the Lord.[54] He is to be not merely invited but drawn into the guest chamber of our heart by the violence of our prayers and the vehemence of our fervor. The gospel tells us of the two disciples to give us an example of this. Indeed if sometimes he makes as though he would go farther,[55] he does so for no other reason than that he may prove the zeal of your love, just as the two angels whom Lot adored and begged to enter. They dissembled saying: "No, we will remain in

42. Ps 84:14.   43. Ps 17:37.
44. Ps 118:28. Cf. St Benedict's Rule for Monasteries (Hereafter RB), Prol. 49. (The verses are cited according to the edition of E. Manning [Westmalle, 1962] who follows Lentini.)
45. Cf. RB Prol., 47.   46. Prov 8:20.   47. Sir 15:1f.
48. Wis 6:17.
49. Prov 19:3 as it is found in the Septuagint version.
50. Cf. Rev 3:20.   51. Song 5:2.   52. Ps 80:11.
53. Ps 118:131.   54. Lam 4:20.   55. Lk 24:28.

the street." But what does Scripture tell us? "He pressed them very much to turn in unto him."[56] Loving violence, by which the heavenly kingdom is borne away;[57] matchless importunity that wins as guest Christ or angels.

But what does it mean, you say, that Jesus makes as though he would go further? What else than what Ecclesiastes tells us of himself: "I have said, I will be wise, and it departed farther from me."[58] The Spouse speaks more explicitly when, giving voice to our daily complaint, she says: "I rose up to open to my beloved, but he had turned aside and was gone. I sought him, and found him not, I called, and he did not answer me,"[59] just as he did not answer the Canaanite woman either.[60] You too are wont to call on the Spirit of wisdom, you are accustomed to seek the Spirit of grace in prayer. If it seems that he draws farther away from you, do not despair but be more importunate in your pleading until you hear him answer you: "Great is your faith, be it done to you as you will."[61]

4. But when you invite Jesus take care that you do not invite the God of majesty into an unclean and unworthy dwelling where a wrangling wife or clouds of smoke or a dripping roof would not allow even yourself to dwell in peace.[62] For his place is in peace[63] and nowhere else. Right and justice are the pillars of his throne.[64] "Now they seek me," he says, "from day to day, and desire to know my ways as a nation that has done justice and has not forsaken the will of their God."[65] "Right," he says, "and justice are the pillars of his throne." Do not plead that it is a lavish dwelling you have to prepare for so great and so powerful a guest and that it is beyond the limits of your poverty. You have the means at hand. I speak in human terms because of the infirmity of your flesh,[66] or rather because of the narrowness of your mind. Make a perfect confession of your past life, have a good will in respect to all else (for there is peace to men of good will),[67] and in this way you will have prepared with right and justice a throne for the Most High.

56. Gen 19:2f.
57. Mt 11:12.
58. Eccles 7:24.
59. Song 5:5f.
60. Mt 15:22ff.
61. Mt 15:28.
62. Prov 19:13; 27:15.
63. Ps 75:3.
64. Ps 88:15.
65. Is 58:2.
66. Rom 6:19.
67. Lk 2:14.

The Third Sermon for Advent

Do you want to hear more explicitly about the confession you should make in preparation for the coming of the Lord? "A just man is the first to accuse himself," says the Scripture.[68] And what follows? His Friend comes, who before the accusation was withdrawing farther away, estranged. For when he said: "I will confess against myself my injustice to the Lord,"[69] the Lord forgave him. "He comes and shall search him."[70] Indeed he shall search him like a strong draught searching the heart and the reins,[71] reaching into the division of the soul and the spirit,[72] drawing out all impurity from the recesses of the soul and the deep caverns of the mind, purging love that it may bring forth more fruit.[73] God the Father, the husbandman,[74] rejoices already over the first-fruits of that confession.

However, he who after such confession is present, sometimes even before he is called on, at other times waits for you to invite him. And in order to increase your merits he often dissimulates for a long time so that by being more attentive at the psalmody[75] and more instant in prayer you may in your gentle violence compel him to enter. If you do not, the prophet laments that the cities of the south are shut up, with none to enter them.[76] When therefore you can say: "My heart is ready, O God,"[77] because it is emptied of evil, "my heart is ready," because it is full of holy desires, then busy yourself with what follows: "I will sing and recite a psalm."[78] And whatever may be your voice, singing or reciting, let this intention be in your mind: "Arise, my Glory, arise at my coming, for as far as in me lies I have gone to meet you."[79]

O good Jesus, how swift and prompt, how full of joy and gladness are you in running to greet such devotion as this. How cheerful do

---

68. Prov 18:17.
69. Ps 31:5.
70. Prov 18:17.
71. Ps 7:10.
72. Heb 4:12.
73. Jn 15:2.
74. Jn 15:1.
75. The reference is to the public or community prayer of the monks where they chanted psalms at great length, ordinarily at least forty in the course of the day.
76. Jer 13:19.
77. Ps 107:2.
78. Ps 26:6.
79. Ps 107:3.

you show yourself in these ways.[80] As Isaiah says: "You have met him that rejoices and does justice: in your ways they shall remember you."[81] For if you sing wisely in the way of integrity,[82] coming he will come and will bring to light what is hidden from you[83] so that you may understand the mysteries of the Scriptures you do not at present know. Then it will be as you say: "I will sing and I will understand in the unspotted way when you shall come to me."[84] Stir up, Lord, your power, which at your coming stirs up our sluggishness, and come to save us,[85] O Savior of the world, who live and reign God for ever and ever. Amen.

---

80. Wis 6:17.   81. Is 64:5.   82. Ps 100:2.
83. Ps 46:8; Hab 2:3.   84. Ps 100:1f.   85. Ps 79:3.

SERMON 4

THE FOURTH SERMON FOR ADVENT

"A VOICE of one crying in the wilderness: Prepare the way of the Lord."[1] Before anything else I think we should consider the grace of the desert, the blessedness of the desert, which right from the beginning of grace has deserved to be consecrated to the repose of the saints. The voice of one crying in the wilderness,[2] John preaching and bestowing the baptism of repentance in the desert, certainly consecrated for us his dwelling-place in the wilderness. Yet even before him the solitude had always been dearly loved by the holiest of the prophets as a place where they could listen to the Holy Spirit.[3] But a far greater and more divine grace came to the desert to sanctify it when Jesus took the place of John. Even before he began to preach to those doing penance he prepared a place for penitents.[4] For forty days while he was living in the wilderness, purifying it and dedicating it as a new place for the new life, he conquered the tyrant who brooded there and all his malice and subtlety, not so much for himself as for those who would be its future inhabitants.

If then you have fled away to remain in the solitude[5] continue to stay there; wait there for the One who will save you "from pusillanimity of spirit and the storm."[6] However much the storm of

---

1. Is 40:3; Mk 1:3. This is found in the pericope used for the Fourth Sunday of Advent.
2. Mk 1:3f. 3. See I Kings 17:2ff.; 19:3ff. 4. Mt 4:1f.
5. Ps 54:8. 6. Ps 54:9.

22

battles may assail you, however much you may feel the lack even of sustenance in the desert, do not because of pusillanimity of spirit return in mind to Egypt. The desert will feed you more abundantly with manna, that is, the bread of angels, than Egypt with its fleshpots.[7] Jesus himself fasted indeed in the wilderness[8] but the multitude that followed him into the desert he fed often and in a wonderful manner.[9] And much more frequently and in an even more wonderful way will he satisfy the needs of all you who have followed him into the desert and whose service is all the more pleasing since your purpose is so much holier.

When you think Jesus has forgotten you for rather too long, he himself, not unmindful of his goodness, will console you and say to you: "I remember the devotion of your youth, your love as a bride, how you followed me in the wilderness."[10] Then will he make your wilderness like the garden of delight,[11] and you yourself will confess that the glory of Lebanon has been given to it, the majesty of Carmel and Sharon.[12] For just as in many places today we are seeing fulfilled to the letter the prophecy: "The beautiful places of the wilderness shall grow fertile,[13] strangers shall eat in the deserts become fruitful;"[14] so places in Scripture which previously seemed fruitless and dry will quite suddenly be filled for you at the blessing of God with a wondrous and spiritual abundance, so that from the fullness of your heart you will sing a hymn of praise, saying: "Let them praise the Lord for his mercy, for his wonderful works to the sons of men, for he satisfied him who is thirsty and the hungry he filled with good things."[15]

2. By the wonderful favor of God's loving care, in this solitude of ours we have the peace of solitude and yet we do not lack the consolation and comfort of holy companionship. It is possible for each of us to sit alone and be silent,[16] because we have no one to disturb us with interruptions, and yet it cannot be said of us: "Woe

---

7. Ex 16:3f.
8. Mt 4:2.
9. Mt 14:13ff.; 15:39ff.
10. Jer 2:2.
11. Is 51:3.
12. Is 35:2.
13. Ps 64:13.
14. Is 5:17.
15. Ps 106:8f. Cf. Lk 1:53.
16. Lam 3:28.

to him who is alone, since he has nobody to console him or if he should fall has none to lift him up."[17] We are surrounded by companions, yet we are not in a crowd. We live as it were in a city, yet we have to contend with no tumult, so that the voice of one crying in the wilderness[18] can be heard by us, provided only that we have interior silence to correspond to the exterior silence that surrounds us. "The words of the wise heard in quiet," Solomon says, "are better than the shouting of a ruler among fools."[19] And now if the depths of your soul were to keep a quiet silence, the all-powerful Word would flow secretly into you from the Father's throne.[20] Happy then is the man who has so fled the world's tumult, who has so withdrawn into the solitude and secrecy of interior peace that he can hear not only the Voice of the Word but the Word himself: not John but Jesus.

Meanwhile let us hear what the Voice of the Word calls to us, so that one day we may progress from the Voice to the Word. "Prepare the way of the Lord," he says, "make straight his paths."[21] He prepares the way who amends his life; he makes straight the path who directs his footsteps along the narrow way. An amended life is certainly the straight road by which the Lord, who in this very conversion is already there before us, may come to us. For indeed it is by the Lord that the steps of a man are directed,[22] and he wants the road to be such that coming along it joyfully towards man he may continually walk with him. For unless he who is the Life, the Truth and the Way[23] anticipates his own advent to us, our way cannot be corrected according to the model of truth, and so cannot be directed

---

17. Eccles 4:10. William of St Thierry, who seems more eremitically inclined, applies this text to his relation with God: " 'Woe to him who is alone,' says Solomon. Woe indeed to me if I be alone, if you be not with me, nor I with you."—Meditation 2:1 (trans. Sr Penelope, *The Works of William of St Thierry*, vol. 1, Cistercian Fathers 3). See also Meditation 4:3. But the Cistercian Fathers more commonly, like Guerric, take the text in its literal sense and apply it to the horizontal relations within the cenobitic life. See e.g. St Bernard, Sermon 33:10 on the Song of Songs (*The Works of Bernard of Clairvaux*, vol. 3, Cistercian Fathers 7).

| 18. Is 40:3; Mk 1:3. | 19. Eccles 9:17. | 20. Wis 18:14f. |
| 21. Mk 1:3. | 22. Ps 36:23. | 23. Jn 14:6. |

to the way of eternity. By what does a young man correct his way, if not by observing his words,[24] if not by following in the footsteps of him who made himself the Way by which we might come to him? O that my ways may be directed to keeping your ways,[25] O Lord, so that because of the words from your lips I may follow even difficult ways. And if they should seem hard to the flesh that is weak they will seem sweet and pleasant to the spirit if it is resolute. "His ways are pleasant ways and all his paths make for peace,"[26] says the inspired writer. The ways of Wisdom are not only at peace, they bring peace; for when the ways of man please the Lord he even makes his enemies aspire to peace.[27] "If only Israel had walked in my ways," he says, "I would have humbled its enemies for nothing and turned my hand against its foes."[28] For why is there grief and misfortune in their ways if not because they have not known the way of peace?[29]

And so, when I have seen a restless, pig-headed and quarrelsome man vexed with grave temptation or tormented by worry, I remember that proverb: "An evil man always seeks rebellion, but a cruel angel will be sent against him"[30] and he is handed over to him for the destruction of the flesh that the spirit may be saved in the day of the Lord.[31] But if sometimes the way of the wicked prospers, do not be jealous of him who prospers in his way, of the man who carries out evil devices,[32] since this way of theirs is a stumbling-block to them,[33] so that the less the road they walk is fenced in for them so much more freely they run to death. It is of such men that Wisdom says: "The way of sinners is made plain with stones, but their end is hell and darkness and pains."[34] They spend their days in prosperity, but in a trice they go down to hell.[35] Blessed therefore are they whose way is blameless, who walk in the law of the Lord,[36] because even if they drink from the brook by the way they shall on that account lift up their head,[37] for their Head, whom they follow

---

24. Ps 118:9.
25. Ps 118:5.
26. Prov 3:17.
27. Prov 16:7.
28. Ps 80:15.
29. Ps 13:3.
30. Prov 17:11.
31. Cf. 1 Cor 5:5.
32. Ps 36:7.
33. Ps 48:14.
34. Sir 21:11.
35. Job 21:13.
36. Cf. Ps 118:1.
37. Ps 109:7.

through the way of his passion, they will accompany at the end of their exile.

3. And so, my brothers, whatever happens to you on the way of the Lord, run the way of God's commandments[38] with a joyful and generous heart, because though the way seems narrow to the fainthearted, still it is straight, and though it seems difficult it is blameless. Indeed, blessed are the blameless on the way,[39] who so travel the way of the world with blameless step that they do not soil their garments or at least if they have dirtied them they do not lose the second chance for happiness but wash their garments in the baptism of penance by which John baptized in the desert, preparing the way of the Lord.[40]

The pure way is surely chastity; the pleasing way along which the Lord of grace advances. Of him the prophet sings: "This is my God, his way is perfect."[41] Perfect was the chastity of the Virgin, by which he entered her womb, perfect must be the chastity of man by which he may enter his soul. Happy is the conscience of whom it can be said: "God girded me with the strength of continence and made my way pure."[42]

But in order that you might not boast of chastity without the other virtues, as if you had already prepared a clean way for the Lord, understand that it is still necessary for this road to be straight and level; it must not be dark and slippery: for the way of the wicked is dark and slippery with the angel of the Lord pursuing them,[43] and the way of the wicked is like deep darkness, they do not know over what they stumble.[44] Do we think, brothers, that somewhere in us is still to be found a certain crookedness of will, roughness of character, darkness through lack of understanding and slipperiness through inconsistent behavior? But how will we fulfill what the Scripture says about preparing the way unless we do what is written there, so that the crooked ways may be straight and the rough ways smooth.[45]

---

38. Ps 118:32. Cf. RB, Prol. 49.   39. Ps 1:1.   40. Mk 1:3f.
41. Ps 17:31.   42. Ps 17:33.   43. Ps 34:6.
44. Prov 4:19.   45. Is 40:4; Lk 3:5.

4. And so in the first place, if our will is crooked and twisted it must be rectified and corrected to the pattern of the Divine Will. Otherwise we will seem to say, as the wicked say: "The way of the Lord is not straight."[46] But immediately the inviolable Truth rebuts us and his terrible severity thunders: "Are my ways not straight? Is it not rather your ways that are crooked?"[47] Therefore you who hasten to prepare the way of the Lord, before all else let your will be good, since Wisdom will not enter into a malicious soul.[48]

And when you have thus made the crooked straight, understand that it is no less necessary to make the rough ways plain, that is, to even out harshness of character and diffuse a certain equanimity in your life with others, lest that meek and gentle traveler be shocked at the roughness of the road and draw back. Why should he not draw back, he who is meek and humble of heart[49] and who only rests with the gentle and humble, when even every human feeling draws back in horror from a man who is angry and cross-grained?

And even if you have advanced so far on the way of the Lord, that the road you follow is straight and your life is ordered by gentleness, you have indeed advanced, but you have not yet reached your destination unless the Word of God is a lamp to your feet and a light on your path.[50] "For in the path where I walk they have hidden a trap for me,"[51] says the Psalmist, and "there are ways which seem right to men, but their end leads to the depths of hell."[52] "The way of the wicked is like deep darkness," as Solomon says, "they do not know over what they stumble."[53] And the Lord says: "He who walks in darkness does not know where he goes."[54]

Certainly the commandment is a lamp, and teaching a light, and the reproofs of discipline the way of life;[55] for he who rejects reproof goes astray.[56] And so if you are wise you will not be your own teacher and guide in the way along which you have never walked;

---

46. Ezek 33:20. 47. Ezek 18:25. 48. Wis 1:4.
49. Mt 11:29. 50. Ps 118:105. 51. Ps 141:4.
52. Prov 16:25. 53. Prov 4:19. 54. Jn 12:35.
55. Prov 6:23. 56. Prov 10:17.

but you will incline your ear to masters[57] and acquiesce in their reproofs and advice and give yourself to the task of learning and reading[58] lest repenting too late you say: "Why did I hate discipline and my heart despise reproof? I did not listen to the voice of my teachers or incline my ear to the instructors. I was at the point of utter ruin in the assembled congregation."[59] Listen to David saying that a knowledge of the law frees from traps: "The wicked have laid a snare for me, but I have not strayed from your precepts."[60]

How have you done that? "Because your testimonies are my inheritance and in the way of your testimonies I delighted as much as in all riches.[61] Sinners laid in wait to destroy me, but I passed through the danger because I understood your testimonies."[62] "The law of God is in the heart of the righteous," he says, "and because of this his steps will not slip."[63] For this reason his son Solomon says: "With his mouth the godless man would destroy his friend but by knowledge the righteous is delivered."[64]

5. But this way in which we must meet with salvation and the Savior, just as it is not now darkened through ignorance of the truth, so it should not be slippery from inconstancy in work. Yet like Balaam, who fell down with his eyes open,[65] so we too see with wide-open eyes because of knowledge and we fall from negligence. Willingly and knowingly we commit sin and freely we fall. Nor can we make the excuse that the road is slippery; the fault is rather with the intention of the mind, that is, the foot we stand on. For who is not walking in slime while he is in the world, while he is living in his body of clay? Therefore it is not so much the road that is at fault as the foot which is not set firmly enough on the way of God.

---

57. Cf. RB, Prol. 1.

58. It is difficult to find a suitable English equivalent for the word *lectio* as it is understood in monastic tradition. It is not simply reading. Its nature may vary from quite serious study to little more than holding an open book in one's hand while the mind dwells in God. What is distinctive about it is that it is directly ordered to and wholly impregnated by the quest for God, contact with him, experience of him.

59. Prov 5:12ff.   60. Ps 118:110f.   61. Ps 118:14.
62. Ps 118:95.   63. Ps 36:31.   64. Prov 11:9.
65. Num 24:16.

But the man who falls, shall he not rise again?[66] A righteous man falls seven times a day and rises each time,[67] for the Lord lifts up those who are bowed down and the Lord guides the righteous.[68] "For if I said: 'My foot is slipping, your mercy, O Lord, helped me up'."[69] So when you cannot do otherwise, walk along the road, falling and rising, constantly crying out to him whom you desire to follow and to reach: "Keep my steps on your paths so that my feet may not slip.[70] And if there is any wicked way in me, that is, any human frailty, lead me in the everlasting way,[71] since it is through you, the Way and the Truth, that I shall come to you, the Life eternal.[72] Glory to you for endless ages." Amen.

66. Ps 40:8.
69. Ps 93:18.
72. Jn 14:6.
67. Prov 24:16.
70. Ps 16:5.
68. Ps 145:8.
71. Ps 138:24.

SERMON 5

THE FIFTH SERMON FOR ADVENT

"PREPARE A WAY for the Lord."[1] Brethren, we prepare the way of the Lord as we are bidden to do by walking along it; and we can walk along it only by preparing it. However far you journey along it, the way is always waiting to be prepared, so that you must start afresh from the place you have reached and advance along what lies ahead. You are led to do so because at every stage you meet the Lord for whose coming you are preparing the way, and each time you see him in a completely new way and as a much greater figure than you have met before. The just man has the right prayer when he says: "Set your way which justifies as a law for me, Lord, and I will always seek after it."[2]

It is therefore eternal life which is probably meant, because although a man can study his route with foresight and determine just how far he can go, from the very nature of goodness there is no limit to the way along which you travel. And so, when the wise and indefatigable traveler has reached his goal he will begin again; forgetting, that is, what lies behind him,[3] so that each day he can say to himself: "Now I begin."[4] He bounds on like a giant, whom nothing deters from pursuing the way of God's commandments.[5]

---

1. Is 40:3; Mk 1:3. This is taken from the pericope which is read on the Fourth Sunday of Advent.
2. Ps 118:33.
3. Phil 3:13.
4. Ps 76:11.
5. Ps 18:6.

Like another Jeduthun[6] with the speed of his running he jumps easily over the lazy who lie in his path. Even though he comes at the last hour of the day he achieves in a short time what takes others long,[7] so that suddenly first, where before he was the last, he receives his crown among the first.

2. But if only we who speak of the course of this way could understand even the beginning of it. As far as I can see a man who has begun has already gone far, provided he begins properly and finds the way to the inhabitable city.[8] "How few there are," Truth says, "who find it."[9] And how many go astray in the wilderness: all those in fact who are isolated, that is, all the proud who think of themselves alone. None of them can yet say: "Now I begin; this change is from the right hand of the Most High."[10] There is no change wrought in them so that they cease to be what they were, because they have not feared God.[11] For "the fear of the Lord is the beginning of wisdom."[12] If the beginning of wisdom, then surely it is also the beginning of the way of goodness. After all, it is this fear of the Lord which always puts into the heart of a man that timely counsel by which he can say: "I have considered my ways and turned my path to your decrees."[13] The fear of the Lord encourages the praise which the Psalmist teaches is the beginning of good works: "Begin for the Lord," he says, "with praise."[14] It also moves the proud man to penance, so that he hears the voice of him crying in the wilderness, ordering the preparation of the way and thus showing how to begin it. "Do penance, for the kingdom of heaven is at hand."[15] Solomon's advice agrees with this when, teaching the simple with unmistakable clarity, he says: "The beginning of the way of goodness is to do what is right."[16] And are

---

6. Jeduthun or Idithun, a prophetical musician of the tribe of Levi whose sons served the temple especially as musicians and gatekeepers, is mentioned several times in the Chronicles and also in Nehemiah and the Psalter, but it is not evident why Guerric attributes to him speed in running.

7. Wis 4:13.	8. Ps 106:4.	9. Mt 7:14.
10. Ps 76:11.	11. Ps 54:20.	12. Ps 110:10.
13. Ps 118:59.	14. Ps 146:7 as it is in the Septuagint version.
15. Mt 3:2; 4:17.	16. Prov 16:5.

we not doing what is right when we do penance? When we take from ourselves what we owe to God and return what we have stolen? This is the righteousness which walks before the Lord and prepares a way pleasing to him, as it is written: "Righteousness will go before him and make his footsteps a way."[17]

Just as John came before Jesus, so does penance come before grace, before that grace of reconciliation which receives us into the kiss of peace after we have made satisfaction. For in this way of penance righteousness and peace kiss each other[18] and run with eager and lighthearted step to meet him. The righteousness, that is, of the man who does penance and the peace of God who forgives; both celebrate with a holy kiss the happy and joyful pact of reconciliation.

Finally, do not think that this righteousness of a man who does what is just and right[19] is of little value, nor presume to compare the insignificant prayers and promises of the lazy with the labors of the penitents. Listen rather to what Solomon says: "The beginning of the way of goodness is to do what is just; this is more acceptable to God than the sacrifice of victims."[20]

If therefore you see a man who has professed this life of penance and who prefers little prayers to the holy labors which he has promised to perform, put before him this statement of the Wise Man: "The beginning of the way of goodness is to do what is just; this is more acceptable to God than the sacrifice of victims."[21] Similarly if you see a man whose brother holds something against him offering at the altar[22] a gift of praise or the sacraments, even there repeat to him the same sentence: "The beginning of the way to goodness is to do what is just, so that you can be reconciled with your brother: this is more acceptable to God than the sacrifice of victims." This also means that a man about to give alms should first of all make restitution if he has defrauded anybody, at least of what he has taken.[23] Nor should you yourselves think the voluntary offerings of your lips are pleasing to God[24]—I mean those psalms

17. Ps 84:14.
18. Ps 84:11.
19. Ps 118:121.
20. Prov 16:5.
21. *Ibid.*
22. Mt 5:23.
23. Cf. Lk 19:8.
24. Ps 118:108.

and prayers which you offer to him secretly—if they prevent you from saying attentively the number of psalms laid down by the Rule.[25] Do you not sin, even though you truly sacrifice, if you do not choose the right victims?[26] "Make his paths straight," he says, "you who prepare the ways of the Lord."[27]

3. O Lord, you have laid down guide-lines for us,[28] if only we would walk properly according to them. You have laid down a law for us, the way of your statutes,[29] through him whom you have given as the Legislator of this holy way of life.[30] "This is the way," you say, "walk along it, swerving neither to the right nor to the left."[31] Clearly this is the way the prophet had promised: "A straight way for us, so that no fool can wander from it."[32] I was young once, I am now old,[33] and if I remember rightly I have not seen a foolish man go astray because of it, though I have hardly seen any wise man able to keep straight along it. Woe to you who are wise in your own eyes and prudent in your own estimation.[34] Your wisdom leads you astray from the way of salvation and does not let you follow the foolishness of the Savior. He who was a fool for Christ's sake[35] was not unaware what evil this earthly, animal, diabolic wisdom could bring about: "If anyone seems wise in this world, he should become foolish so that he can be wise before God."[36] We should strive after the foolishness which is considered wisdom in God's sight, the foolishness which does not let a man wander from the way. Unless I am mistaken such foolishness is that

---

25. St Benedict's Rule for Monasteries gives detailed directions for the arrangement of the psalms at the celebration of the divine office (RB 9ff.). However, it concludes with this statement: "We strongly recommend, however, that if this distribution of the psalms is displeasing to anyone, he should arrange them otherwise, in whatever way he considers better, but taking care in any case that the Psalter with its full number of 150 psalms be chanted every week. . . ." trans. Doyle (Collegeville: Liturgical Press, 1947), p. 40.
26. Gen 4:7 as it is found in the Septuagint version.
27. Mt 3:3. 28. Ps 98:4. 29. Ps 118:33.
30. The reference is to St Benedict. 31. Is 30:21.
32. Is 35:8. 33. Ps 36:25. 34. Is 5:21.
35. St Paul. See 1 Cor 4:10. 36. 1 Cor 3:18.

wisdom which comes from above, pure, peaceful, gentle, open to reason, consenting to what is good;[37] if only we had never learnt from experience to what an extent a man despises these, who is wise in his own eyes. If we are saddened by the arrogance or obstinacy of people who are wise in this fashion, let us take comfort more readily from the peace and courtesy of people who are fools like us, people who are more easily persuaded to consent to what is good the more they distrust themselves. Fools such as these do not wander easily from the way of God, but as the prophet says, they always listen to the voice of him who gives his warning in the ear: "This is the way, walk along it, swerving neither to the right nor to the left,"[38] that is, do not exceed the measure through fervor, nor fall short of it through tepidity, and thus forsake the law you received, the royal road.[39] The spirit stands to the right and the flesh to the left. These are opposed to each other in deadly combat so that we may not do whatever one or the other wishes. In this way we avoid falling to the right by following the impulse of the spirit more than we ought or falling to the left by attending to the flesh more than is due.

4. And now, with your indulgence, I cannot resist recalling the praises with which Isaiah foretold this way of the Lord's precepts, this way of truth which you have chosen.[40] And there will be there, he says, that is, in the ancient lairs of dragons, in the terrible trackless wastes, a path and a way; and today we see in uncouth and uncultivated men who used to live without a law, a life of order and control. And it shall be called, he says, the holy way;[41] holy, because it is the sanctification of sinners and the salvation of those who were lost. The prophet then shows to what extent this way stands out, because of the help it offers and the reverence its holiness demands; he says, the unclean shall not pass over it.[42]

But surely, Isaiah, those who are unclean will not therefore have to travel by another way? Certainly not: all must come to this one way and travel by it. For Christ, who came to seek and save what

37. Jas 3:17. 38. Is 30:21. 39. Num 21:22.
40. Ps 118:27, 30. 41. Is 35:1, 7, 8. 42. *Ibid.*

had fallen[43] by the ways of this world, has laid down this way especially for the unclean. Does this mean then that the unclean will travel along the holy way? Not at all. However unclean a man is when he reaches it, he will no longer be unclean when he travels along it because once he starts along it he is already cleansed. The holy way does admit a man defiled, but immediately cleanses all admitted to it, because it cleanses the faults that have been committed like another baptism of repentance. The one who baptizes here with the baptism of penance[44] is clearly not John but Jesus. Here a fountain is opened for the house of David to cleanse them from sin and uncleanness.[45] And that is why this way admits the defiled but does not let him travel along it in that state. The way is constricted[46] and is like the narrow hole to which the snake can come with his slough when he wants to cast it off but through which he cannot pass with it on. And when he has passed through the narrow opening he puts on in his nakedness a new and better skin, leaving behind the old and shabby skin he had brought. It is good that we are invited to imitate the snake's astuteness, since we cannot renew ourselves in any other way than by forcing ourselves through the narrow way.

5. When Isaiah mentioned in connection with this way that: "No lion shall be there nor shall any ravenous beast come upon it, and they shall not be found there,"[47] he clearly assures us that we can avoid the guile of the ancient serpent if by this narrow way we follow the example of this new one. We are safe then,[48] if we do not stray from the way. That lion who roams abroad seeking his prey[49] is able to place stumbling-blocks beside the road,[50] hide traps and terrify travelers by his bellowing, but he cannot harm those who persevere on the way because for him the way is a torment and

---

43. Lk 19:10.   44. Jn 1:33.   45. Zech 13:1.
46. Mt 7:14. See RB, Prol., 48.   47. Is 35:9.
48. The critical edition here has the subjunctive: *Securi ergo simus*, but the reading of Brussel's II 977 has been adopted in the translation: *Securi ergo sumus*, as it seems to fit better into the context.
49. 1 Pet 5:8.   50. Ps 139:6.

terror. The way of the Lord, after all, is the strength of the straightforward and the fear of those who work evil.[51]

If you are on the way then fear only one thing: lest you leave it, lest you offend the Lord who leads you along it so that he would abandon you to wander in the way of your own heart.[52] Apart from him fear no one. If you feel that the way is too narrow look forward to the end to which it leads you. If you were to see how everything is to be attained, then you would say without hesitation: "Broad indeed is your command."[53] If you cannot see so far, believe Isaiah who could; he is your eye. He must have seen, for he described the consequences: "Behold," he says, "the redeemed shall walk by this way and the ransomed of the Lord shall return and come to Sion with singing; everlasting joy shall be upon their heads. They shall obtain also joy and gladness, and sorrow and sighing shall flee away."[54] The man who dwells sufficiently on this end I think will not only make the way easier for himself but also grow wings so that he no longer walks but flies.

Always therefore, brethren, bear in mind the prizes which await us, and then you will run eagerly with all your might along the way of God's commandments.[55] May he who is the track of the runners and the reward of the winners lead and guide you along it; to him, Christ Jesus, be honor and glory for ever. Amen.

---

51. Prov 10:29.
52. Is 57:17.
53. Ps 118:96.
54. Is 35:9f.
55. RB, Prol., 49.

SERMON 6

THE FIRST SERMON FOR CHRISTMAS

"UNTO US a Child is born."[1] A Child who is the ancient of days.[2] Child in bodily form and age; ancient of days in the Word's eternity past understanding. And though, as the ancient of days, he is not a child, still he is always new; indeed he is just as new as newness itself which remains always in him and renews all things.[3] Every single thing grows old just so much as it recedes from him, and is renewed in the degree that it returns. And, in a way unheard of, the reason for his youth and age is one and the same, for his eternity has no beginning in birth nor decline in old age. For him, his very newness is ancient and his antiquity new. But in another way the newness of this temporal birth is that the Child is born to renew us, he who as God is born eternally to beatify the angels. The eternal birth certainly is more full of glory, but the temporal more lavish in mercy, in that it is on my behalf who needed mercy. I was besieged by misery, misery I could not expiate.[4]

Show your mercy to us[5] who are not yet fit to see your glory; let the kindness and humanity of God, our Savior, appear to us,[6] so that through it we may be made fit and worthy for the majesty and divinity of God, our Creator, to appear to us too. Show us, Lord, your mercy,[7] cloaked in our misery and working the cure of the

---

1. Is 9:6. The opening words of the mass celebrated on Christmas Day are used by Guerric as the theme of this first Christmas Sermon.
2. Dan 7:9.   3. Wis 7:27.   4. Is 47:11.
5. Ps 84:8.   6. Tit 3:4.   7. Ps 84:8.

miserable by a new kind of mercy drawn from our very misery. For this, the art of mercy, has blended God's beatitude and man's misery in making them one in the Mediator, that by dint of the mystery of this unity, in virtue of his resurrection,[8] beatitude may absorb misery, life swallow up death and the whole man pass glorified into fellowship with the divine nature.[9] The divine dignity accepted all the weakness of the flesh to which human nature because of its guilt is subject, without of course the guilt. He went so far that he neither avoided the hurts of childhood nor wanted to share any other beginning than is the common lot of man; save, of course, being born of the Holy Spirit, immaculate from her who was immaculate, he washed away our origin's sins and granted us the mystery of a second birth.

2. Unto us therefore a little Child is born,[10] and "emptying out"[11] his majesty God has taken on himself not merely the earthly body of mortal men but even the weakness and insignificance of children. O blessed childhood, whose weakness and foolishness is stronger and wiser than any man; for it is the strength and wisdom of God[12] that does his work in us, does the work of God in men. It is the very weakness of this Child that triumphs over the prince of this world, binds the strong man armed,[13] takes the cruel tyrant captive, looses our captivity and sets us free. This Child's seeming dumbness, his childhood's simplicity, makes the tongues of children eloquent,[14] makes them speak with the tongues of men and angels,[15] dividing the tongues of fire. It is he, who seems to know nothing, who teaches knowledge to men[16] and angels, for he is the very God of all knowledge, the Wisdom of God, the Word. O sweet and sacred childhood, which brought back man's true innocence, by which men of every age can return to blessed childhood[17] and be conformed to you, not in physical weakness but in humility of heart and holiness of life.

In a word then you sons of Adam, who are exceedingly great in

8. Phil 3:10.
9. 2 Pet 1:4.
10. Is 9:6.
11. Phil 2:7.
12. 1 Cor 1:24f.
13. Lk 11:21.
14. Wis 10:21.
15. 1 Cor 13:1.
16. Ps 93:10.
17. 1 Pet 2:2.

your own eyes and have grown by pride into giants,[18] unless you are converted and become like this little Child, you shall not enter into the kingdom of Heaven.[19] "I am the Gate of the Kingdom,"[20] this little Child says, and unless man's proud head is bowed the doorway of humility will not let him in. Without doubt then he will shake the self-confidence of many men upon the earth,[21] and those who approach him with heads held high will fall back again, thrust away, heads beaten down.

What is this? Are you still proud, earth and ashes, even after God has humbled himself? Still great in your own eyes, even after God has made himself a little Child under those very eyes of yours? He has emptied himself[22] so as to seem very nearly nothing at all, yet nothing at all was made without him;[23] and you are hugely puffed up and exalted, thinking yourselves to be something or other, whereas in very truth you are nothing at all. It is yourselves you are leading astray,[24] as the Apostle declares to you, since if you would be something greater than you are you must be so much the more humble. Wisdom says: However great you are be humble in everything and you shall find grace before God[25] who resists the proud and gives grace to the humble[26] and who, although the greatest of all, made himself the humblest and least of all, to be an example to you. It was not enough for him that he should become less than the angels[27] by assuming mortal nature; he would become less even than grown men by adopting the state of helpless infancy. Let the holy and the humble see this then and glory in it, while the wicked and proud see it and are confounded. Let them, I say, see the great God made a tiny child, a little child to be worshiped: an amazing mystery, the redemption of the holy and the glory of the humble, the judgment of the wicked and the ruin of the proud.

What a mystery to inspire worship and fear. How holy and how terrible your name is,[28] a fountain of mercies and an abyss of

---

18. Gen 6:4.
19. Mt 18:3f.
20. Jn 10:9.
21. Ps 109:6.
22. Phil 2:7.
23. Jn 1:3.
24. Gal 6:3.
25. Sir 3:20.
26. Jas 4:6.
27. Ps 8:6.
28. Ps 110:9.

judgments. Who is there who has drunk from this fountain and not loved you, or who has thought of this abyss and not trembled? He who has not loved is evil and wicked; he who has not trembled is foolish and stupid. But there is no reason at all for getting frightened of judgment unless you have set yourself up in haughtiness against mercy. And true enough, he much prefers to be loved than to be feared with servility, and he gives greater approval to filial affection freely and voluntarily offered than to servile fear extorted under compulsion. And so now when he shows himself to mortal men for the first time he prefers to present himself as a child, in order to inspire love rather than fear. For he came to save us, not to pass judgment on us,[29] so he displayed what would provoke our love, putting off till later what could compel our fear.

3. Let us now then come up to the throne of his grace with confidence,[30] even though formerly we used not to be able to think of his throne of glory without trembling. Here is nothing frightening, nothing severe, to make you tremble, but every sort of kindness and gentleness to give you confidence. And if he really has terrifying power,[31] for the moment he hides it while he pardons the penitent and hears his plea. Nor will he be exact with you in proportion to the gravity of your offences. As a child, though offended, he does not know how to be angry, or if he does get angry he can be easily pleased again. And indeed nothing is more easy to please than the soul of this Child, who himself makes the first overtures of peace and satisfaction, sending on in front messengers of peace, so that you who are the guilty party may want to make reconciliation. You have only to want this, to want it truly and perfectly, and he will not only grant you pardon but heap grace upon you too. Not only that, but, not reckoning by halves the gain of having recovered a lost sheep, he will keep high festival with the angels.[32] The state of innocent and simple childhood accords perfectly then with the divine gentleness; and it was quite suitable and appropriate that he should have begun the salvation of sinners from such a state, so that

29. Jn 3:17.   30. Heb 4:16.   31. Job 25:2.
32. Lk 15:3ff.

those whose consciences were terrified by their state of guilt might be consoled by the hope of a pardon not hard to obtain.

4. O most sweet Child, good Jesus, how great is the abundance of your sweetness which you have hidden for those who fear you, which you bring to its fullness in those who trust you.[33] You have shown so much of it to those who do not yet know you. What incomparable sweetness and loving kindness, that I should see the God who made me[34] himself made a child for my sake; that the God of all majesty[35] and glory should become not only like me in true bodily form but show himself even wretched and, as it were, devoid of all strength in the weakness of his infancy. Truly you are the Child-God, my Champion and my God.[36] You are all that is sweet and desirable, yet your soft tender body makes you even more sweet to me. Indeed it is this which makes you so easily comprehensible to the senses and feelings of children who are still not fit to receive you as solid food.[37]

So for us now it is sweet to think and to think again of this Child-God, sweet and utterly delicious; more, for him to be in us is a most effective remedy for curing and sweetening our rancor of soul, bitterness of speech and harshness of manners. For I cannot believe that where there is awareness and remembrance of his divine sweetness room can be found for anger or sadness, but every trace of anger and bitterness and every other source of evil shall be taken away from us.[38] So it will be that like new-born babes[39] we shall worthily praise the new-born Infant Lord, and in the complete accord of our lives and voices, out of the mouths of babes and sucklings shall perfect praise[40] be given to the Babe and Suckling, our Lord Jesus Christ, to whom with the Father and the Holy Ghost be praise and rejoicing throughout endless ages. Amen.

---

33. Ps 30:20.
34. Sir 24:12.
35. Ps 28:3.
36. Ps 41:6f.; 42:5.
37. Heb 5:14.
38. Eph 4:31.
39. 1 Pet 2:2.
40. Ps 8:3.

SERMON 7

THE SECOND SERMON FOR CHRISTMAS

"A CHILD IS BORN for us, a son is given to us."[1] That he was born for us is proved by the fact that he was given to us; for he can rightly be said to be born only for those to whom he has been manifestly given. Everyone has been offered the graces of this birth, but not all have accepted them; for not everyone has faith.[2] He came to his own people and they did not accept him.[3]

His birth would have been quite useless had he not also been freely given: he would have been made the Son of Man in vain had he not also been accepted by the sons of men to whom he was giving the power to become the sons of God.[4] Woe to you, Jewry, so unbelieving, so ungrateful, and so little sensitive to spiritual values: God's kingdom has been taken away from you and given to a people who will bear fruit.[5] Rejected by the Synagogue,[6] Jesus has been accepted by the Church: rescued from the quibbling of the Jews, he has been firmly established over the Gentiles. The people he did not know to be his own have paid him homage,[7] the instant they heard him they obeyed. It is to you, children turned strangers, children turned robbers and murderers of your own kith and kin, that your loving Father addresses his complaint: "The children I nourished and brought up have come to despise me.[8] But will not

---

1. Is 9:6. This is sung as a verse and response at Vespers on Christmas Day and repeated throughout the octave.
2. 2 Thess 3:2.   3. Jn 1:11.   4. Jn 1:12.   5. Mt 21:43.
6. Lk 4:29.   7. Ps 17:44f.   8. Is 1:2.

he who despises me be despised in turn?"[9] It was for the Apostle to say: "Very well, since you have repudiated God's word and reckoned yourselves to be unworthy of eternal life we are turning away from you to peoples outside."[10]

What good fortune for the outsider. See, Jesus is offered to you: run to him open-handed, throw out your arms and enfold him in your embrace. Prove your devotion in love and deed: take him to yourself without a qualm, this Son who is given you; embrace him lovingly and linger with him always pressed to your heart.[11]

I seem to hear a jubilant song of praise[12] welling up from every corner of the earth: praises to the Just One from farthest lands. It is the sound of teeming millions, the sound of God's army on the march,[13] joining in one loud voice of praise:[14] "The Child is born for us, the Son is given to us." Without a doubt it is the Church, filling the whole wide world with joy and praise[15] at the Son who has been born for her, given to her, and whom she enfolds in her embrace; her prize, of whom she sees the Jews deprived because of their unbelief. Give praise then, you who could not bear a child: give full vent to your praise and jubilation, you who could not bring a son to birth, for through this Son who has been given to you, you who were all alone shall have many children[16] in place of her who seemed to be the Lord's espoused, bound as she was to his law in troth. Then your heart will throb with wonder,[17] puzzled at the thought: "By whom were these borne and bred for me? For I was barren and childless, I was a prisoner and an exile; who has brought these up for me? I was abandoned and all alone; where were these then?"[18]

O virgin and mother, in utter purity conceiving, they are your gift from the Son who was given you. For he is the Son of God Most High[19] and his Father has adopted them for him, to shape them to his pattern, so as to make him the eldest of many brothers.[20]

9. Is 33:1.
10. Acts 13:46.
11. Song 1:12.
12. Ps 41:5.
13. Ezek 1:24.
14. Lk 2:13.
15. Is 35:2.
16. Is 54:1.
17. Is 60:5.
18. Is 49:21.
19. Lk 1:32.
20. Rom 8:29.

Throw wide then your outposts from east to west, across the seven seas, for you will advance in all directions; every nation will become a heritage for your children.[21] For Mary's only son is the first to be born of all creation,[22] and the Father has told him: "Ask me for anything; I am ready to give you every nation for your heritage and the farthest lands for your estate."[23]

2. Although she was formerly unable even to conceive, the Church has, in her reception of God's Son, given birth to many children and grown the stronger thereby; while the Synagogue, her rival, has, in her rejection of him, grown so much the weaker in bringing sons to birth.[24] Today the Church can fill high heaven with her song of praise and thanks, grateful as she is for this gift of her Son; but the Synagogue sits hunched in dumb darkness and wearies even the devil with her wailing. Blind and forlorn, why does she not see how, plainly, her God has passed her by for us;[25] how, clearly, her engagement has been broken off; and she is left with but the legal form,[26] the writ, I mean, which proclaims her own adultery? All her would-be dowry the Bridegroom has bestowed upon his freshly-chosen Bride. See: it is we who have in our hands the marriage contract, written in two Testaments. More still, we have the sacramental oils, the royal honor, the priestly rank, the holy ministry, the rite of temple and of altar and the very truth of every sacrifice. True indeed, every glimmer of her erstwhile glory has been taken from her[27] and focused upon us; for this Son who has been given us is the cause and truth of everything that is. He tilted the cup of the law, which he proffers in his hands,[28] from Jewish lips to Christian, and decanted out for us every last drop of the pure and true wine it contained. Only the dregs which were not emptied out[29] remained for the Jews: they must needs drink them for these are their share of this cup.[30]

3. But why take up time with talk? Nobody could possibly give the details of everything that has been granted us together with this

---

21. Is 54:2f. 22. Col 1:15. 23. Ps 2:8. 24. 1 Sam 2:5.
25. Ps 49:3. 26. Deut 24:1. 27. 1 Sam 4:2 28. Gal 3:19.
29. Ps 74:9. 30. Ps 10:7.

Son who is given to us: for has not every choicest gift, every perfect present, come down to us from him[31] and with him, at one and the same time? Has he not with his own Person brought us the whole armory of heaven, all the treasures of God? But all this must the while be secret and lie hidden in himself; still, even now would he scatter his largesse, sharing out the spoils, it would seem, of a battle as yet unfought, though not thereby detracting from the fullness of reward set aside for conquering heroes.

Who could count up such an abundant grant of munitions for every sort of spiritual warfare: the whole assortment of our weapons; the supporting arms of the sacraments, the basic rations of the Scriptures, officers in orders and other ranks too, in the holy ministry, drawn from every age and sex and state of life, of every people and of every language, to form their several divisions; the martyrs with their trophies, the standard-bearers, men of blameless life, the virgins with their crowns? Should you be wondering, says the Church, where this rich throng has come from, so manifold in glory, to me but lately so wretched and so poor, remember it is God's Son who is given to us, the God of grace, the Lord of might, the King of glory.[32] More wonder it would be were such a wealth of good not to follow upon our Lord, for he is all-good himself. "Those who seek the Lord," she says, "lack no good thing;"[33] how much more so those who find.

If you are surprised at what has been given us through this Son I will amaze you more by adding that every single thing that is has been bestowed upon us with him. For when the Father granted us his Son, through whom and in whom everything abides, how could he not grant us everything else together with him?[34] With the Apostle she can say: "Every single thing is ours,"[35] for he is ours too who shaped them and remains their liege-Lord, so though we may seem almost to have nothing at all, we yet find ourselves to possess everything.[36]

So you see what a vast sort of thing this gift of the Son turns out

---

31. Jas 1:17.　　32. Ps 23:10.　　33. Ps 33:11.
34. Rom 8:32.　　35. 1 Cor 3:22.　　36. 2 Cor 6:10.

to be; and how fittingly it is told of Wisdom, who truly is but himself: "Every kind of good came along with her, and honors without number by her help."[37]

But why, my brethren, should I emphasize this so much? Simply so that you may learn to glory in this Son that is given to us;[38] and reckon whatever the world can give or promise you not only as cheap and worthless in comparison with him but even as loss for his sake.[39] He does not make you gifts in the way the world does.[40] Be very grateful[41] that he has been given to you and make every effort that the gift within you may be brought to full perfection. Once he was given to the world shaped in flesh; and on certain days, at set times, he is offered to the faithful in the likeness of bread: the food, I mean, of his own Sacrament; but to his devoted friends he is quite often granted at unexpected moments by the delicious breath of his Spirit. The first of these gifts then was to save us, the second to furnish us with the means of holiness, the third to bring us comfort. For the first he demands a sure faith, for the second a pure conscience, for the third a ready love that bestirs the mind, melts the heart, throws wide the gates of love to make way for grace to enter in abundance. Not only such a touch as this, but every kind of grace there is, may he heap upon you,[42] he who is the God of all grace,[43] the Son who is given to us, the Son who is God, the All-Blessed, throughout endless ages. Amen.[44]

---

37. Wis 7:11.   38. Is 9:6.   39. Phil 3:8.   40. Jn 14:27.
41. Col 3:15.   42. 2 Cor 9:8.   43. 1 Pet 5:10.   44. Rom 9:5.

SERMON 8

THE THIRD SERMON FOR CHRISTMAS

"A CHILD IS BORN for us."[1] For us indeed; not for himself, not for the angels. He was not born, I say, for himself. This birth did not confer being on him, did not bring him any improvement in his condition.[2] Before he was born in time he existed from all eternity and was his own perfect beatitude. For he was born perfect God of perfect God. He was not born for the angels. Those who were faithful to the truth did not need redemption. Those who fell were beyond redemption. Therefore he does not make himself the angel's champion, no sign of that; it is the sons of Abraham that he champions.[3] Born as God for himself, he has been born as a child for us, leaving himself behind as it were and passing over the angels. Coming all the way to us, he has become one of us and, emptying himself out,[4] made less than the angels, he has become our equal. Born in eternity he was beatitude for himself and for the angels: born in time he has become redemption for us, for it was we alone he saw burdened with the ancient condemnation arising from our birth.

1. Is 9:6. See note 1, Ser. 7, above.
2. A trace of the influence that the rising scholasticism has had on Guerric is evident here in his use of the distinction: *esse* and *melius esse*.
3. Heb 2:16.
4. Phil 2:7. One of the facets of the Incarnation which seems to have most intrigued the Cistercian Fathers is that of the "humility of God"—the self-emptying involved in becoming man. Cf. e.g., Bernard of Clairvaux's First Sermon for Christmas (Cistercian Fathers Series, 10); Aelred of Rievaulx's Sermon for Christmas (Cistercian Fathers Series, 23).

How happy, how lovable is your birth, Child Jesus, which repairs everyone's birth, reforms his condition, does away with the condemnation, cancels the deed which passed sentence on his nature.[5] If anyone is ashamed at being born under condemnation he can be born again in utmost happiness. For to all those who received you, you gave the power to become the sons of God.[6] Thank you for the free gift of your gracious birth, God, Son of Man, through which we have access to that grace in which we stand and in which we are confident of attaining glory as the sons of God.[7] It is indeed an admirable commerce[8] to take flesh and bestow divinity; a commerce of charity, not one undertaken out of the desire for gain; one bringing glory to your indulgence, abundant profit to my indigence. Truly you are a compassionate child; it is compassion alone that has made you a child, although compassion and truth alike have met in you.[9] Truly you have been born for us and not for yourself as a compassionate child. When you were born of us it was our profit, not your gain, that you sought. Your sole purpose in deigning to be born was to promote our welfare by your own lessening, to glorify us by your humiliation. Emptied yourself you filled us, for you transfused all the fullness of your divinity[10] into man. You transfused it, but you did not confuse the two.[11] I would not say that God had been transfused into man, rather I would deduce that the Spirit had been given to this man to a limited extent,[12] if any residue of all his fullness had remained with God which he had not poured out into the human nature with which he was united.

2. Rightly then is the name of the God-man oil poured out,[13] or

---

5. Col 2:14.   6. Jn 1:12.   7. Rom 5:2.
8. "Admirable commerce"—*admirabile commercium*, the opening words of the first antiphon at vespers on the octave day of Christmas. The Cistercians used this antiphon daily at Lauds of the little office of the Blessed Virgin Mary.
9. Ps 84:11.   10. Col 2:9.
11. Although the critical edition here maintains the reading *effudisti*, many of the manuscripts give the reading *confudisti* (see the apparatus in the critical edition) which we have followed here since it gives a better reading and fits in better with the context which a few lines later insists on the necessity of God having been poured out (*effudisset*).
12. Jn 3:34.   13. Song 1:2.

rather ointment wholly emptied out,[14] since God has been so thoroughly poured out into man that the Apostle in his faith declares he emptied himself out.[15]

Yet he emptied himself out in such a way as not to diminish or change anything in himself. No other emptying out of an unchangeable nature was possible than the taking to itself of our nature, earth, empty and void that it is.[16] Great indeed is this emptying out in the eyes of those who see it; the radiance of his Father's splendor and the full expression of his being[17] chose rather only the form of a slave, and even in it he had no comeliness or beauty.[18] For as if he was emptied out too little if he only became man, he so thoroughly brought to nothing in himself the glory of human flesh, made its wisdom foolish, weakened its strength and diminished its greatness as to show himself in his birth the least of men and in his passion the last of men, for which reason they made little of him.[19]

Do you wish to see God emptied of himself? See him lying in the manger.[20] "Behold our God," says Isaiah[21] who from such a distance saw and recognized his Lord's manger,[22] or rather his God in the manger. "Behold our God," he says. "Where?" I ask. "In that manger," he says. It is an infant I find there.[23] Do you mean to say that this is he who declares: "I fill heaven and earth,"[24] for whose majesty the whole breadth of heaven is narrow? I see a child wrapped in swaddling clothes.[25] Do you mean to say this is he who is clad in the glory and beauty of unapproachable light, clothed with unbounded light as with a garment?[26] I hear him crying. Is this he who thunders in the heavens, at the sound of whose thunder the angelic powers lower their wings?[27] "So it is," says another prophet, taking Isaiah's place, "so indeed it is. This is our God;[28] but he has been emptied out in order to fill you, and he has willed to fall short of himself as it were in order to restore you." The whole choir of the prophets joins in with one spirit and one mind, although some use different words: "So it is: this is our God, and no one else besides

14. Cf. Mt 26f and parallels.	15. Phil 2:7.	16. Gen 1:2.
17. Heb 1:3.	18. Is 53:2.	19. Is 53:3.	20. Lk 2:7.
21. Is 25:9.	22. Is 1:3.	23. Lk 2:12.	24. Jer 23:24.
25. Lk 2:12.	26. Ps 103:1f.	27. Ezek 1:25.	28. Bar 3:36.

him shall enter into account; for there is no one else besides him."[29]

"But I know," says David, "I know that the wicked and adulterous race of the Jews will not believe this sign; they will contradict it. Proclaim him, you apostles, to the peoples of other nations."[30] Why? Because this Child, at whom the Jew does not even look as he lies in the manger, whom he despises as he hangs on the Cross, whom he does not see when he is wonderfully born, whom he envies when he works miracles,[31] whom he mocks when he suffers torments, this, I say, is our God for all eternity and for endless ages: he shall rule us for ever.[32]

3. And now behold the apostles preach, the prophets bear witness: although the fleece remained dry, all the breadth of the threshing-floor was moistened;[33] although the ivy-plant withered, Nineveh was saved;[34] and the Jews' loss became the wealth of the world and the salvation of nations.[35] All the kings of the earth adore the little one who is born for us; all nations serve him;[36] for if there are any who do not or will not serve him, before him they are as if they were not.[37] The nation and the kingdom which will not serve him will perish.[38] Yet already we rejoice to see fulfilled what was promised by the Father through Isaiah: "Men of stature will pass over to you and be yours; they will walk after you, they will bow down to you and make supplication to you." And he rightly says that: "In you alone is God and apart from you there is no God. Truly you are a hidden God, God of Israel, the Savior."[39] If Jesus could ever have been called God more plainly, more expressly, let the Jew never believe. Or at least if he pleads that these things were not said of Jesus, let him point to someone else in whom God is and who is God, and besides him there is no God. He does not confess the Trinity of Persons, and so cannot show a God in whom God is in such a way that there is no God beside him.[40]

29. Deut 4:34.   30. Ps 47:14.
31. In the artful counterpoise of words here Guerric reveals himself as a true disciple and follower of Bernard of Clairvaux: *jacentem . . . respicit, pendentem . . . despicit, . . . nacsitur non videt, . . . operatur invidet.*
32. Ps 47:15.   33. Judg 6:37ff.   34. Jon 3:10; 4:7.   35. Rom 11:11, 15.
36. Ps 71:11.   37. Is 40:17.   38. Is 60:12.   39. Is 45:14f.
40. Deut 32:39.

Sermon 8:3-4

But what ought to have led to devotion is for you, faithless man, a scandal, that a God hidden in man was applied to eyes, like the mud made from spittle,[41] to enlighten blind man so that he could see God. This, I say, is a scandal to you: that God's strength has been hidden in the weakness of the flesh,[42] that the strength of the God-man has been hidden in the weakness of the Cross; that his appearance among men was without glory and his form inglorious among the sons of men. Wherefore you made little of him,[43] thought him to be as a leper and struck by God and brought low, while God placed on him the iniquities of us all.[44] For he would have taken yours too upon himself if you had been willing to lay it down even at the last moment. But, wretch that you are, you do not lay it down: you add iniquity to iniquity,[45] to the blood of prophets, the blood of God's Son and of the apostles.[46] Place then, since you so desire, place the yoke of your iniquities[47] on yourself and on your sons. I would rather bear Christ's yoke,[48] that he may bear my iniquities. Do you bear the bundles of impiety, the heavy burdens;[49] let me bear the bundle of myrrh[50] which Mary has tied together for me and, wrapped in swaddling clothes, laid in the manger.[51]

4. You then, my brethren, who have known the manger of your Lord and your Lord in the manger, whom Israel did not know;[52] you, I say, who did not think the worse of your Savior because he willed to show compassion, but cherished him the more tenderly the more insignificant he appeared: sing and exult and chant:[53] "A child is born for us: a son is given to us."[54] Sing to the Lord a new song, for he has done wonderful things. The Lord has made known his salvation;[55] so much so that the ass from the nations knows in the manger his Lord become grass for him; for all flesh is grass.[56]

In the sight of the nations he has revealed his justice[57] which the Jew does not recognize, still having a veil upon his face.[58] He has a veil because he holds on to jealousy and therefore does not see what

---

41. Jn 9:6f. 42. Hab 3:4. 43. Is 52:14. 44. Is 53:3ff.
45. Ps 68:28. 46. Acts 8:2. 47. Lam 1:14. 48. Mt 11:29f.
49. Is 58:6. 50. Song 1:12. 51. Lk 2:12. 52. Is 1:3.
53. Ps 97:4. 54. Is 9:6. 55. Ps 97:1f. 56. Is 1:3; 40:6.
57. Ps 97:2. 58. 2 Cor 3:14f.

is true but is moved to envy because a child is born for us, a son is given to us. He does not envy because he desires to have him for himself but because he desires him to perish both for me and for himself. The evil harlot in her rivalry would rather the infant were killed than given to me alive, but the judgment of our Solomon, whose word is more penetrating than any two-edged sword, searching heart and minds,[59] made no mistake in finding the mother. Give to the Church, he says, the living infant, for she is its mother.[60] Whoever does his will, he is his mother and brother and sister.[61]

Lord Solomon, you call me mother. I profess myself to be a handmaid. I am Christ's handmaid; be it done to me according to your word.[62] And indeed I will show myself a mother by love and anxious care to the best of my ability; but I will always be mindful of my condition.

5. Brethren, this name of mother is not restricted to prelates, although they are charged in a special way with maternal solicitude and devotion: it is shared by you too who do the Lord's will. Yes, you too are mothers of the Child who has been born for you and in you, that is, since you conceived from the fear of the Lord and gave birth to the spirit of salvation. Keep watch then, holy mother, keep watch in your care for the new-born child until Christ is formed in you[63] who was born for you; for the more tender he is, the more easily he can perish for you, he who never perishes for himself. If the spirit which is in you is extinguished for you, it returns to God who gave it.[64]

Keep watch, I say, in your care for the new-born child, remembering that your rival as she slept smothered the son that was given her.[65] For who is she but the carnal soul that extinguishes the spirit by negligence and sluggishness? Although men of this sort have lost the fervor of religion they claim its glory and its name for themselves. Hence the disputes of the carnal with the spiritual, even in Chapter meetings where the true Solomon presides invisibly as judge. "My son," the carnal say, "is alive and yours is dead.[66] I have

---

59. Ps 7:10.   60. 1 Kings 3:16ff.   61. Mt 12:50.   62. Lk 1:38.
63. Gal 4:19.   64. Eccles 12:7.   65. 1 Kings 3:19. 66. 1 Kings 3:22

the Spirit of God,[67] you have not; the love of God is alive in me, it is dead in you." They strive to make their own the authority of religion, the true substance of which is possessed by the spiritual, so that by depriving them of authority they may introduce customs to suit their own wanton desires. And in fact the mother wishes the child to be given alive and whole to her rival: she does not begrudge glory to her as long as she possesses virtue. But the other says: "Let it be neither mine nor yours, but let it be divided,"[68] because she desires to keep for herself the honor of holiness and leave to others the toil. But the judge makes no mistake, although he sometimes pretends not to notice. Solomon's sword finds the mother and allots to her undivided both the affection of charity and the effect of power, both fervor in working and favor in commanding.

So you, brethren, in whom the faith that works through love[69] has been born of the Holy Spirit, preserve it, feed it, nourish it like the little Jesus until there is formed in you the Child who is born for us; who not only by being born but also by living and dying gave us a form to be the model of our formation. He remembered that he was born only for us and he willed to live only for us, to die only for us: for himself he had no need. And that in order that we might be reborn through him, live according to him, die in him, who lives and reigns for ever and ever. Amen.

---

67. 1 Cor 7:40.   68. 1 Kings 3:26.   69. Gal 5:6.

SERMON 9

THE FOURTH SERMON FOR CHRISTMAS

BEHOLD THE FULLNESS OF TIME has now come.[1] St Paul understands this fullness of time as abundance of grace, or as fulfillment of preceding prophecy, or as the greater maturity of faith which has come of age. Let us consider these aspects one by one.

Christ the Lord is the fullness of all good things, he who is full of all the treasures of God's wisdom and knowledge[2] and of all grace, he indeed in whom all the fullness of the godhead dwells in bodily form.[3] The apostles saw him full of grace and truth and of his fullness they all received,[4] to the point that the last of them all, one born out of due time,[5] Paul, the vessel of election,[6] from the fullness which he had received spread abroad everywhere the fullness of grace and truth, crying out and saying: Behold the fullness of time has now come. For since the author of time was born in time full of all good things, how should he not have brought the fullness of time? When the heavens dropped down dew from above and the clouds rained the Just One and the earth brought forth a Savior,[7] how should such wealth of heavenly blessing not bestow fecundity on all lands? You have blessed, Lord, your land; you have given your kindness and our land has given its fruit.[8] From one grain of corn which a virgin's womb brought forth an abundant harvest of

---

1. Gal 4:4. This text is used in the First Vespers for Christmas as the fourth antiphon.
2. Col 2:3.   3. Col 2:9.   4. Jn 1:14, 16.   5. 1 Cor 15:8.
6. Acts 9:15.   7. Is 45:8.   8. Ps 84:2, 13.

faithful souls has grown up all over the world. For I would not have you look for this fullness of time in plenty of temporal goods, but of eternal, not in the produce of the fields but of heaven. If heaven drops down dew from above and the clouds rain the Just One, if the earth brings forth a Savior and justice arises at the same time,[9] if finally there arises in the days of the Lord not only justice but also abundance of peace,[10] do not seek happier times, since the kingdom of God too is nothing other than justice and peace, and joy in the Holy Spirit[11] which proceeds from them. In our times also things are judged to be best and finest when justice disciplines behavior, and plenty together with peace affords a quiet life and happiness. In short the earth is full of the Lord's mercy[12] and the Lord has blessed the crown of the year with his bounty, while his fields are filled with the wealth[13] of all spiritual grace. Who but an ungrateful man would deny the fullness of the time? What golden age ever had anything that resembled the fullness of this time, when the bread of angels, endowed with every savor of sweetness and every pleasure[14] is set even before beasts and not only men but beasts too are fed with food from heaven? Men and beasts you will save, Lord, as you have multiplied your compassion, God.[15] Multiplied without limit is this compassion of yours, God; you who are the bread of angels not only enrich and gladden the tables of men but also, become grass, fill the mangers of beasts. You confess, Lord, compassionate Wisdom, that you are a debtor to the wise and to the foolish.[16] You made both and for both you provided the food they need. You save both men and beasts, both the spiritual and the natural, each in his own rank and order. Let them give thanks to the Lord for his steadfast love, for his wonderful deeds to the sons of men.[17] For he has sent his Word made flesh, medicine and food for all, in order that even they who are unable to receive the Word may be healed and satiated by the flesh of the Word. So let the poor eat and take their fill[18] and confess that the blessed fullness of time has come,[19] when they find even in their mangers bread from heaven prepared without the sweat of

---

9. Is 45:8.   10. Ps 71:7.   11. Rom 14:17.   12. Ps 32:5.
13. Ps 64:12.   14. Wis 16:20.   15. Ps 35:7.   16. Rom 1:14.
17. Ps 106:8, 15, 22, 32.   18. Ps 21:27.   19. Gal 4:4.

their brow.[20] Will the ox low, when the manger he stands before is thus filled?[21] Let him low, but for joy of spirit and jubilation of heart, because he has come to know the manger of his Lord[22] or rather his Lord in the manger.

2. It is good to consider still more plainly what fullness of time Christ brought when he came from heaven, at how easy and slight a price he decreed every precious thing could be obtained. With two farthings[23] or a cup of cold water[24] or indeed with good will alone the kingdom of heaven is now purchased in his days; although even now it will scarcely find a buyer amongst such a large number of rich men. Shame upon us, even we ourselves who have already begun to buy, already made out the deed of purchase, already received the pledge of our inheritance,[25] even we, I say, so often repudiate our agreement and, almost with satisfaction, complain and murmur as if we had been cheated in the transaction, as if that almost nothing which is asked of us were a great sum. Well did Scripture prophecy of us: "A poor thing, a poor thing, says every buyer; then off he goes and boasts of it."[26] Will he not be able rightly to boast who has obtained that measureless and eternal weight of glory at the price of this light and momentary affliction,[27] who has paid nothing for his salvation?[28] But now you may hear every day on all sides complaints and irksome murmurings: this is bad, that is bad; this is burdensome, that is unbearable; who would put up with so much and of such a kind? So there is practically no one who judges the matter worthily and as it deserves, saying: "The sufferings of this time are not worthy to be compared with the future glory that is to be revealed in us,"[29] unless then when at last it begins to be revealed. Then indeed he, who now paints a gloomy picture and moans that the price is burdensome, will boast when he leaves the market-place of this world where the contract is made and returns to his eternal home with an object so valuable bought at so slight a price. A man after God's heart was that man, simple, without complaint, who knew nothing of this art or rather

20. Gen 3:19.   21. Cf. Job 6:5.   22. Is 1:3.   23. Lk 21:1f.
24. Mt 10:42. 25. Eph 1:14.   26. Prov 20:14. 27. 2 Cor 4:17.
28. Ps 55:8.   29. Rom 8:18.

Sermon 9:2-3

laziness and infidelity of buyers. I mean David, who said: "Because I did not know business, Lord, I will remember your justice alone.[30] In no wise will I remember my own justice, so as to exaggerate my labors, make much of my merits; rather I will remember your justice alone who did freely bind yourself to me by your promise. In your fidelity hearken to me, in your justice, and do not enter into judgment with your servant."[31] If I will to justify myself my own mouth will condemn me.[32] "Through this," he says, "I will come to the mighty deeds of the Lord,"[33] that is, because I will not set up my own works of justice; through this he will make me powerful both now in battle and then in the kingdom, because I will always confess my weaknesses. For when I am weak, then I am powerful.[34] Therefore he conducts his case prudently before God who, reckoning nothing of his own justice, commits everything to mercy; so also he buys prudently who refuses to have anything to do with the pretence and avarice of business. When he finds that precious pearl he spends not only all his property[35] but himself, too, freely and eagerly. But we, lukewarm, false, ungrateful, undedicated, lovers of our pleasures rather than of God, can scarcely be restrained from uttering that faithless and most wicked complaint: "A poor thing, a poor thing;"[36] even after we have tasted and seen, as it is written of the valiant woman, that our business is profitable.[37]

3. I would be carried away still further by an unrelenting wrath against the ingratitude and faithlessness of this time of ours, but I am called back by the theme I chose for my sermon, the holy and blessed fullness of Christ's time, with which you should be fed more fully today. Yet these two times run in conjunction and are borne along side by side, as different as they are opposed, the time of grace and the time of wickedness, although only one time is found belonging to both. For if now was not the time of grace the Apostle would not say: "Behold now is the acceptable time, behold now is the day of salvation."[38] And again if now was not the time of

30. Ps 70:15f.   31. Ps 142:1f.   32. Job 9:2.
33. Ps 70:16.   34. 2 Cor 12:10. 35. Mt 13:46.
36. Prov 20:14. 37. Prov 31:10, 18. 38. 2 Cor 6:2.

wickedness, the same Apostle would not say: "Hoard the opportunity that is given you in evil times like these."[39] So grace and ingratitude compete in one time as in one racecourse. For a long time now Wisdom has been fighting against wickedness and for that reason it comes down now, too, into the arena of this world. He fights, I say, refusing to be overcome by evil but wishing to overcome evil by good.[40] Iniquity abounded, and although men's charity was frozen solid that of God did not grow cold.[41] Great was the ardor of that charity; indeed, as it is written, it could not be extinguished by many waters.[42] Although the multitude of sins called for the last judgment already, God sent his Son not to judge the world but that it might be saved through him.[43]

So when the world's wickedness had almost reached its term and was calling for an end of time, the coming of the Redeemer infused a new and unhoped-for fullness of time into the affairs of men. When the world had grown old and was near to perishing[44] by reason of its age, suddenly at the coming of its Creator it was renewed by a new and unexpected springtime of virtue and by a certain youthful warmth of faith. Of that faith the earliest period, its childhood as it were, was the age of the patriarchs who arose in the early morning of the Church that was coming to birth. Its youth was the age of the prophets. It grew to the fullness of manly vigor in the age of the apostles when it exhibited the warmth of its virtue for the world to gaze upon in the glorious and doughty triumphs of countless martyrs. This adult and mature age of faith is what the Apostle calls the fullness of time,[45] that is, when they who were under the tutorship of the Law and in nothing differed from slaves while they were little,[46] have now grown up and received the liberty of sons through the Only-begotten of the Father. In order that no fullness might be lacking to his time he came full both of grace and of truth,[47] so that through grace he could make the commandments of the Law to be fulfilled and through truth himself fulfill God's promises. Whatever was done or said in mystery during all the centuries which had

---

39. Eph 5:16.
40. Rom 12:21.
41. Mt 24:12.
42. Song 8:7.
43. Jn 3:17.
44. Heb 8:13.
45. Gal 4:4.
46. Gal 3:25; 4:1.
47. Jn 1:14.

preceded was to be more truly and more completely fulfilled in this fullness of time. This very day has manifested so many mysteries, so many oracles, summed up as it were in brief, that those words can be truly said of him: "Being perfected in a short time, he fulfilled long years."[48]

4. Since therefore it is clear in so many ways that the blessed fullness of time has come, Solomon was right in checking the complaints of the foolish with the words: "Do not say: What is the reason, do you think, that past times were better than these present? This sort of question is stupid."[49] Obviously it is God's grace that made the happiest of times for men, while men's ingratitude made the times to be the worst for themselves. O acceptable time,[50] which this day has inaugurated under such blessed and favorable auspices. This is the day on which the eternal Creator of time was born and introduced eternity to mortal men. Truly this day is a day of salvation,[51] this day on which the salvation of the world was born and made himself a saving draught for the sick. O brethren: it was of this day, if I am not mistaken, that the Wise Man spoke to his son: "Do not be defrauded of the good day."[52] And he explains what it is to be defrauded: "Do not let a crumb of the goodly gift escape you."[53] He calls it the good day because today the goodly gift, indeed the best gift, has been given, the perfect gift which comes down from the Father of lights.[54] Of what sort it is no one knows except him who receives it.[55]

But you, brethren, have received the Spirit which is of God, that you may know what has been given you by God.[56] It is with heartfelt praise you sing: "A Son is given to us."[57] This Son is the bread of sons: of himself today he makes a blessed and solemn feast for the whole family of the Father.

5. Thanks be to you, Father of mercies, who give us today our daily bread, and have opened your hand with such generosity to fill every living thing with blessing[58] that even their manger is found to be full of that blessing.

48. Wis 4:13. 49. Eccles 7:11. 50. 2 Cor 6:2. 51. *Ibid.*
52. Sir 14:14. 53. *Ibid.* 54. Jas 1:17. 55. Rev 2:17.
56. 2 Cor 2:12. 57. Is 9:6. 58. Ps 144:16.

How wretched, how brutish and unfeeling, even more how harmful and grudging to himself is he who defrauds himself of this day, so that he loses his portion of the goodly gift.[59] He has no share in the heavenly grace which has been set before him, and passes the day of all refreshment and joy with a sad and fasting heart. For him it is as if the most abundant fullness of time had not come yet and bread from heaven had not filled the mangers of the simple and the humble. Wisdom brands such a man as harmful and grudging to himself, ungrateful and insulting to God, in the words: "An eye jaundiced with its own passions, and never a full meal, but always he must sit hungry and pensive at his own table."[60] Therefore, Wisdom says, his soul will not be filled with good things[61] because his eye is jaundiced; and his eye will not return to a healthy state[62] so as to consider with devotion and faith the things which are set before it on the rich man's great table. "A diseased eye has the niggard that will turn away its face and despise its own soul."[63]

Without doubt, brethren, if we do not turn away our face from the consideration of him who lies in the manger, we can feed most happily on the very look and we shall say: "The Lord feeds me and I lack nothing; he has settled me in a place of pasture."[64] Then indeed we shall know that the fullness of time yearning with desire has come, in which God has sent his Son,[65] through whom we are already filled with such a plentitude of good things. To him be blessing and thanksgiving now and throughout unlimited ages. Amen.

---

59. Sir 14:5, 6, 14.   60. Sir 14:10.   61. Prov 13:2.
62. Job 7:7.   63. Sir 14:8.   64. Ps 22:1f.   65. Gal 4:4.

SERMON 10

THE FIFTH SERMON FOR CHRISTMAS

YOU HAVE COME together, brethren, to hear the Word of God. But God has provided something better for us. Today it is given to us not only to hear but also to see the Word of God, if only "we will make our way to Bethlehem and see this Word which the Lord has made and shown to us."[1] God knew that men's minds were incapable of perceiving invisible things, unwilling to be taught about the things of heaven, slow to yield their faith unless the object itself in which they were asked to believe was visibly borne in on the senses to convince them. For although faith comes from hearing[2] it comes much more readily and promptly from sight, as we are taught by the example of him who was told: "Because you have seen me you have believed," you who were unbelieving when you heard.[3] Because it is more difficult to believe in what is only heard, not seen, the faith of those who have not seen is rightly declared blessed by the Lord, because they have attributed more to the authority of the Word than to the experience

---

1. Lk 2:15. This is the opening line of the gospel which is sung at the second Christmas mass, the mass which is celebrated at dawn and, because of this gospel, referred to as the shepherds' mass. Therefore the monks would have heard this gospel sung a short time before gathering in the chapter for this sermon by their abbot. However, there would have intervened an "interval" (as the Cistercians have customarily called those periods of the day when they are free for personal prayer, reading and meditation) and the office of prime, during which they and the speaker would have had time to meditate on the text.

2. Rom 10:17.   3. The apostle, Thomas. Jn 20:29.

of their own senses or reason. Yet God wishes to satisfy our slowness in everything. His Word, which previously he had made to be heard, today he makes visible to us, indeed even tangible.[4] So some of us could say: "Our message concerns that Word, who is life; what he was from the beginning, what we have heard about him, what our own eyes have seen of him; what it was that met our gaze and the touch of our hands."[5] He was from the beginning of that eternity which is without a beginning; we heard him promised from the beginning of time; we saw him and handled him shown to us at the end of time.

Elsewhere you will find that the Word of God has been made not only an object of sight and touch but also of taste and smell.[6] He sought an entrance for himself to the soul through all the ways of the senses, so that as death had entered through the senses life too might return through the same. If then the Word was made flesh[7] it was for us who are wholly flesh, so that as we had previously only been able to hear the Word of God, we might now be able to see him and taste him made flesh, summoning all the senses to witness to hearing. All our senses should confess with one agreement and one voice: "As we heard, so we have seen."[8]

Yet incomparably more is now granted to sight than was ever granted to hearing. Now the Word which is God[9] is seen, whereas before it was considered extraordinary to hear any word which came from God. As for the word which comes from God, brethren, I have on occasion seen it heard without interest. But surely the Word which is God can only be seen with joy. I will pass sentence on myself first: when the Word which is God offers himself to me today to be seen in that which I am, if it does not gladden me I am godless, if it does not edify me I am reprobate.

---

4. Guerric here elaborates on the theme which is found in the Preface to the Eucharistic Prayer which is used on Christmas and the following days: ". . . through the mystery of the incarnation of the Word a new ray of the divine brightness illuminates the eyes of our minds so that knowing God visibly we might be drawn to the love of what is invisible."

5. 1 Jn 1:1.   6. Ps 33:11; Song 4:11.   7. Jn 1:14.
8. Ps 47:9.   9. Jn 1:1.

2. If then any brother is found among us who is troubled with spiritual lassitude I do not wish that his ears should be wearied any longer by our contemptible sermon. Let him make his way to Bethlehem and there let him look upon that Word of God upon which the angels yearn to look,[10] that Word which the Lord has shown to us.[11] Let him picture in his mind what the living and creative[12] Word of God is like as he lies there in the manger. If only piety enlightens the eye of him who looks, what can there be so delightful to see, so wholesome to think about? What so edifies behavior, strengthens hope, inflames charity?

Truly it is a trustworthy word and deserving of every welcome,[13] your almighty Word, Lord, which in such deep silence made its way down from the Father's royal throne[14] into the mangers of animals and meanwhile speaks to us better by its silence. Let him who has ears to hear, hear[15] what this loving and mysterious silence of the eternal Word speaks to us. For, unless hearing deceives me, among the other things which he speaks he speaks peace for the holy people[16] upon whom reverence for him and his example impose a religious silence.[17] And most rightly was it imposed. For what recommends the discipline of silence with such weight and such authority, what checks the evil of restless tongues and the storms of words, as the Word of God silent in the midst of men? There is no word on my tongue,[18] the almighty Word seems to confess while he is subject to his mother.[19] What madness then will prompt us to say: "With our tongues we can do great things; our lips are good friends to us; we own no master."[20] If I were allowed I would gladly be dumb and be brought low, and be silent even from good things,[21] that I might be able the more attentively and diligently to apply my

---

10. 1 Pet 1:12. 11. Lk 2:15. 12. Heb 4:12.
13. 1 Tim 1:15. 14. Wis 18:14f. 15. Mt 11:15.
16. Ps 84:9.

17. Although the Cistercians never made a vow of silence as has sometimes been alleged, they have traditionally interpreted the sixth chapter of the Rule of St Benedict with considerable strictness. Guerric here gives some of what we might call the theology behind this Cistercian interpretation.

18. Ps 138:4. 19. Lk 2:51. 20. Ps 11:5. 21. Ps 38:3. Cf. RB 6:2.

ear to the secret utterances and sacred meaning of this divine silence, learning in silence in the school of the Word if only for as long as the Word himself was silent under the instruction of his mother.

3. O brethren, if we listen devoutly and diligently to this word which the Lord has made and shown to us today,[22] how much and how easily we can be taught by it. It is an abbreviated word, yet in such a way that in it every word which makes for salvation is summed up: for it is "a word that sums up and abbreviates with equity."[23] And this abbreviated summing-up has overflowed with justice, as you remember was promised through Isaiah, since from its own fullness it has overflowed with justice upon those who partake of it.[24] Thus their justice may abound more than that of the Scribes and Pharisees,[25] even though these latter exercise themselves in manifold justifications of the Law while the former are content with the brief and simple word of faith.

But is it surprising that the Word should have abbreviated all his words to us when he willed to be abbreviated himself and after a fashion diminished, to the point that he contracted himself from his incomprehensible immensity to the narrow straits of the womb and he who contains the world suffered himself to be contained in a manger? In heaven this Word strikes awe into the angelic powers by his dreadful sublimity; in the manger he feeds the simple and the stupid. There he is unsearchable to the keenest intellects of the angels; here he is to be touched by even the dull senses of men. Because God could not speak to us as spiritual men but only as carnal[26] his Word was made flesh[27] so that all flesh might be able not only to hear but also to see that the mouth of the Lord has spoken.[28] And since in its wisdom the world did not know God's wisdom, by an unspeakable condescension the same Wisdom of God made itself foolishness.[29] It offered itself to be learned by men however uneducated or stupid, and through the folly of preaching saved those who believed.[30] "I give you thanks, Father, Lord of heaven

---

22. Lk 2:15. 23. Rom 9:28. 24. Is 10:22f.
25. Mt 5:20. 26. 1 Cor 3:1. 27. Jn 1:14.
28. Is 40:5. 29. 1 Cor 1:21, 23. 30. *Ibid.*

and earth, because you have hidden your wisdom from the wise and prudent and revealed it to little ones. Even so, Father, so it was your good pleasure"[31] that to little ones should be given the little one who is born for us.[32] The loftiness of the proud is too far removed from the humility of this little one. What is lofty among men is abominable to him, who although he is lofty in very truth, has become a little one for us. It is only with little ones that this little one agrees, only in the humble and the quiet that he rests. Therefore as the little ones glory in him and sing: "A little one is born for us,"[33] so he too glories in them: "Behold me," he says, "and my children which God has given me."[34] For in order that the Father might give his little Son companions among those of his own age, the glory of martyrdom was at once inaugurated in the innocence of little ones before all others.[35] By this the Holy Spirit gave to understand that it is only to such that the kingdom of heaven belongs.[36]

4. If we wish to be made such, again and again let us make our way to Bethlehem[37] and let us look with all earnestness upon this Word which has been made flesh, the immense God who has been made a little one. In this visible and abbreviated Word[38] we may learn the Wisdom of God which in its entirety has been made humility. In this virtue that all-embracing Virtue has for the time being found its expression: that supreme Wisdom has willed for the time being to know nothing else but that humility of which he willed afterwards to declare himself a teacher. And he indeed—I say this to my own confusion—he, I say, was worthily and justly made a teacher of humility. Although he knew it well, by origin from his mother and naturally from his Father, none the less from the very

---

31. Mt 11:25. 32. Is 9:6.

33. *Ibid.* This is solemnly sung as the opening (introit) of the mass which is celebrated on Christmas day itself.

34. Is 8:18; Heb 2:13.

35. Mt 1:16. A feast is celebrated in honor of these little ones on the third day after Christmas: the Feast of the Holy Innocents.

36. Mt 19:14. 37. Lk 2:15.

38. Is 10:23; Rom 9:28.

womb of his mother he learned it from the things he suffered.[39] He was born in a travelers' inn in order that we might learn from his example and confess ourselves to be strangers and travelers upon earth.[40] There too he chose the last place and was put in a manger in order that we might learn by this act of his what those words of David mean: "I chose to be of no account in the house of my God rather than to dwell in the tents of sinners."[41] He was wrapped in swaddling clothes[42] that we might be content to have just enough to cover us.[43] In everything he was content with his mother's poverty and in everything he was subject to his mother. The whole pattern of a religious life seems already to have been born at his birth.

Blessed is the faith of the simple shepherds. Although it found an infant wrapped in swaddling clothes[44] it was not at all scandalized by them so as to refuse belief and think the less of him. Rather its devotion was increased so as to be more grateful for such condescension. For the more deeply humiliated and completely emptied out for them that majesty showed itself, the more easily and fully (if we wish to entertain a worthy opinion of them) love of him took possession of and claimed for itself the whole of their affections.

5. Brethren, you also will find today an infant wrapped in swaddling clothes and laid in the manger of the altar. Take care that the poverty of the covering does not offend or disturb the gaze of your faith as it beholds the reality of that august body beneath the appearance of other things. For as his mother Mary wrapped the infant in swaddling clothes, so our mother grace hides from us the reality of the same sacred body by covering it with certain outward appearances which are in keeping with the economy of salvation. So too mother wisdom covers the hidden majesty of the divine Word with riddles and figures, in order that in the one case the simplicity of faith and in the other the exercise of study may accumulate merit for itself unto salvation.

For when I too, brethren, declare to you in my own words the truth which is Christ what else am I doing but wrapping Christ in

39. Heb 5:8.
40. Heb 11:13.
41. Ps 83:11.
42. Lk 2:12.
43. 1 Tim 6:8.
44. Lk 2:12.

rather mean swaddling clothes? Yet blessed is he to whom Christ is no meaner even in these swaddling clothes. So a prudent man does not value precious wares less highly because they are packed in old sacking. Christ it is whom I desire to give you in my sermons, however poor they may be, so that according to the words of the apostle Peter you may enthrone him as Lord in your hearts.[45] Be patient and cherish that word implanted in you which can bring salvation to your souls.[46] May all the wealth of Christ's world dwell in you,[47] love, that is, and remembrance of the incarnate Word, so that you may sing both happily and faithfully: "The Word was made flesh and dwelt amongst us."[48] With complete devotion then let us think of Christ in the swaddling clothes with which his mother wrapped him, so that with eternal happiness we may see the glory and beauty[49] with which his Father has clothed him, glory as of the Only-begotten of the Father,[50] with whom and with the Holy Spirit may honor and glory be his for ever and ever. Amen.

---

45. 1 Pet 3:15. 46. Jas 1:21. 47. Col 3:16.
48. Jn 1.14.   49. Ps 20:6.   50. Jn 1:14.

SERMON 11

THE FIRST SERMON FOR THE EPIPHANY

"BRING TO THE LORD, ye sons of God."[1] It is better to bring to him than to the leech, that is, to concupiscence, whose two daughters, pleasure and vanity, give her no rest day and night as they clamor: "Bring, bring."[2] What then shall we bring to the Lord? Bring to the Lord glory of gold and honor of incense; bring to the Lord glory for his name,[3] myrrh for his burial.[4] But Christ's disciple, Peter's son, tells me: "Silver and gold I have none,[5] nor bags of those foreign wares, myrrh and incense." Will you then appear empty-handed in the Lord's sight and not honor the cradle of the new king with any presents? O rich poverty, O wealthy nakedness—provided it is Christian and freely willed.[6] With what riches do you not abound, not only gold but the very best gold, gold that has been fired, not only myrrh and incense but also all the fragrant powders of the merchant.[7] Indeed who else can abound in riches of this sort but the poor of Christ? "I walk in the ways of justice," he says, "endowing with wealth those who love me and filling their treasures."[8] And he does not lack the where-

---

1. Ps 28:1. These are the opening words of the first psalm sung at the Vigils on the Feast of the Epiphany.

2. Prov 30:15.   3. Ps 28:2.
4. Mt 2:11; Jn 19:39.   5. Acts 3:6.

6. Bernard of Clairvaux brings out the same doctrine in his First Sermon for the Feast of All Saints, n. 8, where he teaches that poverty is not a beatitude unless it is voluntarily embraced from a will to please God and save souls.

7. Song 3:6.   8. Prov 8:20f.

withal: "Riches and glory are with me, proud wealth and justice."⁹ Goodly wealth indeed, the riches of salvation, which inspire a pride that does not fail in justice.

Brethren, this pride is the glory of men who exult in the Lord and scoff at the world because it has nothing precious enough to compare with the poverty of the saints. O you who are fainthearted, why do you not take pride with me in these riches? The Master of humility does not condemn this pride; he rewards it, provided you are magnanimous enough in your contempt of the world to look down as from a lofty height upon all its glory and rate it as nothing for the love and honor of your nakedness. You are altogether rich if you pride yourself on poverty;¹⁰ and for you too the Apostle will give thanks in those words of congratulation: "I give thanks to my God that you have become rich, through him, in every way, in eloquence and in knowledge, so that there is no gift in which you are lacking."¹¹ It is in quite a different strain that the Lord speaks to the man who was congratulating himself on all that he possessed in this world: "I am rich, you say, nothing now is wanting to me; and all the while it is you who are wretched, you who are to be pitied: you are a beggar, blind and naked."¹²

2. Among riches of this sort, on which the apostle Paul congratulates his disciples, I do not doubt that gold, incense and myrrh can be found to be offered to the newborn Christ as a worthy and pleasing gift.

But I am not aware, you will say, that I have received anything of the sort, or that anything so precious as gold, incense and myrrh is to be found in my possession. For I am a man well acquainted with poverty,¹³ finding it hard to beg my daily bread, leading an impoverished life. You think, you say, that you have not received any such thing. Is it not rather that you have squandered in riotous living the inheritance you received from your father?¹⁴ But I pass over that. As the Wise Man says, "One who turns away from sin to become wise is not to be reproved."¹⁵ Rather I would wish that you

---

9. Prov 8:18.   10. Sir 10:34.   11. 1 Cor 1:4ff.   12. Rev 3:17.
13. Lam 3:1.   14. Cf. Lk 15:13.   15. Sir 8:6.

had the energy to examine if there be not some slight remnant of your paternal inheritance in your hands with which you could begin to recover the whole. I would wish you to dig within yourself, for valuable treasures are wont to lie hidden in the recesses of the earth. That treasure, the desire of which drove a man to sell all he had, was hidden in a field.[16] The ten Israelite men who escaped the murderer's sword did so by declaring that they had treasures hidden in a field.[17]

O what treasures of good works, what riches of devotion lie hidden in the field of man's body; and how many more in the depths of the heart, if only a man will take the trouble to dig. I am not saying what Plato taught, that before the soul came into the body it learned arts which were then buried by forgetfulness and the weight of the body and have to be dug up by hard work;[18] but that man's reason and natural endowments, with the help of grace, are a seed-bed of all the virtues. If then you will ponder in your heart[19] and train your body,[20] you need not doubt that you will find worthwhile treasures—if not of gold or incense at the very beginning, certainly of myrrh, and that is not useless. It is not for you to describe as useless what Christ accepts as a gift. With this he willed that the burial of his body should not only be foreshadowed when it was offered to him[21] but also be completed when he was embalmed with it.[22]

3. If you would have plainer language, myrrh in your heart is sorrow, myrrh in your body is work, provided that the one and the other come of repentance. That both are myrrh is proved not only by the etymology of the name or by its taste but also by the effects of its medicinal power. For myrrh, even by its very name, has a very bitter taste, but its effect, apart from other useful qualities, is to withstand corruption. What more bitter to the taste, what more wholesome in its effect than the sorrow which moves a sinner to

---

16. Mt 14:44.   17. Jer 41:8.
18. Plato teaches this most explicitly in *Meno*, 86 (*The Dialogues of Plato*, trans. B. Jowett [New York: Random House, 1937], vol. 1, p. 366) and *Phaedo*, 73 (*Ibid.*, p. 456).
19. Is 46:8.   20. 1 Tim 4:8.   21. Mt 2:11.   22. Jn 19:39f.

repentance? He passes his life in review in the bitterness of his soul,[23] imploring God not to condemn him,[24] but all this bitterness is nothing other than myrrh preserving him from the corruption both of the wantonness in which he has grown rotten and of the undying worms which he has deserved. Though it is not so much myrrh as a bundle of myrrh[25]. If we are to believe those who have just come in from the world, the regular fasts and vigils, the daily manual labor, the rough clothes and practically everything are bitter to them because they are unaccustomed to them. These things are bound together as it were into one bundle which has to be taken up and carried. And indeed it would be with exceeding bitterness that they would carry this bundle of myrrh were it not that, although they do not as yet rejoice to share the sufferings of him they love, so as to say: "He whom I love is a bundle of myrrh to me,"[26] yet they find some sweetness in mitigating the bitterness of their heart by outward bitterness, as they might relieve a stomach ache by drinking absinth. For just as the stomach, spoilt by immoderate indulgence in sweet things, is purged by a dose of something bitter, so the soured conscience of those who have lived in pleasure is never better cured than by the opposite, that is, austerity of life and rule—and this especially if they are often given to drink the myrrh-spiced wine of the Lord's Passion, that is to say, if they are dosed with the wine of compunction[27] which is all the more wholesome for the sinner as it is bitter on account of sin remembered. Jesus refused to drink the spiced wine[28] because he had not committed the sin which the men who crucified him ascribed to him. He was given to drink the bitterness of a vine not his own, but he was to drink new wine, of the fruit of the true vine, with his friends in the Father's kingdom.[29]

4. Although in comparison with piety training of the body avails but little for the perfect, such as Timothy,[30] how useful it is for the rough and imperfect such as we. You yourselves, brethren, bear

23. Is 38:10. 24. Job 10:2. 25. Song 1:12.
26. Ibid. 27. Ps 59:5. 28. Mt 27:34.
29. Mt 26:29. 30. 1 Tim 4:8.

witness to yourselves. You know how the bitterness of a scant diet and hard work redeems our life from corruption.³¹ For you yourselves know how your hearts, how your bodies would be creeping with worms if it were not for the myrrh distilled day by day from manual labor.³² Is not wantonness a worm? I know of no other more harmful. It creeps in by its enticements, it bites by its smile, it pierces by causing pleasure, it destroys by the will's consent. Are not spiritual weariness³³ and sadness a worm? "As the moth to a garment and as the worm to wood, so does a man's sadness harm his heart."³⁴ What are all evil desires? Are not they too worms? But every idle man is a prey to desires; and "the desires of the sluggard kill him."³⁵

Happy then is he whose own hands drip myrrh all over him to kill worms of this sort and who anticipates now the anointing of his body for burial.³⁶ But shall I say his body or that of Jesus? Surely that of Jesus, too. For that man's body is a member of Jesus.³⁷ Whoever he is who is so anointed need not fear the worm which dies not,³⁸ because the worm from which that worm takes its origin he has already done to death.

5. You too then, a king yourself, have offered to the Lord with the kings myrrh, choice myrrh of the highest quality,³⁹ if for the time being, while your means do not suffice to offer the gold of wisdom or the incense of devotion, you have consecrated to the Lord at least a contrite heart and an afflicted body, together with the bitterness of penance.

For I think, without excluding a better interpretation, that myrrh is the first offering of beginners, then incense that of those who are making progress, while gold is the offering of the perfect. When the

---

31. Jon 2:7.   32. Song 5:5.
33. This is what monastic tradition has referred to as *acedia*, and has usually listed among the capital sins. Cassian made a great deal of this vice in his writings, devoting a full book of the *Institutes*, Book 10, to it (*The Institutes of John Cassian*, trans. E. Gibson, in *The Nicene and Post-Nicene Fathers*, second series, vol. 11 [Grand Rapids, Mich.: Eerdmans, 1955,] pp. 266ff.), as well as touching on it often in the *Conferences*, e.g., Conf. 5:9 (*Ibid.*, pp. 342f.), 24:4 (*Ibid.*, p. 533).
34. Prov 25:20.   35. Prov 21:25.   36. Mk 14:8.
37. 1 Cor 6:15.   38. Mk 9:43.   39. Sir 24:20; Song 5:5.

Evangelist lists these more precious and valuable things, the order in which they are named is determined by their relative worth.[40] Elsewhere, according to stages of progress, you will find myrrh put before incense, as in the text: "Like a column of smoke perfumed with myrrh and incense,"[41] and "I will go to the mountain of myrrh and to the hill of incense."[42]

Indeed it is no slight progress to advance from myrrh to incense, from what is used for human weakness to what is reserved for festival sacrifices offered to God. The man who was wont to offer the sacrifice of a crushed spirit[43] and a humiliated body, not without the myrrh of bitterness, now offers the sacrifice of praise together with the incense of devotion. As the Lord promised, such great consolation is accorded to the mourners of Sion that he gives them a garland instead of ashes, the oil of gladness instead of mourning, the mantle of praise instead of a grieving spirit.[44] Then he who used to mourn sings: "You have changed my lamentation into joy; you have torn off my sackcloth (the spirit of grief), and clothed me with gladness (the mantle of praise), so that my glory may sing to you and no longer be sad.[45] For right gladly will I rejoice in the Lord and my soul shall exult in my God, because he has clad me in the garments of salvation and put on me the clothes of rejoicing.[46]

6. O brethren, you who find the clothes of your poverty insufficient in the bitter cold of this winter, you who say: "Who can bear this cold?"[47] why do you not put on, I ask you, this garment of gladness, this mantle of praise? If it praises the Lord, in the Lord shall our soul be praised;[48] and he who is greatly to be praised will cover you too with the mantle of praise which covers him; he will cherish you as does the hen her chickens under her wings,[49] if only you are willing. How often he wished to do so—but you were unwilling. For is this mantle too short to cover both?[50] "You are not restricted," he says, "by us but you are restricted in your own affec-

---

40. Mt 2:11.
41. Song 3:6.
42. Song 4:6.
43. Ps 50:19.
44. Is 61:3.
45. Ps 29:12f.
46. Is 61:10.
47. Ps 147:6.
48. Ps 33:3.
49. Mt 23:37.
50. Is 28:20.

tions."⁵¹ Expand your hearts,⁵² and the mantle will be extended to cover you also. His hand is not shortened so as not to be able to save us.⁵³ It is an easy matter for him to console us, did not our perversity prevent him. O you who are freezing, this mantle is warm, because it is warmth, able to warm not only internally but externally also. Are not your garments warm when the south wind blows through your land?⁵⁴ Indeed is not fire kindled in your bones,⁵⁵ does it not blaze up? With this fire burn that incense which you offered together with the kings, so that your prayer may go up as incense in the sight of the Lord⁵⁶ and when he smells the sweet fragrance of your sacrifice⁵⁷ he may say to you: "The fragrance of your garments is like the fragrance of incense."⁵⁸

7. But with regard to the gold of wisdom, which, as we said, is the offering of the perfect, let him speak to you of it who has obtained it, for only the man who receives it knows what it is.⁵⁹ Let the man then who has learned wisdom speak wisdom among the perfect⁶⁰ and with the gold which he possesses let him fashion golden ornaments for your ears.⁶¹ For I do not consider that I have obtained this, yet I press on in the hope that I may obtain it.⁶² Great indeed and happy is he who has found wisdom and abounds in prudence; wisdom in the contemplation of things eternal, prudence in the administration of temporalities; or, to define the wise man more moderately, he who is able to rule both himself and another. This gold is more precious than all riches, even than incense and myrrh; and all the virtues and graces that might be desired are as nothing in comparison with this. To be sure, the wise man, man of virtues as he is and rich in everything, although his principal concern is to offer gold in sublime contemplation or prudent administration, does not neglect to offer incense as he devoutly fulfills the Work of God or myrrh by mortifying himself.

For ourselves then, brethren, let us offer what we have to the glory

51. 2 Cor 6:12.	52. 2 Cor 6:13.	53. Is 59:1.
54. Job 37:17.	55. Lam 1:13.	56. Ps 140:2.
57. Gen 8:21.	58. Song 4:11.	59. Rev 2:17.
60. 1 Cor 2:6.	61. Song 1:10.	62. Phil 3:12f.

Sermon 11:7

of the new King; what we have not got, let us ask for it from him to whom we desire to offer it. Is there someone who lacks wisdom? Let him ask God for it. God gives to all freely and ungrudgingly.[63] "They are my gifts, my presents," says the Father of lights, from whom come whatever gifts are worth having, whatever endowments are perfect of their kind.[64] To him be glory for ever and ever. Amen.[65]

---

63. Jas 1:5. 64. Jas 1:17.

65. The critical latin edition does not have an *Amen* at the end of this sermon, as is the case with a number of others, but we have added it in every case in the translated text for the sake of consistency. As it was the common practice of the times to end with a doxology and an *Amen*, the inconsistency in the manuscripts probably does not correspond to the actuality. As will be noted, the two Lenten Sermons are exceptional.

SERMON 12

THE SECOND SERMON FOR THE EPIPHANY

"ARISE, BE ENLIGHTENED, Jerusalem, for your Light has come."[1] This present day of lights has been enlightened for us and consecrated by the Light of Light. He had lain hidden and unknown, but today he has vouchsafed to reveal himself to the world for the enlightenment of all nations. For today he revealed himself to the Chaldeans by the sign of a new star, dedicating in them as in first-fruits the faith of all nations.[2] Today he revealed himself to the Jews, by the witness not only of John but also of the Father and of the Holy Spirit, when, baptised in the Jordan, he consecrated the baptism of all.[3] Today he manifested his glory before his disciples when by the changing of water into wine he prefigured that ineffable mystery in which by his word the substances of things are changed.[4] The Holy Spirit, foreseeing that the Church's faith was to be enlightened by all these appearances of God, speaks to it under the figure and name of Jerusalem in the words: "Arise, be enlightened, Jerusalem, for your light has come." The Light indeed had come; he was in the world, and the world was made through him, but the world did not know him.[5] He was born but he was not known,[6] until this day of light began to manifest him. So the

---

1. Is 60:1. This might well be called the key text of the Feast of the Epiphany. It is frequently repeated in the celebration of the divine office; both Vespers, First Nocturn, Lauds and Tierce all include it.

2. Mt 2:1ff.   3. Mt 3:13ff.; Jn 1:29ff.   4. Jn 2:1ff.   5. Jn 1:10.

6. We have here an example of Guerric's proclivity to play on words: *Erat natus sed non erat notus.*

Prophet says: "O new Jerusalem, great city of the new king, Mount Sion, at the sides of the north[7] (that is, to be built from both walls, that of circumcision and that of uncircumcision), arise, be enlightened, for your light has come." Arise, you who sit in darkness; look at the light which has risen up in the darkness but is not mastered by the darkness. Draw near to him and be enlightened,[8] in his light you shall see the light;[9] and it will be said to you: "You were once darkness, but now you are light in the Lord."[10] Look upon the Eternal Light which has tempered itself to your gaze, so that he who dwells in inaccessible light[11] affords access even to weak and bleary eyes. See the Light in a lamp of earthenware, the Sun in a cloud, God in man, the Splendor of Glory and Brightness of Eternal Light[12] in the clay vessel of your flesh.

2. Majesty indeed lies hid in human nature, power in lowliness; but signs and prodigies break through the covering and leave no doubt as to their origin. "The works which I do," he says, "bear witness to me.[13] Great indeed is the witness of John, who came to bear witness as a lamp to the light.[14] But much greater is that heavenly witness which the Father and the Holy Spirit bore to the Son, the Father by his voice, the Spirit in the form of a dove; since on the evidence of two witnesses every claim is established.[15] But if even this be not accepted the countless and unimpeachable works which I do bear witness to me." Surely an impartial and unquestionable witness, when unfeeling creation is endowed with a certain feeling to confess its Creator, hearkening to his will and obeying his behest without delay. For what more God-like could be manifested to human senses than the prodigies, which Jesus today exhibited, long before the beginning of his signs? A new-born child cries on earth while in the heavens he creates a new star, so that light may witness to Light, a star to the Sun, and so that kings in the splendor of its rising[16] may be led to the Eternal Splendor which has also risen up. They come from the sunrise to the true Sunrise, that is to

---

7. Ps 47:3.   8. Ps 33:6.   9. Ps 35:10.   10. Eph 5:8.
11. 1 Tim 6:16.   12. Wis 7:26.   13. Jn 5:36.   14. Jn 1:7.
15. Deut 19:15; Mt 18:16.   16. Is 60:3.

the man whose name is Sunrise.[17] They are led by the star not as a star but as a rational animal, going before them on the journey, coming to a halt at the end of the journey and pointing out as with a finger him whom they sought.

Granted, as the unbeliever falsely asserts, that this star is not Christ's work, he must admit that it is the Father's work in witness to the Son. However he will be overwhelmed by the infinite number and greatness of the truly God-like wonders which without any question our Jesus worked in the flesh but not by the power of the flesh.

3. But let darkness cover the earth and shades the peoples[18] who, when the light came into the world, preferred darkness to light,[19] provided you are enlightened, Jerusalem, heavenly city, you who in every land and people are to bear to God sons of Light whom he will transfer from the power of darkness to the kingdom of his brightness, the true light.[20]

Thank you, Father of lights, who have called us out of darkness into your admirable light.[21] Thanks be to you who bade light shine out of darkness and have kindled a light in our hearts whose shining is to make known your glory as you have revealed it in the features of Jesus Christ.[22] This is the true light, indeed eternal life: that we may know you the one God, and him whom you have sent, Jesus Christ.[23] We know indeed through faith, holding on to it as to a trustworthy pledge so that we shall know by sight too. In the meantime increase our faith,[24] leading us on from faith to faith,[25] from brightness to brightness, by your Spirit,[26] so that from day to day we may enter more deeply into the treasures of light, so that faith may become more all-embracing. Thus will knowledge be more full, charity more fervent and expansive, until, through faith, we are led to the vision of your face, as if led by a leading star to our Leader at Bethlehem. Coming forth from Bethlehem he rules Israel[27] and reigns in Jerusalem, not the Jerusalem that killed the

17. Zech 6:12. 18. Is 60:2. 19. Jn 3:19. 20. Col 1:13.
21. 1 Pet 2:9. 22. 2 Cor 4:6. 23. Jn 17:3. 24. Lk 17:5.
25. Rom 1:17. 26. 2 Cor 3:18. 27. Mic 5:2; Mt 2:6.

prophets[28] and the Lord himself of the prophets, but the Jerusalem in which the same Lord crowns those who have been killed, he who is the cause, the power and the glory of martyrs.

4. O with what joy does the faith of the Magi exult there as they look upon him reigning in that Jerusalem, him whom they adored as a crying babe in Bethlehem. Here he was seen in the inn of the poor, there he is seen in the palace of the angels; here in the swaddling clothes of infants, there in the splendors of the saints; here on his mother's lap, there on his Father's throne. Truly the faith of the blessed Magi deserved to be rewarded with so blissful a sight. Their faith, although it saw in him only what was weak and contemptible, could not however find in that a stumbling-block to prevent them from worshiping God in man and man in God. Without doubt a Star out of Jacob[29] had shone in their hearts, the Morning Star, I mean, the Herald of Light which knows no setting, he who from without also had kindled for their hearts a star as a sign of his rising in the morning. What is written in the Book of Proverbs can be very aptly understood of these: "The path of the righteous is like the light of dawn, which shines brighter and brighter until full day."[30] For at first they entered on the path of justice by the light of a dawning star; led by it they advanced to seeing the new rising of early morning Light; and so finally they reached the point where they could contemplate the face of the Midday Sun in all the brilliance of its power.

5. These first-fruits of the nations, then, these beginnings of the new-born Church, aptly and pregnantly prefigure the stages by which faith progresses in individuals: whence it begins, how it advances, whither it arrives, so that the traces of those who are fathers may be recognized in their sons. For just as they began with the sight of the star, advanced to the sight of the Child, arrived at the sight of God, so in us faith is born by the preaching of heavenly luminaries, it is strengthened by the sight of certain images which show us God incarnate, through a confused reflection in a mirror,[31]

28. Mt 23:37.
29. Num 24:17.
30. Prov 4:18.
31. 1 Cor 13:12.

and it will be brought to its consummation when the naked truth of things will be seen as present and we shall contemplate face to face what now is scarcely seen for a fleeting moment now and then, as a confused reflection. Then faith itself will be transformed into knowledge, hope into possession, desire into enjoyment.

For us too stars shine, not one but many—except that the many are one, since they have one heart and one soul,[32] the same faith, a harmonious preaching and a similar life. What are these stars? If you are in doubt, ask Daniel. "They who instruct many unto justice shall shine like stars for all eternity."[33] Paul also calls those men luminaries who shine in the midst of a wicked and perverse nation[34] and contain the word of life, like splendor borrowed from eternal light, with which they seem to enlighten the night of this world. Therefore when the Lord, the source and origin of light, was disposing the moon and the stars to govern the night[35] he told them: "You are the light of the world;"[36] and again: "So let your light shine before men that they may see your good works and glorify your Father who is in heaven."[37] So they shine by their word, they shine by their example, and by these two rays of light they proclaim the rising of eternal Light. They preach with their voices one who is in heaven and commend him also by the resemblance of a heavenly life.

6. Look up, brethren, into heaven, for your true home is in heaven.[38] Look up and direct the eyes of your mind at least on the brilliance of the stars, if you are not able yet to gaze upon the sun's disk. Admire the splendor of the saints, imitate their faith, emulate their holiness. Those stars blaze like a flame and show clearly that the Light of lights has risen. They lead to the cradle of the new King, to the bedchamber of the Virgin Mother, faith's inviolable mystery, indeed they lead to the temple of the King, to the sanctuary of God the Father, faith's reward that surpasses all understanding. In the meantime however, while we are not able to search out the wisdom of God which is hidden in mystery[39] or to contemplate the majesty

---

32. Acts 4:32.　　33. Dan 12:3.　　34. Phil 2:15.
35. Ps 135:9.　　36. Mt 5:14.　　37. Mt 5:16.
38. Phil 3:20.　　39. 1 Cor 2:7.

Sermon 12:6–7

which is to be our reward, let us be content to wonder at the brightness of the saints.

"My son," Scripture says, "have you desired wisdom? Keep the commandments and the Lord will grant it to you."[40] But do not seek what surpasses you, do not search out what is beyond your strength, but observe always what the Lord has commanded.[41] For the Lord's command is full of light, it enlightens the eyes[42]—and with those eyes you will be able afterwards to look on the Light itself, when you have grown accustomed to living in the light of its rays, that is, in the fulfillment of the commandments.

"Light is pleasant," as Solomon says, "and the eyes delight in beholding the sun."[43] Pleasant indeed and delightful, but for those who can bear it. It fosters healthy eyes, but it tortures weak eyes. And whose sight is so healthy and so keen that it is not enfeebled by the vision of that invisible Sun? Who can search out majesty and not be overwhelmed by its glory?[44] Your brightness, Lord, is too wonderful for me, both on its own account and on my account; for it is strengthened against me, while my gaze is weakened in me. I am no longer able to bear it[45] as I could in Adam. Perhaps I may be able to bear the brightness of stars, although I cannot bear the Sun itself. The one will give me strength to bear the other.

7. Come then, my soul, arise, be enlightened, you who sat in darkness.[46] Look up to heaven's luminaries, raise your eyes to the mountains from where help will come to you[47] if you revere him who dwells in the heavens,[48] that is, in the mountains themselves. From the mountains, I mean, help will come to you, for a Light that is beyond your reach[49] enlightens wonderfully from the eternal mountains.[50] The mountains have received a Light for the people[51] and from them it will come down upon the valleys and fields that lie beneath them. So I say this, brethren: to attend to those who are enlightened is an excellent beginning of enlighten-

---

40. Sir 1:33 (Septuagint). 41. Sir 3:22. 42. Ps 18:9.
43. Eccles 11:7. 44. Prov 25:27. 45. Ps 138:6.
46. Is 60:1; Lk 1:79. 47. Ps 120:1. 48. Ps 122:1.
49. 1 Tim 6:16. 50. Ps 75:5. 51. Ps 71:3.

ment and one suited to our weakness. The straightest way to finding Jesus is to follow the guiding light of the fathers who have gone before us. The path of the just has been made straight, the way of the just is straight to walk on.[52] He who follows the just man does not walk in darkness but will have the light of life[53] and not only see it. He will see it for the comforting of his present life, he will have it to possess as an eternal inheritance.

Piety holds promise for the present life and also for the life to come.[54] Let us exercise ourselves in piety and we shall not be disappointed of either by him who of his own free will has made himself our debtor. Let us exercise ourselves in the works of light and he who hides light in his hands[55] and tells his friend that it is his possession and that he can ascend to it, will show it to us now from time to time to encourage us in our work and afterwards will give it us as a reward, he our Light, Christ Jesus, who lives and reigns for ever and ever. Amen.

---

52. Is 26:7.
53. Jn 8:12.
54. 1 Tim 4:8.
55. Job 36:32.

SERMON 13

THE THIRD SERMON FOR THE EPIPHANY

"ARISE, BE ENLIGHTENED, Jerusalem, for your Light has come."[1] Blessed is the Light which has come in the name of the Lord, God the Lord, and has shone upon us.[2] In virtue of it this day also, sanctified by the enlightening of the Church, has shone upon us. Thanks be to you, true Light, you that enlighten every man coming into this world,[3] you who for this very purpose have come into this world as a man. Jerusalem has been enlightened, our mother, mother of all those who have deserved to be enlightened, so that she now shines upon all who are in the world. Thanks be to you, true Light, you who have become a lamp to enlighten Jerusalem and to make God's word a lamp for my feet.[4] Thanks be to you, I say, because Jerusalem itself, enlightened, has become a lamp to shine upon all who are in the house[5] of the great Father. For not only has it been enlightened: it has been raised aloft on a candlestick, one all of gold.[6] The city sits on the mountain of mountains,[7] that city once forsaken and hated; it has been set majestic for ever and ever,[8] so that its gospel may shine out far and wide, as far and as wide as the world's empire spreads.

Although its gospel is veiled it is only veiled for those who are on the road to perdition, those whose unbelieving minds have been blinded by the god this world worships, so that the glorious Church

---

1. Is 60:1. See n. 1, Sermon 12.   2. Ps 117:26f.   3. Jn 1:9.
4. Ps 118:105.   5. Cf. Mt 5:15.   6. Ex 5:31.
7. Is 2:2; Mic 4:1   8. Is 60:15.

of Christ cannot reach them with the rays of its illumination.[9] Yet those who do not see by the rays of its illumination are provoked to envy by those rays; refusing to be enlightened by the Church's grace they are tortured by its glory. But the Church is not proud on account of the glory which brings it prosperity, neither does it begrudge the grace which gives it strength. It begs that the light which it has received may be imparted even to those whom it tolerates as a burden, in the words: "For you have lighted my lamp, Lord my God, enlighten my darkness.[10] Perhaps they are mine, because they are predestined, but they are still darkness, because they are not yet called or justified.[11] Call them too into your wonderful light[12] and they will proclaim your wonderful name together with me."

Yet every just man, every holy man in the Church, for all that he is glad to be enlightened, sees that to a great extent he is still in darkness, and he is saddened by this. Of necessity therefore, although he is enlightened, he asks to be enlightened still more. For the more his lamp is enlightened, the more truly is his darkness revealed to him by the lamp itself. Do not immediately consider as opposed to this the words of incarnate Truth in the gospel: "The lamp of your body is your eye. If your eye is clear your whole body will be lit up."[13] For it does not follow that because the whole of our activity is lit up by the eye of a pure intention all the darkness of our mistaken opinions and ignorant views is immediately enlightened. The measure of our enlightenment is still this, that the man who is able to know his own inadequacy and recognize what is lacking to him is to be judged as having made great progress towards the light of truth. Hence it is that among the wise men of this world whose disquisitions on the subject of knowledge are the most marked by sobriety the first degree of knowledge is reckoned as knowing one's own ignorance.[14]

---

9. 2 Cor 4:3f.   10. Ps 17:29.   11. Rom 8:30.
12. 1 Pet 2:9.   13. Mt 6:22.
14. E.g., Aristotle, *Nic. Eth.*, 1, 4; Socrates in Plato's *Phaedrus*, 235; Cicero, *Pro Cluent*, 31; Livy, *Works*, 22, 29.

2. Brethren, all of you are sons of light and sons of the day. We do not belong to the night or to the darkness.[15] For the night has passed away, the day has drawn near.[16] Although we were once darkness, now we are light in the Lord.[17] None the less if, because we are not darkness nor sons of the darkness, we say that we do not suffer anything of darkness, we are deceiving ourselves and bringing upon ourselves the darkness of death such as does not deserve to be enlightened. For what does the Light of the world say, he who came into this world for judgment, in order that they who do not see may see, and they who see may become blind? "Because you say: We see," he says, "your sin remains."[18] I see to some slight extent, because you enlighten my lamp, O Lord; but since what I see is not much, my God, enlighten my darkness.[19] We see for the most part as in a mirror, in a confused reflection.[20] But this is very far removed from the true clarity and the clear truth which accompany face-to-face vision. That perhaps is why the blind man in St Mark's gospel whom our Lord had begun to enlighten, saw men as trees walking: because he saw only as in a mirror, in a confused reflection. But when Christ laid his hand on him the second time he restored his sight fully, so that he could see everything clearly.[21] This will come about in us when he renews us and gives us perfect health by laying his hands on us a second time: the first time began the process of healing, the second will restore us to perfect clarity.

3. But even this enlightenment, as in a mirror with a confused reflection, to whom or when or for how long can it happen? What a signal act of mercy it would be for me, what a blissful enlightening I would consider it, if I could see my sins, I who must needs bewail every day that evils without number have encompassed me, and that I am unable to see.[22] For who understands transgression?[23] Vice under the deceitful appearance of virtue deals its mortal blow, like an angel of darkness transforming itself into an angel of light.[24]

---

15. 1 Thess 5:5.   16. Rom 13:12.   17. Eph 5:8.
18. Jn 9:39ff.   19. Ps 17:29.   20. 1 Cor 13:12.
21. Mk 8:22ff.   22. Ps 39:18.   23. Ps 18:13.
24. 2 Cor 11:14.

Great indeed and considerably enlightened is the man who can and will understand his transgressions clearly; for the deceitful man neither can nor will understand so as to behave well.[25] God, you who give light to all nations, of you we will sing: "Behold the Lord will come and enlighten the eyes of his servants."[26] Behold, you have come, my light; enlighten my eyes, that I may never fall asleep in death;[27] that mortal sin may not close my eyes by its pleasure nor entice to consent, that it may not find me asleep like Ishbosheth and pierce me through.[28] You have come, O light of the faithful, and behold you have granted us today to rejoice at the enlightening of faith, that is, of our lamp. Grant us also to rejoice always at the enlightening of the darkness that remains to us. You granted us the light of faith: grant us also the light of justice, the light of knowledge, the light of wisdom, too.

4. These are the stages by which you should make progress, this is the way in which I think you should advance, O faithful soul, in order that you may cast off the darkness of this world and arrive at your home country of eternal brightness, where your darkness will be like midday[29] and night will be lit up like day.[30] Then indeed, then you will see and be radiant, your heart will thrill and rejoice,[31] when the whole earth is filled with the majesty of unbounded light and his glory is seen in you.[32] House of Jacob, come and let us walk in the light of the Lord;[33] as sons of light let us walk[34] from brightness to brightness, with the Spirit of the Lord to go before us[35] and by one degree of virtue after another let us enter further and further into the kingdom of brightness.

Let us then who are already in the light through faith go forward from it and through it towards a more ample and a more serene light, first that of justice, then that of knowledge, finally that of wisdom. For what we believe through faith has to be worked out or merited in keeping with our faith through justice, afterwards under-

25. Ps 35:4.
26. Jude 14.
27. Ps 12:14.
28. 2 Sam 4:7.
29. Is 58:10.
30. Ps 138:12.
31. Is 60:5.
32. Is 60:2.
33. Is 2:5.
34. Eph. 5:8.
35. 2 Cor 3:18.

stood through knowledge and finally contemplated through wisdom.

First of all the lamp of faith is lit, so that by it we may work in the night of this world. Therefore it is written in praise of the valiant woman that she rose by night and, working with her hands by day and by night, she did not eat her bread in idleness: her lamp shall not be put out during the night,[36] that is, her faith shall not fail under temptation. By this lamp the works of darkness are not done, rather it is put out when they are done. For he who does evil hates the light;[37] and therefore he extinguishes the lamp of faith, puts behind him mindfulness of God. The fear of God is not before his eyes,[38] and he flatters himself on the darkness, which he has made for himself, and the absence of judges, saying: "Who is there to see me? Darkness surrounds me and walls cover me and no one is looking at me; whom should I fear? The Most High will not remember my transgressions." He does not understand that his eye sees everything.[39] Whereas good works, although to avoid vanity they may be done sometimes secretly, are done in light both from within and from without, that is, under the judgment of faith and the witness of God; because they are works of light, lamps burning in the hands of those who do them as they await the coming of the Bridegroom[40] who will bring forth your justice like the light[41] into the sight of men and angels. As the midday sun is bright[42] so will your deeds be bright, because they are done in God,[43] so that the judgment of all may make God bright in you and you in God.

5. With what great brightness justice shines even in the present, with what great light it gladdens the conscience of the just man. The witness of your own conscience will teach you more familiarly and more pleasantly than the testimony of my tongue. Yet often faith is radiant and justice shines brightly, while the understanding is still in darkness; so that it is unable to unfold the mystery of faith[44] which it venerates, holding it as it were wrapped up. The book of

---

36. Prov 31:15ff. 37. Jn 3:20. 38. Ps 35:2.
39. Sir 23:26f. 40. Lk 12:35. 41. Ps 36:6.
42. Is 18:4. 43. Jn 3:21. 44. 1 Tim 3:9.

Scripture is sealed for it, as if it did not know how to read; neither are its faculties exercised so that they can distinguish between good and evil, true and false.[45] And indeed there are many such in the Church, whose faith is considerable, whose justice abounds, but whose knowledge is little or none.

The Prophet's word however teaches that the merit and the experience of justice kindles the light of knowledge. He had said first: "Sow for yourselves unto justice;"[46] then, to show what first-fruits we should gather in the meantime from this seed, he added: "Light up for yourselves the light of knowledge."[47] So too the Apostle: "Bearing fruit in good works, growing in the knowledge of God."[48] You too, David, sitting in your chair, wisest prince among three,[49] how did you understand better than the aged? "Because I strove after the commandments,"[50] he says. "Through your precepts indeed I have understood,"[51] for all those who cultivate the fear of the Lord have a good understanding.[52] For the Anointing who teaches everything,[53] knowing, indeed, what matters are to be learned and in what order, first teaches goodness and discipline, and afterwards knowledge[54] provided that the man who is to be taught has first of all believed, that is, has learnt the rudiments of the doctrine of justice. That Disciple of the Anointing selected and disposed the terms of his prayer so prudently: "Teach me goodness and discipline and knowledge," he says, "because I have believed in your commandments;"[55]—as if to say: "I have learned the rudiments, that is, unfeigned faith; now teach me what comes next, justice, that is, goodness and discipline, that so finally I may be brought to the knowledge of the saints. You have called me to the grace of faith: now justify me through the goodness of love and the discipline of chaste fear; so that afterwards you may

---

45. Heb 5:14.   46. Hos 10:12.   47. *Ibid.* (Septuagint)
48. Col 1:10.   49. 2 Sam 23:8.   50. Ps 118:100.
51. Ps 118:104.   52. Ps 110:10.

53. 1 Jn 2:27. From John's context it is clear that the Anointing is the Holy Spirit, and it is equally clear from the next paragraph in this Sermon that Guerric so understood it.

54. Ps 118:66.   55. *Ibid.* (Vulgate).

glorify me with the gift of spiritual knowledge." For those whom he called he justified, and those whom he justified he glorified.[56]

6. You must know that, although this is the knowledge of the saints[57] not all the saints are taught it, but only those in whom industry helps grace and grace helps industry, both co-operating in mutual support, so that man is a docile disciple and the Spirit is present as a diligent teacher. However, while this knowledge contains various spiritual gifts, the governing Spirit does not easily bestow them all together but distributes them to individuals according to his will: to one he gives knowledge of mysteries, to another understanding of the Scriptures, to another interpretation of tongues, to another power to test spirits,[58] to another that ability, necessarily a taste as it were, to distinguish and judge between virtues and vices, so that vices may not deceive under the appearance of virtues. "They shall do no harm, neither shall they kill," it is written "in all my holy mountain: for the earth is full of the knowledge of the Lord."[59]

7. Now if a man, after these three things and through them, faith, justice and knowledge, advances to wisdom, that is to the savor and taste of things eternal, so that he can be still and see[60] and, while he sees, taste how sweet is the Lord;[61] and if what the eye has not seen and the ear has not heard and what has not entered into the heart of man [62]is revealed to him through the Spirit—this man indeed I will say is enlightened, magnificently and gloriously, like one who gazes on the Lord's glory with face unveiled[63] and over whom the Lord's glory often rises.[64] To such a man it is no prophet but the Spirit of the prophets who will say: "Arise, be enlightened, Jerusalem, for your light has come and the glory of the Lord has risen over you."[65]

Brethren, we do not all accept this word, but let him who can, take it.[66] He who does not take it is not condemned, but he who does not desire it is accused of tepidity. But he who desires it should

---

56. Rom 8:20.
57. Wis 10:10.
58. 1 Cor 12:10f.
59. Is 11:9.
60. Ps 45:11.
61. Ps 33:9.
62. 1 Cor 2:9f.
63. 2 Cor 3:18.
64. Is 60:1.
65. *Ibid.*
66. Mt 19:12.

know that this light of wisdom is kindled by fervent prayer, just as the light of knowledge is by frequent reading, provided that when you read you use a burning lamp, that is, justice in your deeds and devotion in your sentiments. But do you, Lord, Father of lights, who have sent your only Son, Light born of you, the Light, to enlighten the darkness of mortal men, grant us to come by the way of lights to eternal light, that we may be pleasing to you in the light of the living[67]—you who live and reign for ever and ever. Amen.

---

67. Ps 53:13.

SERMON 14

THE FOURTH SERMON FOR THE EPIPHANY

WE ARE CELEBRATING, brethren, a second birth today, which seems to follow on and be born of the first birth as an effect of its cause. That which we have celebrated up to today is the birth of Christ, that which we celebrate today is our own birth. In the former Christ was born, in the latter Christianity was born. There are three things which make us Christians: faith, baptism and sharing in the altar. This present day brought us the beginning of faith, consecrated baptism and prefigured the wonders of the heavenly table. There is no need for us to teach you now how the first enlightening of the nations marked the beginning of faith for us, how Christ's baptism consecrated our baptism, how that changing of water into wine foreshadowed the changing of the elements in the banquet of the Lord's table. What I think it is worthwhile to impress upon ourselves is that faith in us should not degenerate from its beginnings, that the grace of baptism in us should not be brought to nothing, that our sharing in the chalice of Christ should not involve us in judgment.[1]

2. Our fathers have given us sufficient and abundant doctrine as to what manner of faith was delivered to us today by those Magi who were the first to receive it, and how they conveyed a very great mystery of faith under the hidden forms of their gifts. In this respect no other work remains for us[2] but that of entering into the work of the Fathers.

1. 1 Cor 11:29. 2. Jn 4:38.

The Fourth Sermon for the Epiphany

Again the present state of affairs, or as I should say, the calamities of our times, do not call for any lengthy treatment of the mystery of faith. What rather has to be striven for to the utmost is, as the Apostle says, that the same mystery of faith be possessed with a pure conscience.[3] For behold today if you question people on the mystery of faith you find them practically all out-and-out Christians; if you examine their conscience you will find very few who are truly Christians. The whole world almost confesses verbally that it knows God; but by its deeds it denies him,[4] so much so that those who seem to have the appearance of piety are often found practically to deny its power.[5] What do you think, my brethren; whom do you think I mean to designate when I say that they have the appearance of piety but deny its power? If you understand it of those who tread the wide path of the world,[6] what do they exhibit even of the appearance of piety? They are Christians only in name, they take to themselves in vain the holy name[7] of Christ while they freely devote themselves to the pursuit of the things which are contrary to this name. All their behavior, their whole way of life, marks them out as enemies of Christ's cross.[8] Is this the appearance of piety which we see in them: wanton dress and gait, ribald speech, a shameless eye, a belly worshiped as a god[9] and all that disgraceful living which as it were insults piety to its face, publicly and boastfully? Their secret actions are too shameful even to bear speaking of.[10] Let him who is sent to prophecy to them dig through their wall, so as to see greater abominations still,[11] which neither shame nor reverence prevents them from perpetrating in the presence of that awesome majesty. Why should I who seem to be a monk judge those who are outside this monastery?[12]

Would that I had no need even to judge those who are here inside it. For my own soul is disturbed.[13] I am afraid lest this very appearance of piety which I display after a fashion together with

3. 1 Tim 3:9.
4. Tit 1:16.
5. 2 Tim 3:5.
6. Mt 7:28.
7. Ex 20:7.
8. Phil 3:18.
9. Phil 3:19.
10. Eph 5:12.
11. Ezra 8:6ff.
12. 1 Cor 5:12.
13. Ps 41:7.

you should begin to accuse me the more gravely if it should convict me of failing in actual piety.

3. Truly, brethren, I must be afraid—as for yourselves, it is for you to decide—lest we especially should be the objects of that warning which the Apostle gave when he foretold the last days. Describing the wickedness of the men of that age, such as can now be read manifestly in their lives and behavior, he concluded a long list of evils with the words: "They have the appearance of piety, but they deny its power."[14] For what so exhibits the appearance of piety as what we undertake: this humble tonsure and habit, our sparing food and drink, our almost uninterrupted work and our whole way of life so carefully planned out? Certainly, were it not manifest to all, I would be ashamed to confess how, of the virtue of piety which these outward forms promise, little or nothing can be found in me and those who resemble me. For what is the virtue of piety but unfeigned charity,[15] true humility, long-suffering patience, prompt obedience? I leave it to your own judgment, brethren, to what extent you may boast of these virtues and their like. For my part I confess quite simply that although I know their names I am still ignorant of their flavor. Rightly then this religious habit which I wear, to which is added almost no witness of virtue, fills me with both shame and fear. For can I safely take to myself the name and honor of a monk when I do not possess its merit and virtue; since, as has been said before our time, an affected sanctity is a double iniquity, and the wolf that is caught in sheep's clothing is to be condemned all the more severely?

Therefore in order that you may be able safely to take pride in this outward form of piety with which your bodies are adorned, do, brethren, set your hearts to consider its virtue,[16] so that both the outward form and the virtue in your hearts may make you acceptable to both angels and men, and so it may be as Scripture says: "All who see them will know that they are the seed which the Lord has blessed."[17]

---

14. 2 Tim 3:5. 15. 2 Cor 6:6. 16. Ps 47:14.
17. Is 61:9.

The Fourth Sermon for the Epiphany

4. This, brethren, is the true piety of Christian faith; this is to have the mystery of faith in a pure conscience.[18]

In order that we might faithfully and worthily preserve, unstained and with a pure conscience, the mystery of faith, which the mysterious gifts of the Magi have commended to us today, today likewise Christ, baptized not for himself but for us, has sprinkled our hearts, as the Apostle says, and has washed our bodies clean in hallowed water,[19] so as to purify us from a bad conscience. How happy, brethren, is that soul which has thus taken the bath of salvation and has immediately followed in its Savior's footsteps, so that henceforward keeping close to him it may deserve to hear together with the apostles those words: "He who has bathed only needs to wash his feet: he is clean all over."[20] But as for the man who has cleansed himself after contact with a corpse and then touches it again, of what use is his washing?[21] For myself, after the waters of baptism I handled not just one corpse but one after another for every deadly sin I committed. That proverb which Peter the Apostle used applies to me: "The dog returns to its vomit and the newly-washed sow wallows in the mire."[22] What then shall I do? With what waters shall I further wash away such filth? I hear that, just as there is one faith, so there is one baptism.[23] There is no place for a second baptism, since all we who are baptized are baptized in the death of Christ.[24] As he died once,[25] so too he was baptized once, so as to lay down for us too the measure and form of a sole baptism.

I would consider it perhaps impossible to be cleansed further did not the trustworthy advice of Elisha, from among the other consolations of Scripture, bring me back from despair to hope. Even if I am infected from head to foot with the leprosy of Naaman, the Syrian, and possessed by an incurable lethargy, I can hope. "Go," he says, "and wash seven times in the Jordan, and you will be cleansed."[26] If he had said: "Wash three times and you will be cleansed," I

---

18. 1 Tim 3:9.   19. Heb 10:22.   20. Jn 13:10.
21. Sir 34:30.   22. 2 Pet 2:22; Prov 26:11. 23. Eph 4:5.
24. Rom 6:3.   25. 1 Pet 3:18.   26. 2 Kings 5:10.

would have understood it at once of the threefold submersion by which the baptized are cleansed, and I would say that the whole of that miracle prophesied the grace of baptism; so that already then the Jordan by the power of our Lord's baptism had begun to effect the salvation of the nations. But in fact, since what he says is precisely: "Wash seven times in the Jordan," what does this number seven mean or what is that Jordan? The etymology of Jordan is, they say, "their descent." Whose? Those to be sure who are brought low to repentance, those who, the deeper they descend by the degrees of humility, submerge themselves more completely and wash themselves more thoroughly in the stream of the spiritual Jordan.

5. "My soul is disturbed, O God, mindful of its sins; therefore I will be mindful of you from the land of Jordan"[27]—mindful, that is, of how you cleansed Naaman, the leper, in his humble descent. "He went down," Scripture says, "and washed seven times in the Jordan according to the bidding of the man of God, and he was cleansed."[28] You also, go down, O my soul, from the chariot of pride into the health-giving waters of the Jordan, which from its source in the house of David now flows through the whole world to cleanse the sinner and the woman in her times.[29] This to be sure is the humility of repentance, which flowing at once from Christ's gift and from his example, is now preached throughout the world and purifies the sins of all mankind.

O you, Naamans of Syria, for it is not a question of one man but of countless; O you rich but lepers, proud but sinful, why do you feel so vehement a repugnance to wash in these healing waters? Why does this Jordan of ours seem of such little account in comparison with the rivers of Damascus? For when you happen to seek some salutary advice and you are told to imitate Christ's humility and poverty, you say: "Are not the rivers of Damascus better than all the waters of Israel for me to wash in them and be cleansed?"[30] Is it not better and more efficacious for the purifying of sins to make benefactions daily from one's worldly wealth rather than leave

---

27. Ps 41:7.   28. 2 Kings 5:14.   29. Zech 13:1.   30. 2 Kings 5:12.

everything once and for all and become poor? But listen, Naaman: "Leviathan will swallow up the rivers of Damascus and will not be surprised;" but as for the Jordan, if he trusts that it will flow into his mouth,[31] he will be disappointed in his hope. He does not reckon you as anything very much, however great your virtues, if Christian humility is not among them, since he is confident that he can devour even Christ's poor. But the enemy shall not prevail against them.[32] The name Damascus means "city of blood" and its waters are mixed with blood, for even the good deeds of carnal and worldly men are hardly pure of all sin. And how shall that which is contaminated by blood cleanse blood? In what way shall what is leprous cure leprosy? But our Jordan itself flows pure and the proud will not be able to hurt you if you submerge yourself wholly in it and are as it were buried together with Christ's humility.

6. Listen at least, Naaman, to your servants, your humble friends, your trusty counsellors. Naaman was going back, indignant at the man of God whom he had consulted. But they said: "Father, if the prophet had bidden you do some great thing you certainly would have done it."[33] Trustworthy advice indeed, full of reason and wisdom, as are the suggestions of a man's rational feelings, which God has reserved for himself as witnesses against man himself. "Father," they say, "if the prophet had bidden you do some great thing you certainly would have done it. To refuse belief to a prophet is an offence against God; not to attempt everything for the sake of health is hatred and envy of oneself. For how can a command seem to be asking too much when health is what is promised?" How much more should it not seem anything excessive or difficult to learn of Jesus that he is meek and humble of heart,[34] since in him there is to be found both repose for the soul and healing for our spiritual leprosy, together with the pledge of eternal salvation? In the end the proud sinner is with difficulty prevailed pon to go down and wash in the Jordan. Yet if he washes seven times and submerges himself completely and often, returning

---

31. Job 40:23.   32. Ps 88:23.   33. 2 Kings 5:13.   34. Mt 11:29.

health will not be slow to vindicate the Prophet's word. But, alas, such is the wretchedness of these times of ours that not only the rich but also poor lepers are so sensitive that they can scarcely bear to enter the healing waters up to their ankles; or if they have washed once they straightway seem to themselves to be fully cleansed.

7. But Elisha is not of that opinion: he expressed himself unambiguously: "Wash seven times and you will be cleansed." For he was aware that Christ's humility, which we must imitate if we wish to be perfectly cleansed, is sevenfold in its virtue. Its first virtue is that although he was rich he became poor;[35] its second, that he carried poverty to its extreme limit and was laid in a manger;[36] its third, that he was subject to his mother;[37] its fourth, that today he bent his head beneath a servant's hands;[38] its fifth, that he so bore with a disciple who was a thief and a traitor;[39] its sixth, that he was so meek before an unjust judge;[40] its seventh, that he was so forgiving in interceding with his Father for those who crucified him.[41] You follow in the giant's footsteps in these things, even if from afar, if you love poverty, if you choose its extreme limit among the poor, if you are subject to the monastery's discipline, if you allow one who is less than yourself to command you, if you bear patiently with false brethren, if you overcome with meekness when you are judged,[42] if you requite with charity those who unjustly make you suffer. This humility truly rebaptizes us with no infringement of the sole baptism, for it does not repeat Christ's death but renews the mortification and burial of sins and carries out in very truth what is represented in outward form by that baptism.

This humility opens the heavens, restores the spirit of adoption. The Father recognizes his son, fashioned anew in the innocence and purity of a regenerate child. Hence Scripture does well to say of Naaman that his flesh was restored like the flesh of a little child,[43]

---

35. 2 Cor 8:9.
36. Lk 2:16.
37. Lk 2:51.
38. Lk 3:21.
39. Lk 6:16.
40. Lk 23:3.
41. Lk 23:24.
42. Ps 50:6.
43. 2 Kings 5:14.

meaning, I believe, that those who so wash themselves clean not only recover for their hearts the innocence of little ones but are also given in their bodies, through the mortification of their members, a purity resembling in some measure that of children. So we read of a certain saint[44] that his dead members seemed to have as it were the gracefulness of a seven-year-old child.

Behold, brethren, we have lost the grace of our first baptism by wallowing in such filth: behold the true Jordan, that is the descent of the humble, in which we find that we may be devoutly rebaptized. All that is required is that we should not be reluctant to go down day by day more deeply, be submerged more completely, and be wholly buried together with Christ. Let us give him thanks, whose humility both consecrated the form of baptism today for those who believe and reserved an equivalent grace for those who repent: to him be glory for ever and ever. Amen.[45]

---

44. St Martin of Tours, the first great monastic leader in the West. This statement is made by his classical biographer, Sulpicius Severus. See PL 185:64.
45. Rev 1:6.

SERMON 15

THE FIRST SERMON FOR THE PURIFICATION

"**YOUR LOINS MUST BE GIRT** and your lamps burning in your hands."[1] Our loins must be girt that we may follow the example of Mary's purification; and lamps burning in our hands that by this outward sign we may remind ourselves of the joy of Simeon carrying the Light in his hands. In other words, we must be pure of body and clean of heart, and so portray the purification of Mary: we must be burning with love and radiant with good deeds, and so take up Christ in our hands with Simeon.[2]

But Mary was not purified; rather she put before us the inner meaning of purification. In fulfilling the legal rite[3] she gave it a spiritual meaning. For what could be purified in her who had conceived as a virgin, given birth as a virgin and remained a virgin

---

1. Lk 12:35. This text of Luke is not actually found in the Liturgy of the day, but it aptly expresses one of the significant elements of the day's liturgy: the carrying of lighted candles. The monks received newly-blessed candles which they lighted from the light which had been kept alive in the sanctuary lamp since the lighting and blessing of the new fire on the previous paschal night. They then carried these burning lights in their hands during a procession through the cloisters. This is one of the oldest processions in the Cistercian liturgy, and was perhaps carried on without interruption from the days of Molesme. Finally the monks brought their lighted candles, after the proclamation of the Gospel which brought out their significance, to the altar to be offered in union with the sacrifice. *Consuetudines Ordinis Cisterciensis* (a. 1134), part 1, *Officia Ecclesiastica*, c. 47, *De Purificatione sanctae Mariae*, in *Nomasticon Cisterciense*, ed. H. Séjalon (Solesmes, 1892), pp. 119f.

2. Lk 2:28.   3. Lev 12.

still? Indeed if beforehand her purity lacked anything at all, she was fully purified in this conceiving. What was there to be purified in that conception, the one source of cleansing for those who are conceived unclean?[4] It is he who is revealed today, he who gives rise to the spring in which uncleanness itself can be purified, the spring of the house of David which gushes up unflaggingly to wash away sin and the waste of the womb alike.[5] And the mother of all purity has seemed to be purified by the law so as to show forth, at one and the same time, the strength of all-obedient humility and the truth of the Gospel's purifying power.

Where then is the man so stubbornly and mistakenly presumptuous of his own sanctity as to refuse to undergo the cleansing action of the remedy of penance? Even if he really be holy he cannot surely be as holy as she, the most holy of all the holy, Mary, who gave birth to the Holy of Holies? I only wish, my dear brethren, that we, in our sinfulness, had the same humility as the saints had in their virtue. But we must pass this over now, and continue with the exposition of our subject.

First of all we must deal with that spiritual purification which Mary recommends to us when she offers a pair of turtledoves or two young pigeons for herself and for her son.[6] The meaning here must be what, as you know well, our forefathers brought to light when they discussed its deeper implications. They showed how by the turtledove is meant chastity of body and by the young pigeon, simplicity of mind.[7] And they did not fail to point out too what is a sacrifice of one—either of the turtledove or the young pigeon—and what is a holocaust of the other. But one thing more we can add: the deeper we fathom such mysteries as these, the more strictly and justly is it demanded of us that we respond to them with deeds, for he is indeed a sinner who knows what is right and does not do it.[8] The servant who knows his master's mind and does not do what he ought shall be beaten with many stripes.[9]

2. Leaving then what has been explained well enough let us

4. Job 14:4.   5. Zech 13:1.   6. Lk 2:24.
7. Mt 10:16.   8. Jas 4:17.   9. Lk 12:47.

rather, if it please you, discuss this charming custom of the Church of bearing lights aloft on this feast day, which may be to re-enact the deed once performed, or to bring home to us our own performance of it. I do not imagine that you cannot guess such meanings even if you have never heard them expounded. Could anyone hold up a lighted candle in his hands on this day without at once remembering that old man who on this same day took up in his arms Jesus, God's Word, clothed in flesh like a candle-flame clothed in wax, and affirmed him to be the Light which would be a beacon for the Gentiles?[10] Surely he was that burning and radiant lamp[11] which bore witness to the Light.[12] For this purpose he came in the Spirit, who had filled him, into the temple:[13] that he might receive, O God, your Loving-Kindness in the midst of your temple[14] and declare him to be Loving-Kindness indeed and the Light of your own people. Truly, O holy Simeon, in the quiet contentment of old age you carried this Light not simply in your hands but in the very dispositions of your heart. You were like a lamp-standard, seeing so clearly how much the Gentiles would one day be lit up, while reflecting even then amidst the gloom of Jewish unbelief the bright rays of our faith. Old, yet still sincere, you can now be happy in that you really see what once you but foresaw. Gone is the world's gloom, the Gentiles bask in this Light of yours.[15] The whole earth is full of the glory[16] of that hidden Light you kindly fondled in your arms, or rather by which you enkindled your own fond heart.

O Tinder of Love, so sweet a love and tender to re-enkindle the heart,[17] sweet and tender still when it grieves and tortures; a delightful torture of happiness, like the burning glow of health refreshed. Such a burning heart, brethren, hidden within your breast, does not set your clothes alight; instead it puts out that fire lurking in your breast which can not only scorch your clothes but lay waste too to what is clothed, consume body and soul together. Our God is a consuming fire.[18] It is written that he is a consuming

---

10. Lk 2:28ff. 11. Jn 5:35. 12. Jn 1:17. 13. Lk 2:26.
14. Ps 47:10. 15. Is 60:3. 16. Is 6:3. 17. Lam 1:11. 18. Heb 12:29.

fire because he sets aflame the heart, licks around the mind, makes anew the soul, closes again the mortal wound of love. Simeon was not unaware of the power of this Fire. He rejoiced to carry it in his arms and let it warm his breast, he gave it an old man's gentle caress. How much more carefully and tenderly did this fire warm an old man than did Abishag, the Shunammite, King David[19]— unless maybe Abishag was this same fire, namely Wisdom, in whose embrace not only are the cold warmed but the dead also brought back to life.

3. Embrace God's Wisdom, then, O blessed old man; and may your heart beat high and glow again as it did in youth. Hold God's Loving-Kindness tight to your breast and your grey hairs shall be blessed with love and kindness.[20] "Close to my heart, it is written, shall he lodge,[21] and even when I give him back to his mother he shall remain with me. And when he is snuggled close to his mother's heart he shall none the less linger close to mine. My heart, too, will be drunk with the overflow of his Loving-Kindness, though not so much as his mother's. For she is the one-only Mother of Mercy All-High; so that in a wonderful way she is fruitful with the fruitfulness of the divine mercy. O Full of Grace,[22] you I congratulate and praise. You gave birth to the Loving-Kindness I received; you gave shape to the candle I accepted. You prepared the wax for the touch of the light, O Virgin, the Virgin of Virgins, when as the unblemished mother you clothed the unblemishable Word in unblemished flesh."

Come then, my brethren, give an eye to that candle burning in Simeon's hands. Light your candles too by borrowing from that Light; for these candles I speak of are the lamps which the Lord orders us to have in our hands. Come to him and be enlightened,[23] so as to be not merely carrying lamps but to be very lamps yourselves, shining inside and out, for yourselves and for your neighbors. Be a lamp then in heart, in hand, in lips. The lamp in your heart will shine for you; the lamp in your hand or on your lips will

---

19. 1 Kings 1:2ff.   20. Ps 91:11.   21. Song 1:12.
22. Lk 1:28.   23. Ps 33:6.

shine out for your neighbors. The lamp in the heart is loving faith; the lamp in the hand is the example of good works; the lamp on the lips is edifying speech. But not just before men must we shine by works and word, but before angels too by prayer, and before God himself by pure intention. Our lamp before the angels is the purity of our devotion when in the sight of angels we chant the psalms with care[24] or pray with burning ardor; our lamp before God is the honesty of our intention to please him only whose approval we have won.

4. Do not imagine that in what has been said we have followed the vaporings of mere imagination. We can show quite clearly that in everything we have kept close to the witness of the Scriptures. The Wisdom of Solomon vouches for faith being a lamp, for it is written there of the valiant woman that "all night long her lamp does not go out,"[25] which means, at any rate for us, that whatever the temptation, her faith does not falter. As for charity, which is nothing but faith working through love,[26] we read in Solomon again: "The torch that lights it is a blaze of fire. Yes, love is a fire no waters avail to quench, no floods to drown."[27] But as for good works being a lamp, the very Light of Truth himself tells us so: "Your loins must be girt and your lamps burning in your hands,"[28] and "Your light must shine so brightly before men that they can see your good works."[29]

As for edifying words being a lamp, here are the words of David: "No lamp like your word to guide my feet, to illumine my path."[30] And the apostle Peter, referring to words of prophecy, adds: "It is with good reason that you are paying so much attention to that word; it will go on shining like a lamp in some darkened room."[31] So the revelation of God's words illuminates and gives understanding to the simple;[32] either when the words of the Gospel dispel the shadow of the Law, or when the words of Gospel and Law alike, which were puzzling to the intelligence of simple minds, are now

24. Ps 137:1; 46:8. 25. Prov 31:18. 26. Gal 5:6.
27. Song 8:6f.   28. Lk 12:35.   29. Mt 5:16.
30. Ps 118:105.   31. 2 Pet 1:19. 32. Ps 118:130.

expounded clearly and all of us say in daylight what was said to us in darkness.[33] This is the reason why Philip is likened, as a type of the Church's teachers of every age, to the orifice of an oil-lamp, across whose lips flows the burning word of the Lord to give light to all around.[34] I reckon as God's own word, my brethren, whatever the Holy Spirit in his mercy sees fit to speak within you[35]—every single word which avails to build up faith[36] stirring up love.[37] If you should start to use words that are as it were God's own,[38] so that no bad word, even in private conversation, should cross your lips but rather words that build up faith, gracious words for all who hear,[39] that make them give you grateful thanks, then blessed indeed is the word upon your lips, for your word is a lamp to guide my feet, to illumine my path.[40]

That prayer is this selfsame lamp, flaring up ardently when God breathes his Spirit, we may infer from what Solomon says: "Man's spirit is a lamp the Lord gives, to search out the hidden corners of his being."[41] For the Light revealed to us in our prayers and psalmody streams down like an invigorating breath of fresh air[42] which we may sweetly breathe. Job seems to recall this lamp when, woebegone in his misfortune, he sighs as he conjures up the memory of his former happiness and comfort: "Alas for the changes the months have brought with them," he says, "alas for the old days when God was my protector, when his light shone above me, its rays guiding me through the darkness."[43] As regards the rest of what was said, that this lamp is to search out the hidden corners of his being, or rather of the realm of his mind, God is not here recalling his threat to search with lamps.[44] In that place he would speak of his searching judgment; here of his enlightening grace. It is one thing for him to

---

33. Mt 10:27.

34. It is not certain to which Philip Guerric is referring, Philip the Apostle or Philip the Deacon. Perhaps it is the former, alluding to the *Benedictus* antiphon he shares with James the Less, where they are spoken of as olives and lampstands, whose tongues open the gates of heaven.

35. Mt 10:20.	36. Eph 4:29.	37. Heb 10:24.	38. 1 Pet 4:11.
39. Eph 4:29.	40. Ps 118:105.	41. Prov 20:27.	42. Gen 2:7.
43. Job 29:2f.	44. Zeph 1:12.		

Sermon 15:5

use the doctor's purge; quite another if he takes up the executioner's axe. But as to good intention also called a lamp, no one can argue about it who has any understanding of the gospel phrase: "Your body has the eye for its lamp."[45]

5. There are so many lamps then, my brethren, to lighten your way, if only you will come to the source of all light and be enlightened.[46] Come, I say, to Jesus who shines out to us from Simeon's arms. He will give light to your faith, luster to your works, meaning to your words for men, ardor to your prayer, purity to your intentions. Whether by works, by words or by prayer you will seek to please him only whom you see in the light he gives to those who really live,[47] who by his own lights keeps a watchful eye on Jerusalem[48] and who can measure too what light it is we have. Now, child of light, aflame with all these burning lamps, you will no longer be wandering in the dark of night[49] nor have reason to fear the curse pronounced: "In deepest night the lamp of his hopes shall be quenched, that turns upon father or mother with a curse,"[50]—that is to say, the comfort of this light shall fade away and darkest night come shrouding in from every side, covering the surface and entering deep down to the inmost depths. There are the many lamps then to glow with ardor in these inmost depths of yours, that when this life's lamp is extinguished there will arise a life's light which can never be extinguished, a shimmering, noonday light, arising as it were at the evening of your life; and at the very moment when you think you are burnt out, your wick's flame will arise again[51] and darkest night for you will be as the noonday.[52] No more need of the sun's rays by day nor of the brilliance of the moon to light your way at night: the Lord will be for you an everlasting light,[53] for the Lamb it is who is the lamp of the new Jerusalem,[54] he who is the All-Blessed and Crystal-Clear, throughout endless ages. Amen.[55]

---

45. Mt 6:22. 46. Ps 33:6. 47. Ps 55:13. 48. Zeph 1:12.
49. Jn 8:12. 50. Mt 15:4; Prov 20:20. 51. Job 11:17.
52. Is 58:10. 53. Is 60:19. 54. Rev 21:23. 55. Rev 7:12.

SERMON 16

THE SECOND SERMON FOR THE PURIFICATION

AS THE DAY of Christ's birth, that is, the day of his coming, was greeted by those accents of thanksgiving and praise: "Blessed is he who comes in the name of the Lord,"[1] and the day of his appearance, that is, of our enlightenment, by what follows: "The Lord is God and he has shone upon us;"[2] so also what comes next: "Appoint a festival day with processions up to the horn of the altar,"[3] seems to me to be quite appropriate to this day which we celebrate with solemn assembly, the day, that is, of our Lord's Presentation, when he was solemnly presented at the altar to the Father by his mother. For in what is added: "You are my God and I will praise you, you are my God and I will extol you; I will praise you, because you have hearkened to me and become my salvation,"[4] what can we understand so suitably and properly as the faith and praise of Simeon and Anna, who at that very hour came to give God praise and spoke of the child to all that were awaiting the deliverance of Israel?[5] Our harpist then did well to bid Jerusalem rejoice and hold a gathering on so solemn a day: "Appoint a festival day with processions up to the horn of the altar."[6] No mean assembly that, nor lacking in solemnity, since it brought Jesus and Mary, with a crowd of relatives, carrying in the

---

1. Ps 117:26.   2. Ps 117:27.
3. *Ibid.* It is still the liturgy, with its distinctive procession on this day, which gives Guerric his theme.
4. Ps 117:28.   5. Lk 2:38.   6. Ps 117:27.

Sermon 16:1–2 107

Child, to perform the custom which the Law enjoined concerning him; and it brought Simeon and Anna to meet him, with a crowd of those who were expecting the deliverance of Israel, and to these they bore witness concerning him.[7]

2. For my part I do not believe that it was this solemnity, honored by so devout, so glad a gathering, which made the prophet complain in tears: "The roads of Sion are in mourning and there is no one to come to the solemnity,"[8] unless perhaps he means that so few came of the many people who were in all Judea and Jerusalem. For in comparison with such a multitude there were few who came, and of those few, fewer still, I suppose, received him when they saw the long-awaited one present as the Father had promised through Malachi in the words: "Behold the Lord whom you seek and the messenger of the covenant whom you desire shall come to his temple."[9]

O Jews, behold the Lord whom you seek is present: why do you not receive him when he offers himself to you? You seek, and you do not seek. But if you seek, seek; return and come.[10] You seek one who will redeem you from the power of men, you do not seek one who will redeem you from the power of devils. You seek one who will rescue you from slavery to the Romans, you do not seek one who will rescue you from captivity to your vices. If you truly seek liberty, seek the liberator of your souls who will save his people from their sins. If you seek one on high, seek first one who is lowly, for as Daniel says: "God will establish the lowliest of men over every kingdom."[11] If you seek one who will govern with power, seek first one who will teach justice, for "by justice will his throne be strengthened"[12] and "justice and judgment are the preparation of his seat."[13] Since you do not seek him perfectly you do not find him even when he is present, as he himself foretold of you: "Evil men will seek me and will not find me, because they hate me."[14] They will seek him absent, they will not find him even present,

7. Lk 2:27ff. 8. Lam 1:4. 9. Mal 3:1.
10. Is 21:12. 11. Dan 4:14. 12. Prov 25:5.
13. Ps 88:15. 14. Prov 1:28f. (Septuagint).

because they hate the light which exposes their evil deeds,[15] whereas wisdom can only be sought through love, let alone found.

Because Simeon sought with devout and faithful desire he found him whom he sought and recognized him whom he found without anyone else to point him out, that is, without any human witness. For it is the Spirit who bears witness that Christ is truth.[16] He is the power which proceeds from him, the Anointing which teaches everything, which flows in manifold richness from him who according to his own name is uniquely the Anointed.

3. What are we to think, my brethren? How did this Anointed, who anoints even those whom he does not touch, anoint all over the pure and holy breast of our old man who took him into his arms and pressed him to his breast, eager to enclose him, if only he could, in the inmost depths of his heart? What are we to think, I say; how did he, so lovable and so meek, introduce himself into the chaste bosom of the devout old man? How did he slip into his inmost parts, how delightful and health-giving he was, rather how utterly ineffable, when he entwined himself in his bones, breathed himself into his senses. The Anointed became wholly liquid, dissolved into ointment to fire the love of him who embraced him, so that ointment might teach what reading preaches but only love experiences. What is it you read? "Your name is ointment poured out."[17] For this ointment is poured out when it loses a certain hardness and becomes liquid, not so that its substance flows away but so that its fragrance may be wafted abroad,[18] so that no longer solid it may be felt but not held.

But certainly even more it was the old man's soul which was liquefied at the embrace of the Anointed or Ointment, so that he would say: "My soul was liquefied when my Beloved was poured into me."[19] Thus the pouring in of the ointment bears witness to the Anointed. It was this which bore witness to the old man concerning the Child, to Simeon concerning Christ. Like the Spirit of truth and charity, it was teaching by truth, anointing and kindling by

15. Jn 3:20.
18. Song 4:16.
16. 1 Jn 5:6.
19. Song 5:6.
17. Song 1:2.

Sermon 16:3

charity and making everything within the old man who was chilled with age as if he was filled with boiling ointments.[20] The movement of boiling unguents is the seething of desires; their sound is the glad paean of affections exclaiming with one voice, if indeed they are able to give expression to anything: "You are my God and I will praise you, my God are you and I will extol you;[21] I shall proclaim you the light which shall give revelation to the Gentiles and the glory of your people Israel.[22] I will praise you, I say, because you have hearkened to me[23] as I asked in tears day by day, 'When will you console me?'[24] You have hearkened to me, to Simeon, now at last. You have made me as one whose prayer has been heard[25] for you have become my salvation,[26] gave Jesus to me. He is of the seed of David according to the flesh,[27] but in his divinity he made David and all things. To everyone in general you have become a Savior,[28] to me in particular you have become salvation,[29] anointing all over my diseased breast, stirring up anew the warmth of life, kindling my soul into a blaze once more and enlightening my eyes. My soul had languished for your salvation,[30] O Lord, Father of my Lord Jesus Christ,[31] my eyes had languished for your word, saying: 'When will you console me?' For I had become like a wineskin in the smoke,[32] cold of body, arid of heart, withered in spirit, wholly languid with desire. But because I hoped in the word[33] of your promise that I would not see death until I saw your Christ,[34] I now see what I hoped for, I hold what I desired, I embrace what I yearned for. I see God my Savior in my flesh, and my soul has been saved.[35] My eyes have seen God's salvation[36] and my interior eyes have been enlightened that were growing dim through sorrow.[37] At the touch of this child, of this new man, my youth is wholly renewed as the eagle,[38] as a little while before I had been promising myself, in the words: 'I will go into God's altar, where Mary is

20. Job 41:22. 21. Ps 117:28. 22. Lk 2:32.
23. Ps 117:28. 24. Ps 118:82. 25. Gen 29:33.
26. Ps 117:21. 27. Rom 1:3. 28. Is 63:8.
29. Ps 117:21. 30. Ps 118:81. 31. Eph 1:3. 32. Ps 118:82f.
33. Ps 118:81. 34. Lk 2:26. 35. Job 19:26; Gen 32:30.
36. Lk 2:30. 37. Ps 87:10. 38. Ps 102:5.

offering Jesus to the Father, to God who gladdens my old age, indeed, to God who will renew my youth.' "[39]

4. It was with no less joy perhaps that Anna's heart exulted in the Lord.[40] She was all the more deserving as her way of life was more sublime and her desire more holy than that Anna who was mother of Samuel.[41] The latter was occupied with thoughts of the world, how to please her husband, the former how to please God.[42] The latter sought offspring from the bed of her husband, the former begged a Savior from the bosom of the Father. In anticipation of the excelling grace which came to flower in her life, by which she deserved to recognize and proclaim the grace of the Redeemer, she received the name of *grace*. She was a pattern of true widowhood, a mirror of holiness, and in a dead body the living image of all virtue. Feeling that the end of the Law and the beginning of the gospel was at hand she had begun to exchange Jewish rites for Christian devotion, serving God with fasts and prayers night and day rather than by food and drink and the various washings which were the justification of the flesh[43] rather than of the soul. That was the reason why she had despised the blessing of children which was esteemed highly in the Law and chose the name which is better than sons and daughters.[44] And for eighty-four years now[45] she rejoiced to be a withered tree, and to dwell in a withered tree, like a turtledove that has once lost its partner.

5. Behold you have a pair of turtledoves, the just old man and the widowed old woman, both of them chaste, both cooing in their desire for the Redeemer, for they offered themselves to the Lord and for the Lord, as living victims, holy, pleasing to God.[46] A pair of turtledoves I call them, not wedded but joined together, by a bond not of matrimony but of a more sacred mystery, peers in their faith, equal in chastity, alike in their devotion, partners in the proclaiming of grace, both advanced in age, both perfect in sanctity. Even before the Gospel they dedicated in both sexes the first-fruits of the Gospel's purity and devotion.

39. Ps 42:4.   40. Lk 2:36ff.   41. Cf. 1 Sam 2:1.
42. Cf. 1 Cor 7:32f.   43. Heb 9:10.   44. Is 56:5.
45. Lk 2:37.   46. Phil 4:18.

These two have adorned your bridal chamber, Sion, with the varied beauty of their virtues, to receive Christ the King—not the walls of your temple but the inmost recesses of your heart, the hidden places of your bedchambers. There it is we are bidden to adore the Father in spirit and in truth,[47] there he is welcomed who declares that he does not dwell in houses made by men's hands.[48] In these faithful Sion welcomed Christ, in these she goes, glad and rejoicing, to meet her God. He hardly has anywhere else to lay his head,[49] and as Isaiah says: "He was at a loss, and there is no one to meet him."[50] Yet the fact that these two come to meet him gives abundant ground for solemnity and rejoicing. The fewer to be filled makes justice overflow[51] and the consummate and abounding justice of a few easily makes up for the infidelity of the many.

6. For me this gathering is indeed a matter for celebration, for me this procession is an occasion for solemnity and every kind of festal joy. On the one hand there come the Child and his mother, Jesus and Mary, on the other hand, coming to meet them, are the old man and the widow, Simeon and Anna. On the one hand the Lord and the Lady, on the other hand the servant and the handmaid. On the one hand the Mediator and the Mediatrix, the Son and the Mother; on the other hand such faithful and devout witnesses and ministers to them. In this gathering finally mercy and truth have met,[52] that is, the merciful redemption of Jesus and the truthful witness of the old man and woman. In this meeting justice and peace kissed,[53] when the justice of the devout old man and woman and the peace of him who reconciles the world were united in the kiss of their affections and in spiritual joy.

We rightly believe then that what we sang last night is appropriate to the gladness of this day, with all allowances made for a deeper understanding: "Rejoice, Jerusalem, and keep a festival day all you who love her,"[54] as if to say: "Nazareth rejoiced at the Annunciation, Bethlehem at the Nativity, do you too rejoice, Jerusalem, at the Purification;" for he who was conceived at Nazareth and born at

---

47. Jn 4:23. 48. Acts 7:48. 49. Mt 8:20; Song 1:6. 50. Is 59:16.
51. Is 10:22. 52. Ps 84:11. 53. *Ibid.* 54. Is 66:10.

Bethlehem was welcomed and proclaimed at Jerusalem. "And keep a festival day," Scripture says, "hold a gathering all you who love her," that is, Jerusalem: "assemble with festive devotion in the temple to welcome your Redeemer, all you who await the redemption of Israel."[55]

7. If now, brethren, as is your custom, you seek some moral instruction, consider the four illustrious persons in this procession, whose life not only lights up the churches but also adorns the heavens—I mean Jesus and Mary, Simeon and Anna. And to go from the lower to the higher, in Anna who served God by night and by day in fasting and prayer,[56] fasting and prayer are recommended to us; in Simeon who embraced Jesus with such joy, piety and devotion; in Mary who, although she owed nothing to the Law as regards purification, none the less fulfilled the Law, humility and obedience; in the Lord Jesus who, born of a woman, was also born under the Law in order to redeem those who were under the Law,[57] charity and mercy. The holy virtue of chastity, in the praise of which, as I well know, your purity always delights, shone forth from all of them alike, although not in the same way: in the old man and woman it had been won by the labor of continence, in the maiden it dwelt as a gift of grace, to the Child it belonged by right of nature as his own, not on account of new-born childhood, but of inborn purity.[58]

In him are the source and perfection not only of this virtue but also of all the others, by him they are distributed one by one, through him they are preserved, with him they find their reward. Let us pray to him then, with the merits alike of the Virgin Mary and of Simeon and Anna to intercede for us, that he may grant us the virtue we lack and watch over what he has granted, so that through his watchful care we may keep his deposit intact and when we return it to him may obtain the reward which he gives, who lives and reigns for ever and ever. Amen.

55. Lk 2:38.   56. Lk 2:37.   57. Gal 4:4f.
58. In adding this last phrase Guerric seemed to be unable to forego the opportunity to make one of his typical plays on words: *non pueritiae recens natae sed puritatis innatae.*

SERMON 17

THE THIRD SERMON FOR THE PURIFICATION

"THE OLD MAN carried the child."[1] The old man full of days,[2] the child the ancient of days.[3] God had filled this old man with length of days, so as to show him his salvation[4] in human form; but he was to fill him with the length of still other days, so as to show him his salvation in his own form. Full then with the days of this world he carried the ancient of the days of eternity, and he held reposing in his bosom a most trustworthy pledge of everlasting hope, that is, that that child would add days to the king's days[5] and would renew his youth like the eagle.[6] Although when this old man like Abraham is said to be full of days,[7] I would more readily understand it as meaning full of virtues than of seasons, since the passage of days has no permanence: they come and go, exhausting a man rather than filling him. And it is no great matter, indeed it is rather an evil, to have lived for many days if you have not grown old in virtues, since the child shall die a hundred years old and the sinner a hundred years old shall be accursed.[8] Therefore if a man lives many years, as Solomon says, and rejoices in them all, let him remember the time of darkness and the many days, which when they come will convict the past of vanity.[9] Whereas on the other hand the old age that is venerable

---

1. The opening words of this sermon are taken from the second antiphon sung at Vespers on the Feast of the Purification.
2. 1 Chron 23:1.   3. Dan 7:13.   4. Ps 90:16.   5. Ps 60:7.
6. Ps 102:5.   7. Gen 25:8.   8. Is 65:20.   9. Eccles 11:8.

is not one reckoned by length of time or number of years. It is a man's understanding that gives him white hairs and old age is a life unstained by sin.[10] If Simeon had not grown old together with this old age he would never have deserved to carry the crown of old men, God's Wisdom, Christ.[11] For so it is written: "Old age is a crown of dignity, which is found in the ways of justice."[12] And what is that old age which is found in the ways of justice, which is accorded as a crown to him who finds it, if not God's Wisdom, Christ?[13] For he it is who rewards just works by granting the white-haired a spirit of wisdom, and afterwards he will shape this into a crown of glory for the just.

So the holy old man Simeon, that he might grow old in yet greater holiness, found the old age of the wise or the Wisdom of the old become a child for justice's sake, when he came into the temple led by the Spirit[14] and found him and came to know him in truth.[15] For there was old age in the child at his mother's breast, wisdom in the infant, power in weakness,[16] the Word in flesh. O infancy, O old age, how splendidly you come together in the understanding and behavior of this child. Nothing could be more innocent, yet nothing wiser, nothing more delightful yet nothing more mature, nothing meeker yet nothing more just.

2. To you, O sons of men, to you even then God's Word was speaking by his very silence,[17] so that you might keep the innocence of children with the thoughts of grown men.[18] For some of you, like a dove led astray and without sense,[19] not salting your simplicity with prudence, are left foolish; others are wise at doing evil but know not how to do well, and not sweetening their prudence with goodness are made bitter. Mixing and seasoning are entirely befitting and pleasing to both. This child is the ancient of days, in childhood manifesting his inborn innocence and from the eternity of his days bringing us the wisdom of the first-born of all.

If anyone knows himself to be imperfect in understanding or

---

10. Wis 4:8f. 11. 1 Cor 1:24. 12. Prov 16:31.
13. 1 Cor 1:30. 14. Lk 2:27. 15. Acts 10:34.
16. 2 Cor 12:9. 17. Wis 18:14f. 18. 1 Cor 14:20. 19. Hos 7:11.

unseasoned in his behavior let him come into the temple with Simeon and receive in his hands the child which his mother Mary brings, that is, let him embrace with his affections the Word of God which Mother Church offers. Laid in his bosom this Word will increase his understanding, sweeten his behavior and temper his whole frame of mind and way of life with a pleasing and wholesome gentleness. However, not only is the Church a mother to those who hear but much more is grace a mother to those who pray. Prayer will give you the Child to embrace provided you come to the temple often and devoutly to pray, so as to tell God daily: "I will adore in your holy temple in fear of you."[20] For him whom the Church offers to our ears by its preaching, grace brings into our hearts by its enlightening; and it makes him the more present and the more delightful inasmuch as it conveys naked truth to the understanding. The Truth which is Christ Mary gives us to embrace clothed with flesh; the Church, clothed with words, grace, naked in the inpouring of the Spirit; however, this comes about in various ways, according to the capacity of the soul which receives it or according to the judgment of the mercy which distributes it.

For although it is not easy for us to see the face itself of supreme Truth, and that man is to be considered great to whom it is given to look upon it even in a mirror and in a confused reflection,[21] yet we experience something of its naked self when the Spirit makes his entry into us, and our understanding is stirred to love of it as if by contact with the naked reality. Then indeed we can say with all our heart and sing in gladness: "We have received, O God, your mercy in the midst of your temple."[22] Happy the man who, in order to receive it the more worthily and the more often, prepares a fitting place for it in the interior of his heart. Happy is that Sion which adorns her bridal-chamber diligently and becomingly, so as to receive Christ the King with worthy and acceptable honor.

3. O holy Sion, soul that contemplates things eternal, consider what that majesty is that is to be received, think with what care and

---

20. Ps 5:8.   21. 1 Cor 13:12.   22. Ps 47:10.

diligence it behoves you prepare him a place. If anyone says: "And who can prove himself worthy of this,[23] what decoration can be in keeping with the magnificence and glory of so great a king?"; "it is in vain," says David, "that a man will allege his poverty. His abode has been established in peace and justice and judgment are the preparation of his seat."[24]

Because Simeon adorned his bridal chamber with draperies of this sort he was worthy to receive Christ with much grace. Do you wish to see that he had found a place for the Lord in peace, that he had prepared a seat for him in justice and judgment? "There was a man," we read, "in Jerusalem, whose name was Simeon, and this man was just and God-fearing."[25] Simeon's house was in peace: he dwelt in Jerusalem, that is in the vision and love of peace. Of that Jerusalem he had heard David promise: "He who dwells in Jerusalem shall not be disturbed for ever."[26] That he dwelt in peace and was a lover of peace and sought before all else the peace of that lasting and eternal Jerusalem which nothing can disturb, you can know from this: when he received in his bosom the peace of God and of men, Jesus, who came to bestow peace upon peace, from the breast of the old man who had long been meditating peace there burst forth the song: "Now let your servant depart, Lord, according to your word, in peace, for my eyes have seen your salvation."[27] It is he who is our peace and makes the two one,[28] not only Jew and Gentile but also God and man, and spirit and flesh in man. Now this only is left for your servant to desire, that in peace I may sleep and take my rest[29] and the peace of God which surpasses all our understanding[30] may absorb me wholly into the concord of that supreme and simple unity. The peace for which I waited has come; let him rest in peace who sought peace and was always at pains to follow what was conducive to peace." So Isaiah says: "Let peace come; let him rest in his bed who walked in his uprightness."[31] In peace to be sure Simeon had made his bed. Driving out all other cares he

23. 2 Cor 2:16.
24. Ps 75:3; 88:15.
25. Lk 2:25.
26. Ps 124:1.
27. Lk 2:29f.
28. Eph 2:14.
29. Ps 4:9.
30. Phil 4:7.
31. Is 57:2.

Sermon 17:4–5

meditated in his heart on Jesus alone, and there he laid him to rest when he received him. He had walked in his uprightness, for he was just and God-fearing; and awaiting the deliverance of Israel[32] he went daily in desire to meet him who was coming.

4. When he is called just and God-fearing understand the justice and judgment by which God's seat is prepared.[33] Justice is mentioned by name, while judgment may rightly be considered to be conveyed by the term fear, or fear by that of judgment, inasmuch as fear is not only born of considering the judgment to be but also brings about in us now a certain form and execution of judgment. For while we are forbidden to judge our neighbors prematurely,[34] we are commanded to judge ourselves here and now, so that we may not be judged by the Lord.[35] But this fear is holier when it follows justice than when it precedes it. When it precedes, it initiates into justice; when it follows, it perfects and preserves it. For it does not allow a man to presume on his justice, but makes him scrutinize all his deeds, so that after his judgment of himself he still fears a more searching judgment and says to himself: "It is the Lord who judges me,[36] he who, at the set time he appoints, will judge with justice."[37] The man who is without this fear cannot be justified, as Scripture testifies,[38] for, however much he exercises himself in just works, aliens devour his strength[39] as long as he seeks to set up a justice of his own and does not submit to God's justice.

5. The gospel then speaks carefully when it commends Simeon's perfect justice. It does not say: God-fearing and just, lest we should think it means the fear which is the beginning of justice. What it says is: just and God-fearing, so that from his example we may learn the fear which is an inseparable companion of justice through all its degrees and encourages it and guards it. Neither should it be judged superfluous that the gospel does not say "afraid"[40] but "God-fearing"[41]—meaning that it is not something new, lasting but an hour or superficial, but a fear that had become a habit, that had

---

32. Lk 2:25.　33. Ps 88:15.　34. 1 Cor 4:5.
35. 1 Cor 11:31.　36. 1 Cor 4:4.　37. Ps 74:3.
38. Sir 1:28.　39. Hos 7:9.　40. *Timentem.*　41. *Timoratum.*

sunk deep roots in the man's affections, taken possession of his senses, adorned with modesty and gravity his speech and his countenance, made him moderate his activity with circumspection and in short put its stamp on the man's whole character both within and without. For awaiting the consolation of Israel as he was,[42] he did not relax his mind with empty consolations. This brought him to the summit of his justice, so that he was anxious not only for his own consolation but also for that of the people and remained poised aloft in expectation.

6. Finally, that you may learn more plainly how precious and true was the splendor of the virtues with which that Sion, that is Simeon, had adorned its bridal chamber, and that it was no mere colorful pretence, the gospel says: "The Holy Spirit was in him."[43]

What had that earthly Sion to compare to this in all the manifold pretentiousness and outward show of its bridal chamber, that is its temple? If it had decorated the face of the temple with crowns of gold,[44] what is gold but mud even when it is not compared with virtue? I should say that not even Solomon in all his glory[45] was adorned like Simeon, since the former lost in his old age the wisdom which had been his while the latter welcomed Wisdom in his old age. Faithless Sion, your bridal chamber itself convicts you. You had been forewarned sufficiently: "Behold the Lord whom you seek will come to his temple.[46] Adorn your bridal-chamber, Sion; put on the raiment of your glory, city of the Holy One." Yet you made no addition to the daily worship in the temple when he came: no curtains, no crowns, no extra lamps or victims, no special psalms or canticles. You leave him who had come to save you wholly unhonored, ungreeted. Therefore this bridal chamber of yours, the house of your glory, will be left to you abandoned,[47] indeed there shall not be left a stone upon a stone that shall not be destroyed.[48] For the faith of the nations shall build you, Lord, a

---

42. Lk 2:25. 43. Ibid. 44. 1 Mac 5:57.
45. Mt 6:29. 46. Mal 3:1. 47. Mt 23:38.
48. Mt 24:2.

more august temple, one more spacious and more perfect,[49] the great Church, reaching from the sun's rising to its setting.[50] As your name, O God, so shall your praise be to the ends of the earth.[51] Hence even today we have heard praises, the glory of the Just One,[52] voices of men giving praise and saying: "We have received, God, your mercy in the midst of your temple,"[53] that is, in the fellowship of your holy people.

O brethren, you too have received God's mercy, indeed you have received it more abundantly. Take care lest you receive it in vain,[54] lest you make grace fruitless through ingratitude. Let your devotion then be full of joy. Glorify and carry in your body every day[55] him whom Simeon carried today in his bosom, Jesus Christ, our Lord, to whom be honor and glory for ever and ever. Amen.[56]

49. Heb 9:11.
50. Ps 49:1.
51. Ps 47:11.
52. Is 24:16.
53. Ps 47:10.
54. 2 Cor 6:1.
55. 1 Cor 6:20.
56. Rom 16:27.

SERMON 18

THE FOURTH SERMON FOR THE PURIFICATION

"WHEN THE TIME HAD COME for Mary's purification."[1] When Scripture relates the mysteries of our redemption it describes the historical events which were enacted for us in such a way as to indicate what moral line of action we have to take. So, as we recall today the purification of Blessed Mary, we are clearly admonished as to our own purification. Who will not be moved by the authority of such an example? We see her, the most holy of holy women, although she had nothing to purify, consenting none the less to fulfill the commandment of legal purification.

O immaculate Mother, O Mother untouched, are you not aware of your own purity, aware, that is, that neither conception nor childbirth violated your integrity but that they consecrated it? Why then, as if you had suffered something of what is the common lot of woman in conceiving or giving birth, do you thus seek the remedies of a cleansing which was provided for woman's weakness? "It is right," she says, "that we should so fulfill all justice,[2] so that I who have been chosen as the mother of supreme Justice should be also a mirror and a pattern of all justice. I know the pride of Eve's daughters, which is more ready to excuse their failings than to purify them. I consider it necessary that the vices of our origin in

---

1. Lk 2:22. These are the opening words of the Gospel passage that is proclaimed at the liturgical celebrations on this feast. This passage is also sung solemnly in the third responsory at the Vigils.
2. Mt 3:15.

antiquity should be offset from the very beginning by all the aspects of the new birth. The mother of prevarication sinned and stubbornly defended herself; the mother of redemption will not sin and will make humble satisfaction, so that the sons of men who derive the impulse to sin from the mother of all that is old may obtain humility at least from the mother of all that is new."

2. O sons of men, the time for purification has come when the mother of supreme purity, the festival of whose purification we are keeping, has both brought forth the fountain and set the example by which we must be purified. It is preferable, brethren, and it is less painful to be purified at the fountain than by fire. Certainly those who have not been purified at the fountain now, will need to be purified by fire—if indeed they deserve to be purified at all—when the judge himself "will sit like a refiner's fire, melting and cleansing silver, and will purify the sons of Levi."[3] Now Christ is a water that washes, then he will be a fire that consumes.[4] Now he is an open fountain to wash the sinner and the woman in her times,[5] then he will be a raging flame and a fire that devours even to the marrow of the soul. From the ardor of him who is angry that purifying fire shall blaze forth in his sight[6] and flames shall be emitted upon his enemies round about.[7] "Smoke mounted up in his anger," we read, "and fire blazed forth from his face."[8] Therefore burning coals shall fall upon them[9] to purify them as a punishment who do not use now the burning coals which give health while they afflict, such as, I suppose, was that burning coal which was taken from the altar to purify the prophet's lips.[10] I leave it to you to decide whether these coals were as those of which it was said to someone: "Behold, burning coals are given to you, and you will sit over them; these will be a help to you."[11] But of this I have no doubt, that if the fire which the Lord Jesus cast on the earth[12] has blazed forth vehemently in us, as is the will of him who casts it, then that purifying fire which

3. Mal 3:2f.   4. Heb 12:29; Deut 4:24.   5. Zech 13:1.
6. Ps 49:3.   7. Ps 96:3.   8. Ps 17:9.
9. Ps 139:11.   10. Is 6:6.   11. Is 47:15 (Septuagint)
12. Lk 12:49.

will purge the sons of Levi in judgment will find in us no wood, no grass, no straw[13] to burn. Both fires to be sure are purifying, but in quite different ways. The one purifies by anointing, the other by burning. In the one case there is the refreshment of dew, in the other the spirit of judgment and the spirit of burning, with which the Lord will wash away the filth of the daughters of Sion and cleanse the blood of Jerusalem from its midst.[14]

3. In this itself the Lord shows great clemency towards the daughters of Sion, but much more clemently and more mildly was she purified whom the daughters of Sion proclaim as blessed,[15] she to whom it was said: "The Holy Spirit shall come upon you and the power of the Most High shall overshadow you."[16] This overshadowing by power from on high was Mary's true purification, not that which was celebrated today in outward appearance only by a certain sacramental dispensation. This was indeed the total and true sanctification of mother and Son, as the angel explained to her in the words: "Therefore the Holy One who is to be born of you shall be called the Son of God."[17] For mortal nature had to be purified beforehand in order to conceive God, not afterwards because it had conceived, for to have conceived the Holy of Holies is supreme sanctification and nothing could be holier than she who was made the Mother of Holiness itself.

The daughters of Sion then, who live a softer and more dissipated life and experience perhaps the burning heat of the flesh, are rightly to be purified by the spirit of judgment and the spirit of burning.[18] But she who was ever a virgin and unlike other women, she who by the overshadowing alone of the Spirit conceived God, she was purified by the sole operation of the Spirit of grace and its refreshing dew. Of all the purifications by which man's condition is restored this purification of the Blessed Virgin was the mildest and happiest. The purification of the daughters of Sion, which will be effected by the purgative fire of judgment, will be the most severe of all just as it is the last of all. The one can only be a cause for

13. 1 Cor 3:12.
16. Lk 1:35.
14. Is 4:4.
17. *Ibid.*
15. Song 6:8.
18. Is 4:4.

wonder to us, the other of dread; since we cannot aspire to the one and, if we are wise, we always dread to fall into the other. Yes indeed, if we are wise, we shall always cry, more by improving our behavior than by loud utterance: "Lord, do not accuse me in your fury, do not rebuke me in your anger."[19]

4. It was necessary then for God's loving-kindness to provide us with other kinds of purifications between those two, the highest one to which we do not attain and that ultimate one which we fear. So he granted us a time and place for repentance and saving remedies in large numbers. They are many and various, but it would seem that they can all be grouped into four kinds, lest we should confuse our listener's memory with a disorderly conglomeration. These are the four kinds by which I consider that we can fittingly and conveniently be purified during these days of our purification: contrition of heart, affliction of the body, works of piety and faith and patience in tribulation.

In accord with this you will find four things by which in general Christ purifies the world as he carries out the purgation of sins:[20] water and blood, Spirit and fire. "This is he," says John, "who came through water and blood.[21] This is he who baptizes in the Holy Spirit[22] and in fire." With water he baptized;[23] with water he washed his disciples' feet,[24] dedicating also the baptism of tears which flow from contrition of heart. His blood he shed so that we too, sharing in his passion by bodily mortification, might wash our robes in the blood of the Lamb.[25] The Spirit he gave, in order that the love of God and neighbor might be poured out in our hearts through the Spirit[26] and cover in us a multitude of sins.[27] If our love is less perfect and not sufficient to cover so many and such great sins, then that refiner who purifies the sons of Levi[28] applies his fire of tribulation either in the present life or the next so that at length

---

19. Ps 6:2.   20. Heb 1:3.   21. 1 Jn 5:6.   22. Jn 1:33.
23. See Jn 3:22; however, Jn 4:2 makes it clear that only Jesus' disciples actually were baptizing, not Jesus himself.
24. Jn 13:5ff.   25. Rev 22:14.   26. Rom 5:5.   27. 1 Pet 4:8.
28. Mal 3:3.

they may be able to sing: "We have passed through fire and water and you have led us forth into refreshment."[29] So too this world, first baptized by the water of the flood, then purified by the fire of judgment, will pass into a new state of incorruptibility.

5. Finally, to make some allowance for the tender and delicate, if they have no tears, if they dread hard work, if they cannot bear tribulation, will they refuse that too which Solomon recommends: "By compassion and faith sins are purified"?[30] What is sweeter than compassion; what is more attractive than faith? The one is oil for the members, the other light for the eyes. The one anoints the affections, the other enlightens the understanding and directs your steps so that by its light you may walk in darkness, contemplate things invisible and meditate on the happiness that is to be yours, anticipating it in your mind. It is well said that sins are purified through compassion and faith, for compassion redeems debts by spending what is its own, while faith obtains indulgence even gratis without works. Of compassion the Prophet says: "Redeem your iniquities by deeds of compassion done to the poor;"[31] and the Lord of Prophets: "Give alms and everything is clean for you."[32] Of faith the Apostle says: "By faith he cleanses their hearts;"[33] and the Lord of Apostles, "Go, your faith has made you whole."[34]

However, in this statement of Solomon there could be understood not the faith by which we believe but that by which we show ourselves worthy of credence, keeping faith with God and men. Thus what is said here:" By compassion and faith sins are purified," and what comes shortly afterwards: "Iniquity is redeemed by compassion and by truth,"[35] is the same statement repeated in different words. Rightly then are compassion and truth or faith joined together, since in all our ways unless compassion and truth meet[36] it is to be feared that sins will be increased rather than purified. To say nothing for the moment of other actions, and to speak only of compassion shown to the poor (which the needs of

29. Ps 65:12. 30. Prov 15:27. 31. Dan 4:24.
32. Lk 11:41. 33. Acts 15:9. 34. Mk 10:52.
35. Prov 16:6. 36. Ps 84:11.

these times demand should be shown in greater abundance), is there not an element of sin even in those deeds by which sins should be purified if compassion is lacking faith or faith compassion?

6. Let them hear who have been entrusted with the distribution; let them hear who have not been entrusted with it. These latter lest they should wish to be faithful in such a way as to abandon compassion; the former lest they should wish to be compassionate in such a way as to injure faith. For there are some who wish to be more faithful than it behoves, and there are some who wish to be more compassionate than is lawful for them. Let those then who take to themselves an undue compassion which is contrary to faith listen to Solomon, who says: "Many men are called compassionate; but who shall find a faithful man?"[37] Let those however who neglect due compassion as if for the sake of faith listen to one who is greater than Solomon saying: "What is over give in alms,"[38] so that at least your superfluity may make up for the want of others.[39] He showed great mercy to our weak and puny faith who did not bid our common goods be shared out equally among the brethren, but that alms be given out of what is over and above our own needs. Even if we say nothing of the natural law, which decrees that whatever the earth, parent of all, brings forth should be common to all who dwell on earth, for those who are indifferent to our adoptive kinship and fellowship in a common inheritance, at least how shall that one Bread which our heavenly Father bestows not be shared in common? Yet granted that this is the law of properly-ordered charity, that the gospel in its moderation first allows everyone his own needs, who is the man who will so measure his own needs, who will distinguish fairly between what is necessary and what is superfluous? Let us watch over ourselves, brethren, lest we begin to be judged for the death of our impoverished brethren if we hold back unnecessarily or use for ourselves what could go to support their lives.

And since the purification today of the purest and poorest of virgins has moved us to speak of our own purification, let us

37. Prov 20:6.   38. Lk 11:41.   39. 2 Cor 8:14.

recognize that our purity consists first and foremost in this: that we renounce whatever we have that is superfluous. Thus not only by the holiness of chastity but also by the simplicity of poverty shall we emulate in some measure the poor Mother of the poor Christ, to whom be kingship and empire now and for ever. Amen.

SERMON 19

THE FIFTH SERMON FOR THE PURIFICATION

"WHEN THE DAYS of purification were completed they took Jesus to Jerusalem."[1] O how fortunate is he of whom it can be said: "the days of his purification have been completed," so that nothing remains for him but that they should carry him to the heavenly Jerusalem and offer him to the Lord. Such was Simeon, that old man of ours, as desirable as he was full of desires. Long before, I think, the days of his purification had been completed. Today the days of his expectation are also completed, so that now, according to the Lord's word, nothing remains for him after seeing the Christ of the Lord, Christ the peace of God and man, but to be allowed to depart in peace[2] and sleep in that same peace.[3] This means to be taken to Jerusalem, the vision of eternal peace, and to be set before the Lord[4] to contemplate the peace which surpasses all our understanding.[5] O Simeon, man of desires,[6] your desire of good things is fulfilled.[7] O blessed old man, your youth is renewed like the eagle's.[8] You have gone in now to God's altar, that heavenly and eternal altar all gold, to God who gladdens your youth[9] with the eternal vision of himself, you whose old age he gladdened today by the vision of his Christ. At that invisible altar you are now presented to the Father to whom you presented the Son today at this visible altar. There you enfold in an embrace

---

1. Lk 2:22. See n. 1, Sermon 18. 2. Lk 2:26, 29. 3. Ps 4:9.
4. Lk 2:22.   5. Phil 4:7. 6. Dan 10:11. 7. Ps 102:5.
8. Ibid.   9. Ps 42:4.

which is now eternal and indissoluble the same Son whom you bore today in your bosom.

2. The desire of the blessed old man is, then, fulfilled in good things, for the whole of his expectation and desire was the Expectation of the Nations and he who is desired by them.[10] His youth has been renewed like the eagle's because in a good old age the days of his purification have been completed. Otherwise he could in no way be able to receive that renewal unless he had during these days sedulously purged out what was old.

Brethren, purge out the old leaven[11] while you have time for purging; so that when the time comes for your purgation to be completed you too may be able to receive that joy which now fills Simeon's soul. And indeed whether we will it or not we complete the days which are given us for purging; but woe to us if when the days are completed our purgation is not completed, so that we must needs be purged by that fire than which nothing more painful, keener or more vehement can be imagined in this life. But who is the man so perfect, so holy, that when he departs hence he owes nothing to the fire; who has so thoroughly burned out all the dross of sin[12] in himself that he can boast he has a pure heart, can say: "My heart is clean, I am pure from sin?"[13] Few are chosen[14] but amongst those few very few indeed in my opinion are so perfect as to have fulfilled that purgation of which the wise man says: "Purge yourself of negligence with the few."[15] Truly, if we purified ourselves of negligence we would belong to the few. As it is, since we neglect things not only of the least but also of the greatest importance, we are widely separated from the few of the earth[16] and to us applies what he says who prefers a few saints to a host of negligent souls: "Amongst many they were with me."[17]

3. And what today so clearly marks out and at the same time is so commonly shared by all religious as negligence? To speak of myself, how often do enemies mock my sabbaths?[18] How often does my

---

10. Gen 49:10; Hag 2:8. 11. 1 Cor 5:7. 12. Is 25:1.
13. Prov 20:9. 14. Mt 20:16. 15. Sir 7:34 (Vulgate).
16. Ps 16:14. 17. Ps 54:19. 18. Lam 1:7.

soul fall asleep for weariness[19] while I spend almost the whole day in idleness as if time were not irrevocable? Would that my soul would so fall asleep that I might not with eyes open and watchful conjure up for myself, wretched that I am, vain and illusory dreams. As it is, to misquote a text:[20] "I am awake and my heart sleeps," so heavily too that it can hardly be roused even by the thunder of that rebuke from on high: "How long, sluggard, will you sleep? When will you rise from your sleep? A little sleep, a little slumber, a little folding of the hands to rest: and poverty will come upon you like a vagabond and want like an armed man."[21]

What is most wretched is that today it is considered not a loss but a gain if the days which have been given us for purgation slip away from us in sleep, pass by and perish in neglect. A pagan,[22] it is said, sitting down to table and calling to mind that he had done nothing energetic or worth remembering that day, pushed away his food with a deep groan and in sorrow exclaimed: "Friends, I have lost a day." We today seem to say: "I have gained a day," if it can slip away without any work, wholly in idleness. There is almost no one who values his time, who ponders in himself what one day is worth for winning eternity. Do you suppose there is anyone amongst us who makes himself render account to himself of his days, diligently reckoning up the losses and the gains of each day; so that if he finds he has acted negligently today he will demand satisfaction of himself and behave more carefully in future? Blessed is that servant whom his last day, when it comes,[23] shall find so doing,

4. This would be to purge oneself of negligence with the few: if the days of purgation were completed rightly and usefully, so that eventually access to holy things might be obtained in a wholesome way. Otherwise, as long as a man remains contaminated by the blood of which he should be purified, eternal justice has decreed, as it is written in the law of Moses, that he shall not touch any holy thing nor enter the sanctuary until the days of his purgation are

---

19. Ps 118:28.   20. Song 5:2.   21. Prov 6:9ff.; 24:33f.
22. The Emperor Titus: see Suetonius, *Titus*, c. 8.
23. Lk 12:43.

completed.[24] Let them consider well with what audacity they will enter the sanctuary, with what sort of conscience they will not only touch holy things but also perform and receive the holiest of holy things, who although as yet not freed from the contamination of blood take no trouble to purify themselves. Do they not hear him who protests in the words: "When you stretch forth your hands I will turn my eyes away, for your hands are full of blood."?[25] What use is it if I am clean of another's blood[26] while the Lord sees me weltering in my own blood, as he says of Jerusalem through Ezekiel?[27] What will it profit me if my feet are not quick to shed the blood of my neighbors[28] but my affections are quick to comply with flesh and blood, of which the Apostle says: "Flesh and blood shall not possess the kingdom of God."?[29] Jeremiah says: "Cursed is the man who spares his sword from blood,"[30] that is who is reluctant to cut off from himself the vices of the flesh.

Deliver me from the guilt of blood, God, God of my salvation,[31] lest contaminated by the blood of which I should be purified I should enter the sanctuary or touch holy things[32] and so be found guilty of your body and blood, eating and drinking unworthily.[33] Yet thanks be to you, God, God of my salvation, who did shed your precious blood for this very purpose, to purify the uncleanness of our blood. You did not shrink from the touch of the sinful woman with the issue of blood[34] who longed for healing. You knew that no one can make clean him who was conceived from unclean seed but you who alone are[35] and that it is not the healthy but the sick, desiring to get better, that need the doctor.[36] So to touch the Holy of Holies, just as it brings the sentence of death to those who take pleasure in their sin, it gives healing and salvation to those who desire to be purified, in accord with the prophecy of Simeon that he is destined to bring about the fall and the rise of many.[37]

24. Lev 12:4.
25. Is 1:15.
26. Acts 20:26.
27. Ezek 16:6.
28. Ps 13:3.
29. 1 Cor 15:50.
30. Jer 48:10.
31. Ps 50:16.
32. Lev 12:4.
33. 1 Cor 11:27.
34. Mk 9:20ff.
35. Job 14:4.
36. Mt 9:12.
37. Lk 2:34.

5. Brethren, you too have sinned; but you have been washed clean, you have been purified.[38] But as the just man confesses: even if you have been washed as with snow-water, yet your corrupt state and your weak will at once plunge you in filth,[39] so that fresh filth will always need fresh purification. So astonishing and so miserable is men's neglect of themselves. Although there is no one who supposes he does not stand in need of purification there is scarcely anyone who does not waste the time accorded him for this, as if he were thoroughly cleansed. Brethren, man's days are short,[40] and yet they are very precious. Indeed the shorter they are, the more precious they are; for they are days of purification and immediately afterwards are to be days of retribution. Blessed are they who during these days wash their robes and make them white in the blood of the Lamb,[41] lest afterwards if their raiment is stained with blood it be burned, food for the fire.[42] And not only is there the fear of punishment to urge us on, but also the hope of reward to allure us to attend to our purification with all carefulness and anxiety; so that what the Son of God willed to prefigure in himself today in outward appearance in keeping with the economy of salvation, we may rejoice one day to see fulfilled in us in very truth and substance.

What is that? "When the days of her purification were completed," we read, "they took Jesus to Jerusalem to offer him to the Lord."[43] We too, if the times of purgation appointed by the law are completed by us, will be borne up into the heavenly Jerusalem by the ministry of angels, so that we may stand there before the face of God, a pure and acceptable offering. There finally we shall be wholly purified, both from sin and from the punishment due to sin. There the consummation and the reward of our purification will be one when divine fire turns us wholly into a holocaust to the Lord.

6. However, this most blessed purification, which cannot be explained in its workings, is even now unceasingly imitated by the devotion of holy men insofar as the perishable nature of their bodies and the cares of this exile on earth allow. They go forth in

---

38. 1 Cor 6:11.
39. Job 9:30.
40. Job 14:5.
41. Rev 22:14.
42. Is 9:5.
43. Lk 2:22. See n. 1 above.

132   *The Fifth Sermon for the Purification*

spirit to that Jerusalem, the true place of prayer, and there offer as it were a turtle and a dove in the sight of the Lord for themselves and from their own substance, from their own heart and their flesh. They exult in the living God, because the dove has found a house for itself and the turtle a nest, your altars, Lord of hosts.[44] Now it is my opinion that there is no less merit, and perhaps greater efficacy for purification, if what is granted but rarely and to rare souls to experience as in a mirror and a confused reflection,[45] that is, to be before the Lord in Jerusalem, we carry out at all times through faith; if we keep the Lord always in our sight and bear in mind with ever-watchful faith and unremitting fear that his eyes and his judgments are upon us. Let this faith, brethren, be in you and you will belong to the few; let this fear be in you and you will purify yourselves of negligence with the few, for this fear does not easily neglect anything.

Finally from the beginnings of this faith you will pass on, as the Bridegroom promises the bride, going from virtue to virtue,[46] from splendor to splendor, by the Spirit of the Lord.[47] You will progress from the vision which is through faith to that which is in a mirror and an image, and finally from that which is in the image of the form to that which will be in the very truth of the face or in the face of the truth.[48] For if you constantly attend, through faith, to the presence of the Lord, veiled though it be, eventually you will even contemplate his glory with face unveiled, albeit in a mirror and an image. But when the days of purification are completed and what is perfect comes,[49] you will stand before the Lord in Jerusalem, dwelling with his face, and ceaselessly look upon him face to face,[50] to whom be benediction and glory for ever and ever. Amen.[51]

---

44. Ps 83:3f.   45. 1 Cor 13:12.   46. Ps 83:8.
47. 2 Cor 3:18.   48. 1 Cor 13:12; 2 Cor 3:18.   49. 1 Cor 13:10.
50. 1 Cor 13:12.   51. Rev 7:12.

SERMON 20

THE FIRST SERMON FOR LENT

"BLESSED BE GOD, the Father of mercies and the God of all consolation, who consoles us in all our tribulations.[1] Many are the tribulations of the just, but the Lord will deliver them from all these."[2] We suffer two kinds of tribulations, since not only do we consist of a twofold nature, flesh and spirit, but also we live on two levels, partly according to the flesh, partly according to the spirit. In the world we were wholly carnal, in heaven we shall be wholly spiritual, while now we are partly carnal and partly spiritual. According to our progress in the spirit either we are made more spiritual and less carnal or we remain more carnal and less spiritual. Hence there arises now a two-fold tribulation: for what is carnal in us is grieved by adversity, what is spiritual, by iniquity. If there was nothing carnal in us no adversity would grieve us, indeed there would not be any adversity; if there was nothing spiritual, our iniquity would not grieve us but rather give us pleasure, as is said of certain persons: "They rejoice when they have done evil and exult in wickedness."[3] That sadness of ours which is caused by adversity is then carnal and of the world, whereas the sadness which is caused by iniquity is spiritual and of God. The one leads to death if consolation is lacking, the other leads to salvation[4] if consolation is not lacking. Now it is of great

---

1. 2 Cor 1:3f. The first readings at Vigils on this Sunday are taken from the Second Epistle to the Corinthians.
2. Ps 33:20.   3. Prov 2:14.   4. 2 Cor 7:10.

importance to determine what kind of consolation is given to the afflicted in external adversity, for God threatens the consolation of the rich with eternal woe.[5] For the most part those who could have been made humble by adversity become all the more proud through prosperity, and "from fatness their iniquity comes forth."[6] Indeed they boldly provoke God, although it is he who has put everything in their hands.[7]

2. For ourselves, when temporal consolation abounds, we should be more grateful and more humble, and when it fails, more certain and more happy about eternal reward. When bodily health or fine weather or a plentiful supply of necessaries are to be had we should use them and distribute them with such moderation that they do not become an occasion of sin but rather a help to virtue. We should rather do good with what is good than become evil through what is good. Let my soul refuse to be consoled[8] with the consolation which fosters pleasure or vanity; rather than the brief enjoyment of sin let it choose to be afflicted with Moses and the true Israelites.[9] But whether we are consoled externally or afflicted, blessed be God who has bestowed on our hearts internal and eternal consolation,[10] the joy of hope which persuades us even to glory in tribulations, promising that if we share his sufferings we shall share his kingdom.[11]

As for that tribulation which we suffer interiorly from our iniquity, the greater danger we realize it to be, the more it troubles us. For we are every day in danger of our lives so that we confess in all truth: Unless the Lord helped me my soul would soon have dwelt in hell.[12] Thanks be to you, Lord Jesus. If the dangers are grave the remedies are ready at hand. If I said, "My foot slipped," your mercy, Lord, helped me.[13] What you once foreshadowed in Peter while you were here on earth, you fulfill spiritually in Peter's sons every day. You have bidden us come to you upon the waters,[14]

---

5. Lk 6:24ff.   6. Ps 72:7.   7. Job 12:6.
8. Ps 76:3.   9. Heb 11:25.   10. 2 Thess 2:15.
11. Rom 5:3; 8:17; 2 Tim 2:12.   12. Ps 93:17.   13. Ps 93:18.
14. Cf. Mt 14:28f.

Sermon 20:2-4

that is, this great and wide-spreading sea.[15] Behold, by your power we walk but by our own weight we are impeded and we are often assailed by the onrush of stormy winds so that we even begin to sink,[16] that is, almost directly consent to the tempter. But if we confess quickly that our foot has slipped, that is, our spirit has wavered, and if we call upon your help in faith, you stretch out your hand in mercy, and strengthen and direct our steps.

3. About this the just man sings daily: "I was assailed so as to fall but I did not fall because the Lord held me up."[17]

But "even when he falls he will not be cast headlong, for the Lord is the stay of his hand,"[18] that is, when he sins he will not be condemned because he has Jesus as advocate.[19] Although he falls seven times a day, seven times he rises again.[20] He does not take pleasure in lying where he falls and wallowing in the mire, but rising speedily he shakes off the dust and washes away the dirt by making satisfaction. It is through this that he becomes just; when he opens his mouth he is always the accuser of himself,[21] mindful of God's advice which bids him: "Tell your iniquities in order to be justified."[22] So it comes about that while he judges himself and of himself gives God satisfaction, he obtains as an advocate in his guilt him whom he feared as a just judge. For the Lord is just and loves justice;[23] he cannot uphold or protect unjust causes, he who will judge in justice in due time.[24] And yet he, who threatens to come as the judge of those who proudly presume on their justice, promises to be the advocate of those who humbly confess their sins. With him, in whose sight no man shall be justified,[25] we cannot in any way justify our cause better than by accusing and punishing ourselves and so transfer his justice to ourselves and play the part of judge against the guilty.

4. It may happen that we commit some venial faults, or sin through ignorance, or are overcome by weakness, so that we cannot

---

15. Ps 103:25.
16. Cf. Mt 14:30.
17. Ps 117:13.
18. Ps 36:24.
19. 1 Jn 2:1.
20. Prov 24:16. Cf. Mt 18:21f.
21. Prov 18:17.
22. Is 43:26 (Septuagint).
23. Ps 10:8.
24. Ps 74:3.
25. Ps 142:2.

get the mastery over our Jebusite and exterminate him but must always suffer him to dwell under our eyes in the land with us.[26] Even in this state of imperfection the prophet's word consoles us as he prefigures our plight saying: "Among these were we always and yet we shall be saved."[27] "What is imperfect in me," says the Body of Christ, "your merciful eyes have seen and in your book all men shall be written,"[28] both the perfect and the imperfect. For indeed the Lord, speaking through the prophet Joel, promises to perfect our imperfection: "And I will cleanse their blood which they have not cleansed."[29] Hence Isaiah speaks first of the perfection of the heavenly Jerusalem that is to be: "And it will come about that everyone who is left in Sion and remains over in Jerusalem will be called holy, everyone who has been recorded for life in Jerusalem."[30] Then he goes on to assert that in the weak holiness is only to be perfected by God's purifying action: "When the Lord washes away the filth of Sion's daughters and cleanses the bloodstains of Jerusalem from its midst."[31] The promised washing does indeed console me, but the way in which it is described next terrifies me: "By a spirit of judgment and a spirit of burning."[32] For fire shall test every man's work. If someone's work is burnt up he will be the loser, but he himself will be saved on account of the foundation, yet "as through fire."[33]

5. How much better for us it would be to burn now with delightful love than then in those punishing flames. How much more pleasant it would be for us to be purified now by the fire of love, so that nothing worldly would be left in us to provide fuel for the blaze which will consume the world. As for the three young men the Babylonian furnace would become for us a dew-laden breeze.[34] But if we live tepidly and negligently, heaping up wood, grass and straw for ourselves and taking away with us from here such a mass of combustible material, when we so enter the searching fires of purgatory who of us will be able to bear with the devour-

---

26. Cf. 1 Kings 9:20f. 27. Is 64:5. 28. Ps 138:16.
29. Joel 3:21. 30. Is 4:3. 31. Is 4:4.
32. *Ibid.* 33. 1 Cor 3:13, 15. 34. Dan 3:50.

ing fire? Or who among us shall dwell in the everlasting flames,[35] when even every bloodstained garment will be burnt as food for the fire?[36] This I know, that if I were to be aflame sufficiently with the fire of charity, of me too it would be said: "Many sins are forgiven him because he has loved much."[37]

As it is, if I do not deserve to be purified by the fire of love, would that I might be purified by the fire of some other passion and there would happen to me what the prophet calls down on himself: "May rottenness enter my bones and my steps totter beneath me, that I may rest in the day of tribulation."[38] Would that he who has begun would himself crush me, would let loose his hand and cut me off; this would be my consolation, that he would not be sparing in afflicting me with pain.[39] But you know, Lord, the weakness of my fashioning. What is my strength that I should hold out, what is my end that I should be patient? My strength is not the strength of stones, neither is my flesh of bronze.[40] This indeed I ask first: "Lord, in your fury do not correct me, in your anger do not rebuke me."[41] But since I hear from you: "It is those whom I love I correct and chasten,"[42] and: "Blessed is the man who is rebuked by the Lord,"[43] then rebuke me, Lord, in mercy and not in your fury, lest perhaps you reduce me to nothing[44] and it be said of me: "You have destroyed him by cleansing."[45] Look upon my weakness and moderate your hand accordingly, lest the vehemence of the blow break the heart's patience; instead let tribulation give rise to patience, patience give proof of our faith, faith lead to hope.[46]

But woe to me if I burn daily and am not cleansed, so that to me also the words apply: "With much labor has it been worked upon yet not even through fire has its thick rust been removed. Your uncleanness is execrable, for although I wished to cleanse you you have not been cleansed from your filth, neither will you be cleansed until I have satisfied my indignation against you."[47]

---

35. Is 33:14.
36. Is 9:5.
37. Lk 7:47.
38. Hab 3:16.
39. Job 6:9f.
40. Job 6:11f.
41. Ps 6:2.
42. Rev 3:19.
43. Job 5:17.
44. Jer 10:24.
45. Ps 88:45 (Vulgate).
46. Rom 5:3f.
47. Ezek 24:12f.

6. How I fear that that may apply to us, who are daily burned by our strictness of life as if by some purifying fire and are never cleansed from our iniquity as we ought to be. Perhaps we shall not be cleansed until the judge himself shall sit like fire refining and cleansing silver and shall purify the sons of Levi.[48]

Yet however little that fire might avail now, I would rather suffer it here and now than that it be reserved altogether for later. For in comparison, the former is a merciful medicine, the latter, an avenging wrath. This was the thought of him who said: "Lord, do not correct me in your fury, nor in your anger rebuke me."[49] I know indeed that even then when my soul is disturbed,[50] Lord, in your anger you will be mindful of mercy.[51] I know that even when in mourning and punishment I would console myself with the hope of better things to come. I would answer the enemy, into whose power I had been handed over for a time to be corrected, in the words of the Prophet: "Do not rejoice, my enemy, over me because I have fallen, for I shall rise. Although I sit in darkness the Lord is my light. I will bear the anger of the Lord, because I have sinned against him, until he judges my cause. He will lead me forth into light; I shall see his justice." My enemy will look at me and be covered with confusion.[52] And I shall say on that day: "I will give you thanks, Lord, because you were angry with me; your fury has turned away and you have consoled me."[53]

However, why should I fear on the evil day?[54] Why do I not rather enjoy good things in the good day and take precautions against the evil day? Behold now is the acceptable time, is it not? Behold now is the day of salvation.[55] Why should I not listen to the Wise Man's advice: "Whatever your hand can do, do it sedulously, for there is no counsel or reason or wisdom in the lower regions to which you are hastening,"[56] and those words of the Apostle: "While we have time let us do good to all men."?[57] We began with

---

48. Mal 3:2f.
49. Ps 6:2.
50. Ps 41:7.
51. Hab 3:2.
52. Mic 7:8ff.
53. Is 12:1.
54. Ps 48:6.
55. 2 Cor 6:2.
56. Eccles 9:10.
57. Gal 6:10.

consolations but we have ended up with terrors, for indeed consolation will be useful when it is mixed with terror. We shall walk in your truth, Lord, if our heart rejoices in such a way as to fear your name.[58] Otherwise if we were to make ourselves wholly free from fear it would be said of us too: "My people, those who call you happy deceive you and lead your footsteps astray."[59] We shall be truly happy, if we rightly recognize our wretchedness and devoutly grieve over it. We shall be free from fear in death, if while we live we are always fearful and cautious.[60]

---

58. Ps 85:11.   59. Is 3:12.
60. The Lenten Sermons, this and the following, stand out from the rest of Guerric's sermons because of their brevity and also because of the fact that they do not end with the usual doxology.

SERMON 21

SERMON FOR THE SATURDAY OF THE SECOND WEEK OF LENT

O HAPPY THE HUMILITY of those who repent; O blessed the hope of those who confess. How mighty you are with the Almighty; how easily you conquer the unconquerable; how quickly you turn the dreadful judge into a devoted father. We have heard today[1] to our great edification of the prodigal son's sorrowful journey, tearful repentance and glorious reception. He was so gravely guilty and had not yet confessed but only planned to; had not yet made satisfaction but only bent his mind to it. Yet by merely intending to humble himself he immediately obtained a pardon which others seek for so long a time with such great desire, beg for with such tears, strive for with such diligence. The thief on the cross was absolved by a simple confession,[2] the prodigal by only the will to confess.

"I said," Scripture says, "I will confess my transgression to the Lord; and you did forgive the guilt of my sin."[3] Everywhere mercy precedes.[4] It had preceded the will to confess by inspiring it; it preceded also the words of confession by forgiving what was to be confessed. "When he was still far off," we read, "his father saw him and was moved with compassion, and running to meet him fell upon his neck and kissed him."[5] These words seem to suggest that

---

1. The Gospel passage that is proclaimed at the Eucharistic Liturgy on the Saturday of the Second Week of Lent is that portion of Lk (15:11-32) where Christ recounts the parable of the prodigal son.
2. Lk 23:42f.   3. Ps 31:5.   4. Ps 58:11.   5. Lk 15:20.

the father was even more anxious to pardon his son than the son was to be pardoned. He hastened to absolve the guilty one from what was tormenting his conscience, as if the merciful father suffered more in his compassion for his miserable son than the son did in his own miseries. We do not mean to attribute human feelings to the unchangeable nature of God; we intend rather that our affection should be softened and moved to love that supreme goodness by learning from comparison with human feelings that he loves us more than we love him.

2. See how where sin abounded grace abounds still more.[6] The guilty one could scarcely hope for pardon; the judge, or rather not now the judge but the advocate, heaps up grace. "Quick," he says, "bring forth the best robe and clothe him in it, put a ring on his hand and shoes on his feet; fetch the fatted calf and kill it, let us eat and make merry, for this son of mine who had died has come back to life."[7] To pass over all these: the best robe, that is, the sanctification of the Spirit with which he who is baptized is clothed and the penitent clothed afresh; the ring of faith by which he pledges his loyalty; the shoes by which he is fortified to trample on poisonous serpents or to preach the gospel; the fatted calf which he offers in sacrifice on the altar; those festive joys enjoined for the son's reception and celebrated by all the host of heaven; to say nothing of all these and leave them to be treated by the more learned, let us consider only that embrace and kiss of the devoted father. What a wealth of graciousness and sweetness, what an abundance of most blessed joy, what torrents of most holy delight do they not contain? "He fell upon his neck and kissed him."[8]

When he thus showed his affection for him, what did he do by his embrace and his kiss but take him to his bosom and cast himself into his son's bosom, breathe himself into him, in order that by clinging to his father he might become one spirit with him, just as by clinging to harlots he had been made one body with them?[9] It was not enough for that supreme mercy not to close the bowels of

---

6. Rom 5:20.   7. Lk 15:22f.   8. Lk 15:20.
9. Cf. 1 Cor 6:15.

his compassion to the wretched. He draws them into his very bowels and makes them his members. He could not bind us to himself more closely, could not make us more intimate to himself than by incorporating us into himself. Both by charity and by ineffable power he unites us not only with the body he has assumed but also with his very spirit. If such is the grace accorded to the repentant what will be the glory of those who reign? If such are the consolations of the wretched, what will be the joys of the blessed? And since he gives us so much in advance while we are still on the way, what treasures is he not keeping stored up for us when we arrive in our fatherland? Indeed, what has not entered into the heart of man:[10] that we should be like him[11] and that God should be all in all?[12]

3. Now you, blessed sinner, although not blessed because a sinner but because repentant of sin, what encouragement was yours in your father's embrace and his kiss, when he restored his love to you of whom he had almost despaired, when he made your heart clean again and overwhelmed you with the joy of your salvation?

"And how," he says, "shall speech explain what the mind cannot contain?" Unspeakable are the groans and inexplicable the affections to which the spirit gives birth as if impregnated by the incomprehensible. The human heart is too narrow for them and therefore it is torn and pours itself out. The ardor which it conceives but cannot contain it breathes forth and spreads abroad in what ways it can, by tears, groans, sighs. These things are known better to people who have tasted them often and abundantly.

Now also, I say, when you have been released after those embraces and kisses, when you think over what has passed between you and him, when you consider what your cause was and how it was judged by him, bearing in mind on the one hand the abundance of your offence, on the other hand the superabundance of his grace, to what, I ask, does your thought give birth in you?

"What but this," he says, "that an unbearable fire blazes out in my meditation,[13] on the one hand for sorrow and shame, on the

---

10. 1 Cor 2:9.   11. 1 Jn 3:2.   12. 1 Cor 15:28.   13. Ps 38:4.

other hand for joy and love. I would not consider myself a man but a stone if I were so hard-hearted as not to grieve or be ashamed, or so wicked and ungrateful as not to be wholly liquefied for joy or love of that father."

4. Keep then, O happy sinner, keep carefully and watchfully this spirit of yours, this most fitting affection of humility and devotion by which you may always so think of yourself in humility and of the Lord in goodness.[14] There is nothing greater than it among the gifts of the Holy Spirit, nothing more precious in the treasures of God, nothing more holy among all the charisms, nothing more health-giving in all the sacraments. Keep, I say, if you wish yourself to be kept, the humility of that sentiment and word by which you confess to your father and say: "Father, now I am not worthy to be called your son: make me as one of your hired servants."[15] Nothing so wins your father over as this sentiment, nor is there any better way of making yourself a worthy son than by always confessing yourself unworthy. This humility not only justifies sinners but also perfects the just and brings their justice to fullness if they confess themselves humble servants even when they have done all they were bidden.[16]

Let your sin be present to you always[17] and, according to the Wise Man's advice, do not be without fear even for sin that has been forgiven.[18] God's judgments are uncertain and hidden; they are not rashly to be presumed upon, for we hold nothing more certain in that regard than that in God's sight no man alive shall be justified,[19] except insofar as he judges himself to be a sinner. Otherwise all our justice is like the rag a woman in her times casts away.[20]

Mercy has welcomed you kindly, revived you with lovingkindness. Fear the judgment, lest the grace given to you in your humility be taken away from you in your pride. You have chosen to be of little account in the house of your father;[21] you were content to become as one of the hired servants. Remain in that frame of

---

14. Wis 1:1.
17. Ps 50:5.
20. Is 64:6.

15. Lk 15:19.
18. Sir 5:5.
21. Ps 83:11.

16. Lk 17:10.
19. Ps 142:2.

mind, so that even if you are promoted you may be advanced to greater things still. Always take the last place, or at least desire it. Claim for yourself the servitude of a hired servant rather than freedom. Cherish your father with a son's devotion, aware of what he has deserved of you; but be content with the humble state and work of a hired servant, aware of your own deserts. Never let humility become displeasing to you; through it you began to please and without it you will begin to displease however great the virtues by which you are distinguished, however dutifully you seem to serve your father.

Humility is the greatest of all virtues, although it does not know itself to be a virtue. It is the root and seed-bed, the tinder and incentive, it is the summit and peak, the custody and discipline of almost all the virtues. From it they begin, through it they make progress, in it they are perfected, by it they are preserved. It is humility that makes all the virtues what they are, and if any one of them be lacking or less perfect it is humility that compensates for the loss since it profits by the other's absence.

An analytic index will be found at the end of the second volume.

CISTERCIAN PUBLICATIONS

Cistercian Publications publishes in the following areas:

Monastic Texts in English Translation

- The writings of twelfth and thirteenth century Cistercians
- The works of monastic writers in both the eastern and western Church.

Monastic Life, History, Spirituality, Architecture, and Liturgy

- By monks and nuns
- By scholars
- For those with a personal interest in monastic prayer and lifestyle
- For students exploring and
- For scholars specializing in some aspect of the monastic tradition
- Cistercian music and retreat addresses on compact disc and cassette.

To discover other titles in our series of texts and studies in the monastic tradition, please request our free complete catalogue from Customer Service or visit our website:

www.spencerabbey.org/cistpub

Editorial Offices & Customer Service

- Cistercian Publications
  WMU Station, 1903 West Michigan Avenue
  Kalamazoo, Michigan 49008-5415 USA

  Telephone 616 387 8920
  Fax   616 387 8390
  e-mail   cistpub@wmich.edu

Canada

- Novalis
  49 Front Street East, Second Floor
  Toronto, Ontario M5E 1B3   CANADA

  Telephone 1 800 204 4140
  Fax   416 363 9409

U.K.

- Cistercian Publications UK
  Mount Saint Bernard Abbey
  Coalville, Leicestershire LE67 5UL UK

- UK Customer Service & Book Orders
  Cistercian Publications
  97 Loughborough Road
  Thringstone, Coalville
  Leicestershire LE67 8LQ UK

  Telephone 01530 45 27 24
  Fax   01530 45 02 10
  e-mail   MsbcistP@aol.com

Website & Warehouse

- www.spencerabbey.org/cistpub

- Book Returns (prior permission)
  Cistercian Publications
  Saint Joseph's Abbey
  167 North Spencer Road
  Spencer, Massachusetts 01562-1233   USA

  Telephone 508 885 8730
  Fax   508 885 4687
  e-mail   cistpub@spencerabbey.org

Trade Accounts & Credit Applications

- Cistercian Publications / Accounting
  6219 West Kistler Road
  Ludington, Michigan 49431   USA

  Fax   231 843 8919